'I love this remarkable collection. *Be: Godly Wisdom to Live By* is a treasure chest to dive into each day. You will find jewels of encouragement, peace and hope.'

Rob Parsons, OBE, founder of Care for the Family

'Knowledge and ideas come swirling around us through thousands of images every single day. But real WISDOM is hard to find. And that's what makes this collection of devotionals so very good. Both inspirational and practical – they are wise counsel from women who have practised what they share. The result is wisdom. Read, consider, and practise these devotionals and you'll find rest for your soul.'

Danielle Strickland, author and advocate

'From the moment I read the first page I was captivated; every Scripture was familiar and I could identify with a personal experience of almost each incident described – a spiritually stimulating book, highly recommended!'

Charles Whitehead, KSG, an international speaker and author

'Fiona Castle and her wonderful group of friends have pooled their thoughts on all their years of travelling through the gauntlet of modern-day life – the worry, the laughter, the pain, the fulfilment, the fear and the fight, the joy and the divine pleasure of loving and living. And what they've discovered along the way is that all the knowledge they'll ever need about human nature is to be found in the ancient wise words of the Bible. Love God. Love one another. Be a channel of God's love on earth, now and always. Amen to that!'

Pam Rhodes, author and television presenter

'We live in a world that tells us we can be anything and should be everything. It's exhausting just trying to keep up. This beautiful book of devotions is a breath of fresh air, helping you to simply be who God created you to be, with no pressure to be more.'

Bekah Legg, CEO at Restored, author and speaker

'Our discipleship lies in the daily moments of life, of how we approach family and friends and work and discover Jesus' ways in the midst of dishes and emails and children's conversations. This collection of stories and insights from women at various stages of life captures that dailiness of being with Jesus and his grace-filled and loving ways. In a world that pulls us into the fears and anxieties of our age, the short devotional thoughts from these women encourage us to be present to our lives with God in the given daily moments.'

Lisa Igram, professor and dean at Biola University

'For women juggling multiple demands in their day these bite-size morsels will encourage, sustain and stimulate them to be living for Christ in their everyday lives.'

Ruth Coffey, Foundation Year leader,
Moorlands School of Theology

'Encouraging inspiration for every day – this book is such a treasure trove of brilliant thoughts and stories!'

Ruth Adams, former director of Activate Your Life

'Authentic Christianity is something that can be summed up in two steps: both of which use that little syllable *be*. The first step is to *believe* in Christ, the second to seek to *become* like Christ. In this context of seeking to become like Christ, this book is such a profound help. In those insistent little daily repetitions of '*be*!' it reminds us that we need to press on from just signing up to Christianity (the *believing*) to living out Christian faith (the *becoming*).'

Revd Canon J. John Evangelist, author and speaker

'What excited me was the sheer practicality of the comments on the Scripture verses. The numerous contributors gave a wide interpretation, and it was so relevant. I look forward to having this book by my bedside, as it does not labour the point, but leaves me thinking deep thoughts about one aspect of what our faith means to us – surely no better way to enjoy a good night's sleep!'

Helen Cooke, past president of Activate,
speaker at Keswick Convention

Be

Godly Wisdom to Live By

365 DEVOTIONS FOR WOMEN

Fiona Castle and Friends

Authentic

28 27 26 25 24 23 22 7 6 5 4 3 2 1

First published 2022 by Authentic Media Limited,
PO Box 6326, Bletchley, Milton Keynes, MK1 9GG.
authenticmedia.co.uk

British Library Cataloguing in Publication Data
A catalogue record for this book is available from the British Library.
ISBN: 978-1-78893-239-4
978-1-78893-240-0 (e-book)

Scripture quotations are taken from the *Holy Bible*, New Living Translation,
copyright © 1996, 2004, 2015 by Tyndale House Foundation; Anglicized text
version, © SPCK, 2018.
Used by permission of Tyndale House Publishers, Inc., Carol Stream, Illinois
60188, USA, and SPCK, London, UK.
All rights reserved.

Scripture quotations noted NIV are taken from
The Holy Bible, New International Version Anglicised
Copyright © 1979, 1984, 2011 Biblica
Used by permission of Hodder & Stoughton Ltd, an Hachette UK company.
All rights reserved.
'NIV' is a registered trademark of Biblica
UK trademark number 1448790.

Scripture quotations noted KJV are from The Authorized (King James) Version.
Rights in the Authorized Version in the United Kingdom are vested in the
Crown. Reproduced by permission of the Crown's patentee, Cambridge
University Press

The Activate Team Contributors
Fiona Castle, Mandy Catto, Rhiannon Goulding, Rachel Allcock, Sarah McKerney,
Esther Tregilgas, Jaz Potter, Hayley Nock, Becky Burr, Sarah Jones
activateyourlife.org.uk

Edited by Jan Greenough

Cover design by Mercedes Piñera

Printed and bound by CPI Group (UK) Ltd, Croydon, CR0 4YY

Foreword

I remember one particular day recently, when I was doom-scrolling headline after headline on social media and thinking how overwhelming it is to live in an age of instant information – where a million stories of people's pain or supposed perfection are only a swipe away. Standing at the kitchen sink, phone in hand and waiting for the kettle to boil, I found myself getting lost, trying to figure out if I had it better or worse than the women whose lives I was viewing. Were my kids as well-adjusted as theirs? Was my mental health as robust? Was I eating the right things, thinking the right thoughts, engaging in the right causes, getting the right amount of sleep? And in the midst of all these comparisons, where was I becoming aware of God's loving presence? And how was I sharing with others the wonder of belonging to God?

Our world is awash with attitude. There's no end of people quick to give us their version of events about how we should act, think, be. As cultural moments go, maybe we're collectively feeling the loss of the art of honest, wise chatter that grounds us in something bigger than ourselves, within a community that tells us we're not alone and helps us wisely navigate life to the glory of God.

Be is a joyful book. Dipping into it is like finding yourself in a kind, safe space with a group of friends who get the ups and downs of life, and have an easy way to talk about how everything fits together with Jesus at the centre. Each daily devotion flows from the lives of women who, like you and I, are working out what it means to live as a beloved daughter of God, who seeks to share his incredible love with others. I love that over half of the contributions are from a personal 'shero' of mine, Fiona Castle. I first met Fiona when I was a slightly awkward teenager, unsure how to be me and God's at the same time. In a few short words she spoke something so good and strong into my heart that the benefit of it has never left me. It's so inspiring to hear pearls of wisdom for life from someone whose passion for sharing Jesus has remained radiant and strong through many years of knowing him. It's very typical of Fiona's humility and desire to release women into their calling that hers isn't the only voice you hear in this book.

Reading through the book I felt I could picture Fiona and her friends, jotting down their thoughts on the backs of envelopes or napkins when inspiration hit them! They don't hold back from telling the truth about themselves – sometimes with hilarious results – because they know that God is glorified in the mundane as well as the marvellous. This is wisdom found in the trenches of life; at work, by a hospital bed, on the school run, at the shops, walking through the woods, in the middle of the night when sleep evaded them or the kids wouldn't settle – exactly the same places where you and I need to know God's loving presence so that we can have the courage and grace to share his love with our friends.

So I encourage you to keep this book close. Read it on the bus, in the queue for coffee or while you're waiting for the kettle to boil. Instead of checking Instagram, let these words of wisdom be the ones that linger. Let them become the screen saver of your daily walk with God. Let Fiona, Rachel, Becky, Esther, Mandy, Rhiannon, Sarah, Sarah, Hayley and Jaz speak into your day, and let their love for Jesus and desire to share him with others inspire your heart and embolden your witness.

This book really does contain godly wisdom you can live by. But don't just take my words for it, dive in . . .

Rachel Gardner

Introduction

Long ago, I had a part in the original West End production of *The Sound of Music*. I was reminded recently of some words from one of the songs, where Maria is wisely teaching the teenage Liesl about love. She sings, 'Love in your heart wasn't put there to stay – love isn't love till you give it away.' The theme is romantic love, but it resonates with our purpose in life.

Jesus gave us the greatest love of all. We mustn't simply savour that love but give it away to everyone who hasn't yet discovered such overwhelming love, peace and security through him. My prayer is that you'll be blessed and encouraged by these devotions, so that in turn you will be motivated to give that love away to others. As the Bible says in 1 Thessalonians 3:12, 'And may the Lord make your love for one another and for all people grow and overflow, just as our love for you overflows.'

I'm part of a very honest team who are known for sharing their struggles and embarrassing stories. They are all very different and are much younger than I am, but we share one common purpose: we want to glorify God with our everyday lives. We hope you'll be comforted by our vulnerability, be awestruck by God's love, and be inspired to share your story.

For over 50 years, Activate Your Life has been dedicated to helping women reach their friends for Jesus, in natural, ordinary ways. This book is a response to requests from women who have attended our events and want to take something of the enthusiasm, understanding and sense of fellowship away with them into their daily lives.

You'll find verses from every book of the Bible and hundreds of stories, memories and insights from lessons we've learned along the way. As a team ranging from 18 to 81, we're navigating what it means to be Christian women in today's world, however we spend our days and whatever God's unique purpose is in our lives.

Fiona Castle

Day 1

Be Trusting

Fiona Castle

For you know that when your faith is tested,
your endurance has a chance to grow.
James 1:3

I love to pray while I'm walking in the quiet of the countryside.

One day recently, I was praying for a troubled friend when I stopped by a gnarled old beech tree with twisted, bare lower branches. But as I looked up towards the top of the tree, sunlight shafted through, and I could see that the upper branches had young shoots and pale green leaves.

I believe God was answering my prayer through that tree. He has new life for us in Jesus if we will only turn our eyes away from our problems and up to him, the source of life.

Next to the beech tree was a young sapling, but it was growing straight and tall. It didn't bear the marks of a long life, and it was neither so interesting nor so beautiful.

The problems and difficulties in our lives create a depth of character and a deep trust in God. I know that when all is going well I think I can run my life fine – but as soon as troubles come, I throw myself into God's arms and plead for help. That's when I learn to trust.

Pray

Thank you, Lord, for the assurance that I can trust you to guide me in all circumstances.

Day 2

Be Observant

Rhiannon Goulding

> So be on your guard, not asleep like the others.
> Stay alert and be clearheaded.
> 1 Thessalonians 5:6

On the third phone call with the hospital, and after the third time he was asked the same question, my dad said to the pre-op team, 'Why do you always ask how many pillows I use at home?' The answer came as quite a surprise. It wasn't for his comfort or relaxation, they explained, but they'd found that a request for more pillows can often be an indication of hidden congestive heart failure. Apparently, it's one of the key signs they look out for in the aftermath of a big operation.

This got me thinking. What signs could we look out for to suggest our heart is failing? What telltale signs indicate that we might be growing cold to the things of God or hard towards people in our lives? An increasingly short temper perhaps or a growing irritability? What if we had people around us who would notice these small signs before they progressed? What if we could find out how many pillows we need, and have people around us who love us enough to hold us to account for them?

Pray

Lord, I pray I'll be able to see when things aren't right, and that you'll put trustworthy people in my life who'll tell me so. I pray for the courage to be open and honest with myself, and the strength to bring change.

Day 3

Be Unafraid

Fiona Castle

'I am leaving you with a gift – peace of mind and heart. And the peace I give is a gift the world cannot give. So don't be troubled or afraid.'

John 14:27

I have proved these words to be true. Before I asked Jesus into my life, I was practically a professional worrier! As a mother of four with many responsibilities, which I took very seriously, I was always anxious.

I could hardly believe the amazing peace which invaded every part of me, the moment I gave my life to Jesus. He didn't change my circumstances, but he did change my attitude to my circumstances. That peace has remained with me for more than four decades, through many different challenges.

To worry is human, but when we recognize it, we can overcome it by placing our trust in Jesus and his promises. We have the confident assurance that he will be with us in all the changing circumstances of our lives.

Pray

Lord Jesus, give me the peace that comes from trusting in your love.

Day 4

Be Resourceful

Sarah McKerney

Reaching into his shepherd's bag and taking out a stone, he
hurled it with his sling and hit the Philistine in the forehead.
1 Samuel 17:49

It's the well-known story of the nation of Israel at war with
the Philistines and terrified of their 'giant' Goliath. When the
young boy David stepped up, he knew God was on his side. So
if God was going to intervene, would it be with supernatural
force? Would he just send an army of warrior angels to sort
out this problem? That would be great!

Yet God didn't send David anything new and startling to
resolve the situation. David used the resources already
available to him: his sling and his stone. David trusted that
God was with him, and he recognized that what he already
had would be the thing to use to bring about victory.

We have the victory through Christ, but our victory is rarely
passive. In the Bible, we see again and again that supernatural
intervention is rare and that God's people are seldom passive
bystanders. Generally, God expects us to step up – and then
he uses the resources we already have available to win the
battles we face.

Pray

Lord, open my eyes to see the resources I have available to
me. Help me to use them to overcome my problems with
your help.

Day 5

Be Guided

Fiona Castle

Your own ears will hear him. Right behind you a voice
will say, 'This is the way you should go,' whether to the right
or to the left.
Isaiah 30:21

We all make choices every day. Some are trivial, such as what time to get up, what to wear and what to have for breakfast. Other choices are more important, such as careers, where to live and friendships. Sometimes we make choices without discussion or consideration of the consequences, which can lead to regret.

The most important choice we make in life is to follow Jesus. Once we have made that choice, we can trust him to guide us to make the right decisions for the right reasons.

When we have children, we limit their freedom to make their own choices until we think they are mature enough to take responsibility for themselves. We do that for their good and their protection. So it is with us, when we trust God to guide us his way rather than our own. A right decision is always one that is based on the principles of God's word.

'And you will know the truth, and the truth will set you free' (John 8:32).

Pray

Steady me, Lord, so that I will make wise choices and follow the right path.

Day 6

Be Free

Jaz Potter

> He cancelled the record of the charges against us and took it away by nailing it to the cross. In this way, he disarmed the spiritual rulers and authorities. He shamed them publicly by his victory over them on the cross.
>
> Colossians 2:14–15

If it were possible to plug in a computer lead between your brain and a huge screen in the sky, everybody could read your every thought and deed. We know this isn't possible, but wouldn't it make for some – well – uncomfortable reading?

However, we have to remind ourselves that our past, our sin and shame have all been dealt with for ever. Jesus did it. He took our sin on the cross, and in that one moment as he cried out, he ripped the lead right out of the socket and tore it into a million shreds. There is nothing to read on the screen in the sky, because the screen has been smashed into smithereens.

It's easy to beat ourselves up about the past: we mull over mistakes and spend time regretting them. Yet this should not be our position. Jesus has made us alive with him, so we no longer live under a screen of condemnation but in freedom and with direct access to our Father.

Pray

Dear God, thank you for dealing with our sin, thank you for forgiving us, and thank you for making us alive in you.

Day 7

Be Awestruck

Rachel Allcock

> You clothed me with skin and flesh, and you knit my bones and sinews together. You gave me life and showed me your unfailing love. My life was preserved by your care.
> Job 10:11–12

For a short time, I worked as a cleaner in the product development area of a well-known crisp factory. In the twilight, wielding a mop and cleaning spray, I lingered over the kitchen area to see what amazing new savoury snacks were being conjured up. Without giving away too many secrets, it was a primitive, homely affair: a simple sink with spoons and crumbs strewn around, a microwave and a ring hob. A few ice cream tubs of ingredients lay open.

That glimpse into one of the first stages of product development has stuck with me as if it were yesterday. I really couldn't believe it was so basic! Whatever we understand of God's creation, the Bible has to keep the description pretty simple so it doesn't blow our minds. Here in today's verse, the image of a person being put together is so simple, but also so incredible. We are all different, all unique. One day, maybe we'll have an insight into God's patterns and product development, but for now, I'm just thankful that each aspect of our being was lovingly planned and developed by a Creator God.

Pray

Creator God, I am in awe of your mighty power and incredible design. Thank you.

Day 8

Be Still

Fiona Castle

'Be still, and know that I am God!'
Psalm 46:10

In our busy lives, with so much pressure, it is not easy to be still. Women are known as multi-taskers and, probably, while we are engaged with one task, we are already mentally preparing for another! We tend always to be thinking ahead, so we fail to enjoy the present. This is sad, because we are so keen to get something over and done with that we lose opportunities to relax and enjoy the moment.

Have you ever seen a toddler totally absorbed in watching a butterfly, or a tadpole in a pond? Time is the 'now' for small children, which is a lesson we sometimes need to re-learn.

As you turn the pages of this little book, take a few moments simply to breathe in deeply the love of Jesus and breathe out all the stress, tension and anxiety that might have built up over the past day.

Charles Wesley describes it perfectly in his hymn 'How Do Thy Mercies Close Me Round':

I rest beneath the Almighty's shade;
My griefs expire, my troubles cease;
Thou, Lord, on whom my soul is stayed,
Wilt keep me still in perfect peace.

Pray

Lord, please give me moments of stillness in my life, today and every day.

Day 9

Be Dependent

Mandy Catto

So now, come back to your God. Act with love and justice,
and always depend on him.
Hosea 12:6

One of the earliest phrases a toddler says is, 'Me do it'. The drive to manage without help in putting on shoes or cutting up food develops along with the 'terrible twos'. My son loved to declare that he could tie his laces 'all by myself' and my daughter delighted in choosing her own random clothes. Two pairs of pants, a unicorn bikini and a tutu were challenging in the Scottish winter.

We act like stubborn children when we step away from God's protection and walk our own path. We rely on our own finances, talents and resources for our security instead of trusting in God. As we seek unhealthy independence, we make decisions that are selfish, moving away from just actions and loving conversations.

If we pivot our thinking and focus back on God, everything changes. As we renew our dependence on him, our identity is secure in his love. Then we can truly act with love and justice to others as we follow his commands and ideals.

Perhaps we should practise saying, 'I can't do it, please help me do it,' as we mature in faith – beyond the terrible twos – into a loving dependency on God, thriving in loving relationships.

Pray

Father God, I come back to you. I am completely reliant on you. Only with your help can I be a confident, just person, loving others.

Day 10

Be Confident

Fiona Castle

Let us strip off every weight that slows us down, especially the sin that so easily trips us up. And let us run with endurance the race God has set before us.
Hebrews 12:1

We won't be rewarded for the 'well said', we'll be rewarded for the 'well done'. The risk of risk-free living is the greatest risk of all. We must not end our lives wishing we'd stepped out and followed God's plan. We have to go ahead and do it!

Nothing anywhere guarantees us total safety; we need to take risks, so we mustn't allow the word 'impossible' to stop us. If the people who changed the world had left every seemingly impossible task undone, we'd still be living in the Dark Ages!

It is said that some people see things as they are and ask, 'Why?', while others see things as they have never been and ask, 'Why not?'

Is there something that you have been longing to do for years but have never felt confident enough to take the risk? What can you do today to begin to realize that dream? Don't waste any more time.

Pray

God, grant me the courage to step out and take risks for you today.

Day 11

Be Comforted

Fiona Castle

> Fear not; you will no longer live in shame. Don't be afraid;
> there is no more disgrace for you. You will no longer
> remember the shame of your youth and the sorrows of
> widowhood. For your Creator will be your husband; the LORD
> of Heaven's Armies is his name! He is your Redeemer, the
> Holy One of Israel, the God of all the earth.
> Isaiah 54:4–5

When I was widowed, I found that different emotions attacked me at different times through the grieving process.

One evening, I was acutely aware of the emptiness of my home, with no one to hug me. I felt so alone. But the next morning I opened my *Living Light* (a book of daily Bible verses from the *Living Bible*) and there were the words I needed!

How amazing that the Lord knew exactly how I was feeling and he provided the answer. Tears of relief flowed as I turned to him in my grief. I no longer felt alone.

When we submit to God's will for the circumstances in our lives, we can know his peace and be grateful for his provision for us. 'You have turned my mourning into joyful dancing. You have taken away my clothes of mourning and clothed me with joy' (Psalm 30:11).

Pray

Thank you, Lord, that I never need to feel alone, because you are with me and you understand my needs.

Day 12

Be Patient

Fiona Castle

I waited patiently for the LORD to help me, and he turned to me and heard my cry.
Psalm 40:1

There's a well-known prayer: 'Lord, give me patience, and give it to me now!'

Patience sometimes means waiting for prayers to be answered, and even accepting that they may never be answered at all in the way we hope. If we pray only because we want answers, we will get frustrated with God. We need to accept his timing and even his answer when it's 'no'.

Are you a patient friend, wife, mother or teacher? We learn so much about patience when we discipline children when they're disobedient. Even Jesus longed for an answer to his prayer to his Father, at the Mount of Olives, the night before his crucifixion, saying, 'Father, if you are willing, please take this cup of suffering away from me.' But then he submitted to his Father, by saying, 'Yet I want your will to be done, not mine' (Luke 22:42).

Even in his agony, knowing what lay ahead, he patiently allowed God's purpose to be fulfilled. Jesus' patience in his suffering is the reason we are assured of his love and acceptance today. Let's try to follow his example of patience and trust.

Pray

Lord, help me always to seek your will, not mine.

Day 13

Be an Encourager

Fiona Castle

They drank my words like a refreshing spring rain. When they were discouraged, I smiled at them. My look of approval was precious to them. Like a chief, I told them what to do.
Job 29:23–25

In his pre-teens, my son was a cheeky young lad! He was never wilfully disobedient, but always loved joking and making people laugh. One day his teacher collared me and told me that my son was a nuisance in the class because of his humour and he couldn't cope with him any more. I asked the teacher if there was anything at all for which he could praise him. His answer was a blunt, 'No!'

I replied that if, in the next few days, he could look for something he could praise him for, it might make a difference. Thankfully the teacher agreed to do this and gave my son a few encouraging comments. The change in him was astounding! He worked harder and at the end of the year, his school report was really positive.

I think the results might have given his teacher food for thought, too. How can we bring out the best in others by encouraging them?

Pray

Lord, please help me to see opportunities to encourage others today. Help me to be sensitive to people's needs.

Day 14

Be an Example

Fiona Castle

Throw yourself into your tasks so that everyone will see your progress. Keep a close watch on how you live and on your teaching. Stay true to what is right for the sake of your own salvation and the salvation of those who hear you.
1 Timothy 4:15–16

I was not very bright academically at school and never came top of the class. I always tried hard, aiming to please the teachers, but I never impressed them! The teachers I appreciated most were those who encouraged me with kind words and by their example, but I knew I would never become a good teacher.

However, as a parent I realized that I had to teach my children as much by example as by verbal advice and correction. If I was constantly losing my temper and yelling at them, how could I expect good, calm behaviour from them in response?

Teachers need to be good role models and I need to be a good role model as a Christian, whether at work or around the family, in order to model the love of Christ in my life to others.

Pray

Lord, I pray that I will be a good role model to those I meet each day, so that they will find the love of Christ for themselves.

Day 15

Be Hopeful

Fiona Castle

'For I know the plans I have for you,' says the LORD. 'They are plans for good and not for disaster, to give you a future and a hope.'
Jeremiah 29:11

Have you ever felt utterly hopeless? All your plans have gone awry, or not materialized, and you think you are absolutely useless! Well, I imagine we have all been there at some point in our lives, when we just feel like giving up.

However, God calls on us not to give up hope; rather to put our hope firmly in him, because whatever our circumstances, he knows and understands them and will see us through. Trusting in him gives us a new viewpoint.

No matter how impossible our future seems, we remind ourselves that in Christ we have eternal hope in heaven, where all our problems are gone for ever. Without him, what hope do we have? His hope brings us life and purpose and direction.

'Faith shows the reality of what we hope for; it is the evidence of things we cannot see' (Hebrews 11:1).

He is our HOPE!

Pray

Lord Jesus, my hope is in you, not just for today, but also for eternity.

Day 16

Be Strong

Rhiannon Goulding

'I asked the LORD to give me this boy, and he has granted my request. Now I am giving him to the LORD, and he will belong to the LORD his whole life.' And they worshipped the LORD there.
1 Samuel 1:27–28

How easy it is to dedicate small cute babies to God, and make our promises to bring them up in the faith and plant them in the church! This is what I did with all my children, but as they got older I realized I had a problem. I had dedicated them to God but I kept taking them back. I said I trusted God with them, but then I would think I knew better. When fears for their future, or worry over their friendships and decisions did not link up with 'my plan', my parenting could get controlling.

At that point – or from the point I recognized it – this was my prayer: 'I have prayed for this child. I dedicate them again to you, Lord. I'm sorry for taking them back and thinking I knew better. Help me to parent out of love for you. Help me to once again let go, and trust you and trust them as they create their own paths.'

Pray

Father, sometimes it's so hard to let go, and let God. Help me to be strong.

Day 17

Be Blessed

Fiona Castle

'May the LORD bless you and protect you. May the LORD smile on you and be gracious to you. May the LORD show you his favour and give you his peace.'
Numbers 6:24–26

These are famous verses, known as the Aaronic Blessing. I have always loved it, but one performance of it had a huge impact on me and millions around the world during the coronavirus pandemic. To me, the power was not only the beauty of the music and singing, but of the many singers from all over the country, from churches of all denominations, coming together online to pray a blessing over our nation. It had a very positive effect on many who are not believers and those who are cynical about the differences between churches and traditions.

I long for people to understand the impact Jesus can make on them, changing attitudes and giving renewed confidence and self-worth to those who feel they have wrecked their lives. The Blessing showed that we are all one in Christ Jesus and wanting the best for every individual. Let us pray that Jesus' love will invade every heart and bring revival to our nation.

Pray

Lord, pour your blessings on our nation and renew faith in individuals, so that they might understand and appreciate the reality of your love.

Day 18

Be Thankful

Fiona Castle

*My entire lifetime is just a moment to you; at best, each of us
is but a breath . . . and all our busy rushing ends in nothing.
We heap up wealth, not knowing who will spend it.*
Psalm 39:5–6

I once heard a story of two old men discussing the will of a deceased friend.

'What did he leave?' asked one.

'Everything!' was the reply.

We come into this world with nothing, and we can't take anything with us when we leave it. However, the things we accumulate in between can often be the cause of trouble, stress and unhappiness.

Jesus accumulated nothing during his time on earth and yet God provided for his every need. And he has promised to do the same for us so long as we put him first in our lives. We all have days when everything seems to be against us. But as Christians, we trust that God has a purpose for our lives.

Take a look around today and see what God has provided for you, and as you recognize it, thank him for it. It could take a long time!

Pray

Thank you, Lord, that you have given me everything I need and more. Give me a generous heart towards others.

Day 19

Be Gracious

Fiona Castle

Since God chose you to be the holy people he loves, you
must clothe yourselves with tenderhearted mercy, kindness,
humility, gentleness, and patience.
Colossians 3:12

The first holiday my husband and I took together without our children surprised us. We spent the first three days getting to know one another again, and found ourselves sharing hurts and resentments – misunderstandings which we hadn't taken the time to clear up.

I could scarcely believe there was so much to sort out. It was like a piece of knitting – fine from a distance, but up close I could see dropped stitches. They couldn't be covered up: we had to unravel it to where the mistake was made.

Back home, I realized how easy it would be to slip into our old ways. I'm often quick to react, and I need to check that my replies won't damage the fabric of my relationships. I have to be careful with every stitch.

That's when this verse is useful. It's no use trying to look good, if underneath I'm seething with resentment or self-pity. But how lovely to know that if we allow the love of Jesus to flow through us, our reactions will be ones which are pleasing to God.

Pray

Dear God, help me to be gracious in my responses to people and to allow your love to flow through me to others.

Day 20

Be Forgiving

Fiona Castle

Confess your sins to each other and pray for each other so
that you may be healed.
James 5:16

'Love means never having to say you're sorry.' This platitude
was made famous in an old film called *Love Story* but, as a
Christian, I believe the opposite is true. Love means *always
being able* to say you're sorry, because forgiveness is one of
the most precious gifts God has given us.

We can't hide anything from God. He knows us entirely and,
through Jesus, he freely forgives us if we are sorry for what
we've done.

When I became a Christian, I discovered that to admit my
faults and ask forgiveness was a blessing. I even discovered
that my own children didn't lose respect for me when I asked
for forgiveness, but responded quickly and readily.

I remember saying 'sorry' to our youngest child, then 2 years old.
He didn't say a word but held out his arms and gave me a big
hug! I was glad I wasn't too proud to admit I'd made a mistake.

We need the open arms of Jesus, always ready to forgive, but
we also need the humility to admit we made a mistake.

Try it. It could change your whole outlook.

Pray

Thank you for your forgiveness, Lord Jesus. Give me a
forgiving heart towards others.

Day 21

Be Resolute

Rhiannon Goulding

So let's not get tired of doing what is good. At just the right time we will reap a harvest of blessing if we don't give up.
Galatians 6:9

I loved being a mum to young children. Yes, I was tired, and sleep was always an issue. But I relished the toddler groups and the chance to have mums over for a coffee and chat while the kids played.

When the children reached their teens, life got trickier. You couldn't just take them to the park or give them a hug. Things changed from physically tiring to mentally tiring. Now I wasn't deprived of sleep, but I was having long conversations and dealing with bigger issues. It was a new stage of parenting.

I remember thinking how easy it would be to turn on the computer, let them watch hours of TV, or not open conversations about how they were acting. However, I knew that if I did, that would bring more challenges. My prayer at this time was that I wanted to finish my parenting race well. I didn't want to give up halfway through or when things got tough. I wanted to keep going, keep pushing forward.

Pray

Father, it's tempting to step back when we're tired and things are tough. But I want to step forward into the next stage and finish well. Give me your strength and love to face the challenges in my life.

Day 22

Be a Listener

Fiona Castle

For the word of God is alive and powerful. It is sharper than the sharpest two-edged sword . . . It exposes our innermost thoughts and desires.
Hebrews 4:12

How do you hear God speaking to you? And how do you know if it's him?

I remember once my husband did something that irritated me. It was trivial, but I got back on a familiar train of thought: why should I always be taken for granted? Fortunately, I didn't say anything, but the thought came into my head as clearly as if God had spoken: 'Love is patient and kind.' I tried to carry on with the argument in my head, but those words from 1 Corinthians 13 cut through my pride.

I suppose that's what working out our faith in everyday life means. It's not that we don't have wrong attitudes or reactions any more, but we're equipped to deal with them.

God speaks to us in many ways, but he never fails to give us the answer we need. It's not always the answer we want to hear, because God doesn't give us soft options. But he gives us the truth, and we have to receive it in order to keep the communication lines open.

Pray

Heavenly Father, thank you that you provide the right answers through your word, even though they are not always easy to accept.

Day 23

Be Restful

Becky Burr

> So there is a special rest still waiting for the people of God. For all who have entered into God's rest have rested from their labours, just as God did after creating the world. So let us do our best to enter into that rest.
>
> Hebrews 4:9–11

Rest isn't a popular concept in our culture. It's not productive – it's lazy. There's always more to do and more to achieve! Yet God offers another way. He invites us into rest, just as he rested after he made all of creation. The God of the universe, who has infinite energy, had a day off!

We are commanded to 'do our best' to rest. In other translations, it says to be diligent, to make every effort, to labour. This seems a bit strange, but on reflection, it *is* hard work to rest. There is a struggling, searching, wrestling and agonising in the process of discovering and understanding rest.

This passage is telling us we *need* to wrestle with this to truly become sure that rest is ours, through Jesus Christ and not through our own works. We can only receive rest when we have peace with God and accept his Son. Rest is deeper than the ceasing of works; it is an internal revelation that we can rest in Jesus because of what he did on the cross.

Pray

Lord, thank you that you invite me into rest. Help me to rest in you because of the gift of your Son.

Day 24

Be Honest

Fiona Castle

Because of this, I always try to maintain a clear conscience
before God and all people.
Acts 24:16

Dishonesty means taking something that is not ours – whether through stealing, lying, to rob someone of their reputation or even cheating at a board game! Being honest means being truthful, fair and honourable, which enables us to have a clear conscience.

I remember a wise barrister telling me, 'If you tell the truth you can forget about it, because it always remains the same; but if you tell a lie, you have to remember it all the time, in order to keep covering up.' Eventually lies will be uncovered. Sadly, we often hear of tests revealing that top sports people have taken performance-enhancing drugs. They're disqualified. What a waste of all the years of intensive training.

Proverbs tells us that truth stands the test of time, and we need to earn the respect and trust of others by our honesty. I doubt that anyone can truthfully say they have never been dishonest in some way at some time. But, thankfully, we have a God who forgives us when we own up and repent.

Pray

Lord, thank you for the wisdom of your word. Help me to keep my conscience clear.

Day 25

Be Thankful

Fiona Castle

Do everything without complaining and arguing, so that no one can criticize you. Live clean, innocent lives as children of God, shining like bright lights in a world full of crooked and perverse people.

Philippians 2:14–15

Complaining is generally an expression of dissatisfaction or annoyance with someone or something. It's a self-centred thing to do, and usually happens because people are jealous, or they don't get what they want, or what they expect, or feel they deserve.

Complainers are difficult people to live with and are often unpopular: it can become depressing to listen to their constant griping!

Here in the UK, we generally have little to complain about and much to be grateful for. There are so many people elsewhere in the world who struggle under much more difficult conditions. And, as Christians, when life doesn't go quite as we intended or hoped, it's so much more satisfying to look for something positive to say to someone, rather than criticize or complain. Sometimes mistakes need to be pointed out, but it is possible to do this in a constructive way.

Look within, to recognize that we are far from perfect and look outwards, to seek and encourage the best in others. Count your blessings, not your complaints!

Pray

Thank you, Lord, that I have so many blessings to count each day!

Day 26

Be Holy

Mandy Catto

You must be holy because I, the LORD, am holy. I have set you apart from all other people to be my very own.
Leviticus 20:26

What does it mean to be holy? To be perfect, without sin? We know that God is holy, and sinning less is something we strive for. But our attempts to live perfect lives – for even one day – always fail. We are so grateful that Jesus saves us and makes us holy, fully accepted by God.

So when God asks us four times in Leviticus, and again in 1 Peter 1:13, to be holy because he is holy, how should we react? Perhaps it is helpful to focus on the 'setting apart'. Our lives are different; we have a calling and purpose as followers of Jesus that sets us apart. Our identity as daughters of the Holy God, as his very own, gives us a privileged position as well as a responsibility.

What will this look like today in your life? How will living 'set apart' affect your choices, the way you speak to others, your actions and reactions? Will others see Jesus in you? Can you reflect God's holiness in your relationships and conversations today?

Pray

Lord, you are holy. Help me to live as close to your holy standards as I can – to reflect my identity as your daughter. I pray that I will live a life set apart. May others see you in me today.

Day 27

Be Led

Rhiannon Goulding

Obey your spiritual leaders, and do what they say. Their work
is to watch over your souls, and they are accountable to God.
Give them reason to do this with joy and not with sorrow.
Hebrews 13:17

Recently, my husband and I bought an inflatable boat. An hour later, we were having a debate over whether to paddle left or right and I was getting silently annoyed about the orders coming from the front, 'Right, left, right, hard right!' As my blood boiled I suddenly laughed. This had been my idea, to bring fun and unity into our marriage! But I was at the back and I couldn't see, so I needed to trust the directions and follow with enthusiasm.

How often do we feel we know better, know more? Yet the person in front who's leading, sees what we don't see and needs us to react in ways we may not fully understand. I decided to let go of my organized, control-freak self and enjoy the ride; forget about getting annoyed with directions I didn't understand, but look at where we were going and enjoy the experience! It was time for me to get rowing and enjoy.

We don't always have to be in control; we don't always have to be in charge. We can just enjoy the ride and trust the one who is leading.

Pray

Father, help us to trust in your guiding wisdom, and be humble enough to follow the lead given by others.

Day 28

Be Aware

Jaz Potter

But Mary kept all these things in her heart and thought
about them often.
Luke 2:19

Just before I got married, a good friend of mine gave me
a great piece of advice. She said that after all the months
of meticulous planning, the wedding day itself goes past so
quickly, you almost miss it. She encouraged me to stop now
and again during the day and take some mental photographs –
advice which I heeded. She explained I was unlikely to look
at my wedding album often (it's true, I don't), but she said I
would be able to recall the moments I had stored in my mind
whenever I wanted. She was right – I only have to choose to
recall those memories and I am instantly transported to a
beautiful autumn day, holding hands with my new husband
and enjoying all our guests and celebrations.

One way to enjoy God is to take mental photographs. His
handiwork is all around us – take time to really notice it.
Maybe it's something in creation, or something you see in
another person. Store it up in your heart and recall it when
you want to spend time with God. It's a brilliant way of
starting your prayer time.

Pray

Dear God, help me to encounter you more in the everyday
things. Give me eyes to see what you have done in order to
worship you more.

Day 29

Be Full of Grace

Fiona Castle

May God's grace be eternally upon all who love our Lord
Jesus Christ.
Ephesians 6:24

The word 'grace' reminds me of my dancing years, when a compliment to a beautiful ballerina was that she was graceful. I never attained to such great heights, but I always aimed to be graceful!

However, for Christians the word 'grace' has a totally different meaning. Grace only becomes real when we discover the reality that we are redeemed from death and hell by the saving grace of God, through Jesus. He was willing to pay the price for our sin by his death on the cross, so that we might receive the assurance of eternal life. It hasn't made us sinless or perfect human beings, but we are people who are grateful to have come to the understanding of this truth.

No wonder we want to share this amazing gift with anyone who will listen! This grace has changed our lives and given us a fresh knowledge, as the dictionary describes it, of 'the free and unearned favour of God'. Amazing Grace!

Pray

Dear Lord Jesus, thank you for the joy of knowing you, through the fullness of your grace to us, because of your willingness to give your life for us. Help us to share this wonderful gift with others.

Day 30

Be Praising

Rachel Allcock

> Yet I still dare to hope when I remember this: The faithful love of the LORD never ends! His mercies never cease. Great is his faithfulness; his mercies begin afresh every morning.
> Lamentations 3:21–23

When I was up in the night feeding my baby, I used to be so happy to see the sunrise and know that we had made it through another night. When my mum was in ICU, she said she never really slept properly – the lights were always on, machines were beeping and the nurses were always busy. It was never fully dark and never fully quiet. She missed the regular rhythm of night and day.

Each new sunrise brings the opportunity to start again and discover something new. The majesty of the morning has captivated poets and hymn-writers for centuries. I can think of maybe three or four hymns that must have been inspired by Lamentations, but I was amazed to find that at least 20 common hymns have been based on these few verses. Two of the best known, 'Great Is Thy Faithfulness' and 'Morning Has Broken', are common choices at weddings and funerals. There is something so captivating about both new beginnings and dignified exits. In all our ups and downs, 'Thou changest not, thy compassions they fail not; as thou hast been thou for ever wilt be' ('Great Is Thy Faithfulness', Thomas O. Chisholm).

Pray

Lord, I praise you for the blessing of each new day.

Day 31

Be Genuine

Rhiannon Goulding

The LORD doesn't see things the way you see them.
People judge by outward appearance, but the LORD
looks at the heart.
1 Samuel 16:7

A few years ago, at an Activate weekend away, we gave away beautiful cacti with lovely bright flowers on them. A few of the extra ones ended up back at my house with me. I've been looking after them and watering them and I keep them in a sunny place. They're still alive, but they have never flowered again. I read that if a cactus is truly happy, it will flower. I don't know what I'm doing wrong or how to make it happy enough to flower again.

Recently I walked past a whole display of cacti in a well-known DIY shop. They were incredible! Each sported a vibrant flower, better than any I'd seen on my plants. When I looked closely at the sign, I found out that they were real cacti, but with artificial flowers fixed on.

I couldn't believe it! Even the professional growers couldn't get them to flower naturally, so they resorted to a bit of 'plastic surgery'!

It reminded me of a valuable lesson. If it looks too good to be true, it probably is. I want a genuine flower, and if I can't make it happen, I'll accept that instead of faking it.

Pray

Father, it's tempting to present a 'perfect' image to the world. Help me to be genuine in everything I do.

Day 32

Be Caring

Fiona Castle

Pray in the Spirit at all times and on every occasion. Stay alert and be persistent in your prayers for all believers everywhere.
Ephesians 6:18

The other day I rang a friend whose husband is dying of cancer. I asked how she was – and she burst into tears. She said that in all the time she'd been caring for him, no one had ever asked how she was coping.

I had a similar story. I was totally dedicated to making my husband's last days as comfortable as possible, and I never had time to think about myself. But afterwards I had a new concern for carers. I'd been in their position, and suddenly understood that their lives were 'on hold' as they cared for their loved ones.

There are the parents of sick and disabled children; there are adults caring for parents with dementia; there are partners caring for survivors of trauma with physical or psychological injuries.

Let's look around us with thoughtful sympathy and see where a compassionate word, a cheering gift or the offer of practical help will make a huge difference to someone who is struggling.

And let's hold all those carers in our prayers.

Pray

Lord, I pray for all carers today, that they might know they are loved and upheld by you, even if the world fails to notice them.

Day 33

Be Peaceful

Fiona Castle

And 'don't sin by letting anger control you'. Don't let the sun
go down while you are still angry, for anger gives a foothold
to the devil.
Ephesians 4:26–27

We get angry for many different reasons. Sometimes our
pride is hurt or we feel cheated, or we don't get our own way.
All these can cause a very negative reaction. However, our
anger may be righteous anger when we see someone else
being treated unjustly. We need always to be aware of our
own reactions and motives.

There's always something that causes a change in our mood.
You can think of something that makes you sad, and your
feelings change. Or something that makes you happy, and
your mood lifts. So what makes you angry?

Anger has negative effects, not only on our mood but also on
our judgement and even on our health, so God's word is very
wise. It tells us to deal with it before the day is over.

If something has made you angry, deal with it. Confront the
situation that has caused it and apologize to anyone who
has suffered as a result, and you will experience peace.

Pray

Dear God, I take authority over any spirit in me that causes a
wrong reaction, and cast it out in the powerful name of Jesus.

Day 34

Be Wise

Fiona Castle

Get wisdom; develop good judgement.
Proverbs 4:5

Unlike personality or talent, wisdom is not inherent in us. We learn to be wise through reading, understanding and, even more importantly, applying God's word. This is far more valuable than any academic achievement.

Sometimes we are tempted to follow our worldly desires without asking God to show us the right road to take. That invariably leads us into a trap, which holds us until we recognize it and are willing to repent and begin again. How wonderful that we have a God who understands our weaknesses and who is willing to forgive and let us make a fresh start.

As parents, our purpose is to impart wisdom to our children to help them make wise decisions. When they ignore us and make a mess of things, we try not to say, 'I told you so!' Instead, we go on patiently loving them, guiding them and helping them to learn from their mistakes.

God's commandments on how to live our lives wisely are as vital to us today as they ever were. They guide us in the right ways, and if we pray and reflect on the choices we make, we can learn to grow in his wisdom.

Pray

Lord, teach me your wisdom in the way I live my life today.

Day 35

Be Enthusiastic

Fiona Castle

'Love the LORD your God, walk in all his ways, obey his commands, hold firmly to him, and serve him with all your heart and all your soul.'
Joshua 22:5

I shall always remember a comment I heard once about Christianity: 'If we're not so excited about what we've found that we want everyone to experience it, then we've not found very much.'

I could never forget the life-changing experience I had many years ago when, with the help of a faithful friend, I invited Jesus into my life to be my Lord and Saviour. I did that with serious trepidation, expecting that it would mean I would have to try even harder to be good, and to tick all the appropriate boxes to make myself a worthy believer. However, the opposite was true. I found myself letting go of all the self-effort I had failingly made over the years; instead, I was able to allow Jesus to lead me the way he wanted. The peace I experienced was life transforming and so exciting that I couldn't wait to tell everybody!

Forty-five years later, the excitement has never left me!

Pray

Lord, I thank you for the way you changed my life all those years ago. Help me to continue to share your gift of new life with all who will listen.

Day 36

Be Observant

Rachel Allcock

> He tried to get a look at Jesus, but he was too short to see over the crowd.
> Luke 19:3

The crowd around Jesus didn't care about Zacchaeus. He was a well-known 'baddie' in the neighbourhood and, as history shows, we do love to categorize people. But Jesus always spotted the person in the crowd who needed him. Jesus knew exactly what Zacchaeus needed, because he came to seek and save the lost (Luke 19:10).

Look through the eyes of Jesus. Let's look for those who wave at us this week, and check whether they're waving, or whether in fact they're in danger of drowning. My high-school English teacher had the uneasy words of the Stevie Smith poem 'Not Waving but Drowning' on her wall. You can find it online. The poem is written from the point of view of a drowned man, misunderstood by the crowd who thought he was simply larking about. The poignant words of the last verse have stuck with me and made me aware of the many people who feel they have been 'much too far out' all their lives.

Pray

Lord, open our eyes to those around us who feel they are drowning this week. Help us see behind the casual wave and brave smile of a neighbour, and to illuminate your love through a simple act of kindness.

Day 37

Be Agreeable

Rhiannon Goulding

Take control of what I say, O LORD, and guard my lips.
Psalm 141:3

There was disagreement and I had been hurt. I'd let it go for a while, but now I was going to put it straight. I'd prayed about it and worried about it, but now I was going to face it. I hate confrontation, so my palms were sweating and my voice trembled.

They were coming to stay, so I made food and tidied the house. The game face was on. And then the Holy Spirit said, 'Stop! Show love and hospitality. Be kind.' This was not on my list. I was worried this might be my last opportunity to say what I had to say. But I listened and trusted.

The next day the person in question came downstairs as I was making breakfast, apologized for their behaviour and asked for forgiveness. I couldn't believe it. God had it in hand. He was working on the person's heart. He didn't need my input. Yes, we need to face situations, but sometimes we can trust God and just wait for him to intervene and work in an individual's life.

Pray

Lord, help me to remember that you go ahead of me in every situation. Help me to trust in your love and wisdom.

Day 38

Be Assured

Mandy Catto

But as for me, I know that my Redeemer lives,
and he will stand upon the earth at last.
Job 19:25

Job's story is one of suffering, bereavement and loss. He is full of sorrow and has many questions as he struggles to understand why so much hardship has fallen on him and his family. Job's friends say that the hardship is because of his own sin.

God rebukes his friends and answers Job by unfolding a beautiful picture of his creation and majesty. He doesn't address the problem of suffering; instead, he reminds Job of his lordship and eternal power, and this is the assurance that Job needs to know that God is his Redeemer.

When my sister was diagnosed with a terminal brain tumour, I had many questions, much heartache and few answers. As I watched her physical and emotional struggles, there were many times when I asked God why this had to happen. She knew Jesus as her redeemer and felt the comfort of his presence as she endured surgeries and neared the end. As I wake up each day missing her, I have to continually return to the truth that God has always been faithful. I know he loves my sister and that we will be together in heaven at last.

Pray

Redeemer God, grant me the assurance that you live and that you will endure in your faithfulness until the end.

Day 39

Be a Giver

Fiona Castle

The free gift of God is eternal life through
Christ Jesus our Lord.
Romans 6:23

When it comes to giving gifts, we sometimes tie ourselves in knots. We know 'it's the thought that counts', but somehow we can end up worrying about how much we can afford to spend at Christmas, on birthdays and other occasions.

The gift of Jesus was the greatest gift of all, but it was also given in the humblest circumstances. A baby born in the poorest conditions went on to care for the outcast and the downtrodden, and to bring life to the world.

Why not make a list of gifts to give to people who might not expect them? They need not cost anything but time.

· Contact a forgotten friend
· Spend time with someone lonely
· Offer to babysit for a weary parent
· Invite a neighbour in for coffee.

Giving one of these gifts will do as much for you as for the recipient.

Pray

Thank you, Lord, for the great gift you have given us – our Saviour, Jesus Christ.

Day 40

Be Trusting

Fiona Castle

In him our hearts rejoice, for we trust in his holy name.
Let your unfailing love surround us, LORD, for our hope
is in you alone.
Psalm 33:21–22

The words of this Psalm were certainly true for my husband. He had a simple and very real faith, which he maintained right to the end of his life.

He was interviewed on the radio once about coping with cancer. 'If this is what God wants, then it's all right with me,' he replied. 'You get on the bus and you trust the driver.' And he did! He knew he could trust God, so he wasn't worried about the future.

It's easy to say we believe and trust God, but do we mean it when troubles come our way? Do we get anxious about the journey and try to hop off the bus and do things our own way? We're all on a journey and sometimes the road will be bumpy, with steep hills to climb. The way may be dark ahead, but if we trust the driver, we don't need to be afraid. We will reach our ultimate destination rejoicing.

Pray

Lord, as I travel along the road of life, help me to trust you, wherever you choose to take me.

Day 41

Be Supportive

Rhiannon Goulding

Timothy, my son, here are my instructions for you, based on the prophetic words spoken over you earlier. May they help you fight well in the Lord's battles.

1 Timothy 1:18

I have a Monstera plant and I like it a lot. I wanted to propagate another plant from it, but I was concerned about taking a cutting, because they don't have a good success rate. Then I read about a technique called air layering. You wrap some damp moss around a leaf joint and tie it in place, then wrap it in a clear plastic bag with air holes in it. When roots start growing into the moss, you can cut off the leaf and repot it, and get a new plant.

This made me think about starting new ministries in our church life. So often we just say, 'You look like a strong Christian. Why don't you go there and do that?' Then we place people in a new area and hope they put down roots and thrive.

Paul may have left Timothy on his own in Ephesus, but he kept in touch through his letters, building up Timothy's faith and encouraging him. Maybe we should keep those pioneers still attached to our fellowship, putting provision around them to enable them to put down roots independently, but with the support of the main plant. Then, when they are established and strong, they can successfully go it alone.

Pray

Lord Jesus, show us how to support our leaders and pastors.

Day 42

Be Accepting

Fiona Castle

But the free gift of God is eternal life through
Christ Jesus our Lord.
Romans 6:23

I was thinking about this verse when a parallel occurred to me. What if you opened the door one day and someone offered you a free gift? Your first response would probably be to ask what the catch was! But what if he said there was no catch? That the smart car by the kerb was yours to keep. The only condition was that you had to find the ignition key.

What freedom a car of your own would bring you! You'd scour the local garages trying to get that key.

God offers us a free gift that's far more valuable – and longer lasting – than the most expensive car on the market. The trouble is, hardly anyone bothers to look for the key, so they fail to find the freedom that's being offered by Jesus.

Jesus knocks at doors, but can only wait for people to open them and let him in. When they do, he freely gives them the gift of eternal life. He himself is the key to freedom, and people don't realize the joy and peace (and excitement and novelty!) they're missing unless they're willing to try it.

Pray

Thank you, Jesus, for the best gift anyone could receive, because it's free and it's not just for life – it's eternal!

Day 43

Be Spirit-filled

Rachel Allcock

'If you love me, obey my commandments. And I will ask the Father, and he will give you another Advocate, who will never leave you. He is the Holy Spirit, who leads into all truth.'
John 14:15–17

It's lovely to remember that the Hebrew word for breath is 'spirit' or *ruach*. As we read in Genesis, it was this Spirit that God breathed into Adam's nostrils to make him different from the animals. God was giving Adam his Spirit, his breath.

In the Old Testament, the Spirit visited and helped individual men and women with certain tasks. But people didn't have free access to the Spirit in those days. Everything changed when Jesus came to earth, as he was empowered by the Holy Spirit all the time. Jesus left us his Spirit, his Helper, to live in us for ever. After Pentecost it was said of the apostles that they were, 'filled with joy and with the Holy Spirit' (Acts 13:52). They were the first ones to turn the world upside down!

When you become a Christian, the same Holy Spirit comes to live inside you! The Spirit brings warmth, joy, a fresh understanding of God, healing, and so much more.

Pray

Holy Spirit, thank you that you come to plant your presence deep within all who believe and follow Jesus. I acknowledge you and I pray that I will know how to share my experience of you.

Day 44

Be Appreciative

Fiona Castle

'Look at the lilies of the field and how they grow. They don't work or make their clothing, yet Solomon in all his glory was not dressed as beautifully as they are.'
Matthew 6:28–29

Walking through meadows and woodlands can be so beautiful in springtime, yet how often do we stop to study the delicacy and fragrance of the blossom and flowers?

I remember on a walk when I was very young, sitting down in a park and picking a daisy. I pulled the petals off one by one as my mother said, 'He loves me, he loves me not!' Of course, the last petal had to be, 'He loves me!'

At that young age, I don't think I understood the intricacy and beauty of that little daisy. Flowers have different shapes and colours, but if we stopped to try to count all the petals on one magnolia tree, it would take us a week!

God created them all and their variety is amazing. The next time you go for a walk, stop for a moment to study a flower, each with its own colour and shape and size, and give thanks to God for the beauty of his creation.

Pray

How amazing, Lord, is the beauty of your creation. Open my eyes to it today, I pray.

Day 45

Be Like God

Mandy Catto

Then God said, 'Let us make human beings in our image, to
be like us.'
Genesis 1:26

What does it mean to be like God, to be made in his image?
Three times in the creation account in Genesis, we are told
that we are the only part of God's creation to be made in
this distinctive way. As we are like God – and unlike animals –
we can create, love, think rationally, reflect on spiritual and
moral ideas and make complex choices. We are not made
to look like God in some physical way, but we are the only
creatures with the capacity to ponder our own existence and
that of God. What an amazing privilege and opportunity!

Some people choose to reject the church and religion,
but almost everyone you meet is interested in some kind
of spirituality. Conversations can be sparked when we
remember that every human has been created to search for
meaning, with a God-shaped hole. We may be temporarily
distracted when people look or sound different from us, but
we are reminded to respect and revere everyone, because
they are all image-bearers of God.

Pray

Creator God, thank you for making me in your image. Help
me to reflect you as I enter into conversations with others
who may be searching. May I see you in everyone I meet
today.

Day 46

Be Forgiving

Fiona Castle

Make allowance for each other's faults, and forgive anyone
who offends you.
Colossians 3:13

Remember the Lord forgave you, and that's why you must forgive others. We are called to forgive people when they've wronged us, and called to seek forgiveness when we've wronged others. We pray this every time we pray the Lord's Prayer, but do we really mean it, or do we just say it by rote?

How humbling it is to hear stories of those who have exercised forgiveness after dreadful events like the murder of their loved ones. It's almost an instinct to want revenge. But becoming angry and nursing a grudge only makes things worse – and then we become the losers in the situation. Anger and resentment can cause health issues like high blood pressure and stress – not to mention that a constantly negative attitude makes other people try to avoid us!

If you're feeling bitter or resentful today, take stock. Let go of your pain and place it at the foot of the cross. When Jesus died there, God offered us his forgiveness. And when Jesus rose again, he offered us new life too. God loves us and forgives us.

Pray

Father, forgive my sins, as I forgive those who sin against me.

Day 47

Be Perfected

Fiona Castle

> I don't mean to say that I have already achieved these
> things or that I have already reached perfection. But I press
> on to possess that perfection for which Christ Jesus first
> possessed me.
> Philippians 3:12

Shortly before my husband died, he was asked to write his autobiography. In the last chapter, he wrote:

> This then raises the question. What do you want out of life? What is success? The answers are much clearer once you are told life is just about over. The simple, caring things then score heavily and the greed, selfishness and ego become millstones.

> Roy Castle, *Now and Then*, Robson Books 1998

In a television interview, Alan Titchmarsh asked him what his finest hour was. He answered, 'I think my finest hour is still to come. If I'm still compos mentis and I can look back on my life and smile – that will be my finest hour.'

What can you do today to prevent you looking back with regrets? People often make 'bucket lists' of things they want to do before they 'kick the bucket'. Perhaps today's the day to make a list – one that doesn't include bungee jumping, or travelling, but perhaps resolving a conflict, or contacting a forgotten friend. Let's do our best to live as Jesus teaches, and know the assurance of his peace.

Pray

Jesus, I pray that I will use each day carefully and generously, with you as my perfect example.

Day 48

Be Disciplined

Fiona Castle

To learn, you must love discipline; it is stupid to hate correction.

Proverbs 12:1

We all need discipline, whether it is in the way we live our lives, or the exercise we do, or even the diet we choose.

Discipline doesn't necessarily mean punishment: it can mean a caring and measured way of teaching the best paths to take in life. We discipline our children because we want the best for them, developing good character as well as a sense of self-worth.

In Hebrews 12:11, it says, 'No discipline is enjoyable while it is happening – it's painful! But afterwards there will be a peaceful harvest of right living for those who are trained in this way.' God's discipline is an act of love; even though it can be painful at the time, it is for our ultimate benefit.

A good schoolteacher needs to have discipline in her class, to get every pupil's attention, in order to enable them to listen and learn in an effective way. A child who refuses to obey such discipline can be a distraction to the whole class. We need to remember that our behaviour, good or bad, affects others.

Pray

Teach me, Lord, to love your discipline, even when I feel like opting out.

Day 49

Be Peaceful

Hayley Nock

Now may the Lord of peace himself give you his peace at all times and in every situation. The Lord be with you all.
2 Thessalonians 3:16

A few years ago, I was due to go into hospital for an operation. I am a nurse and I don't know whether that made it worse for me or not. All I know is that I was fearful and scared: I thought I would die. I told my friends of my fear and asked them to pray for me.

The morning of the operation was unbelievable. I woke up feeling totally peaceful. On the ward, I felt as if I was in a bubble of peace. I have never experienced anything like it before. The next thing I knew, they were coming to collect me for my operation, and I wasn't even changed or ready!

This taught me to be open with others and ask for prayer. It taught me that God is the God of Peace.

Is there someone you know who may need you to pray for them? Is there an area in your life you are struggling with? Why not ask others to pray for you?

Pray

Thank you, Lord, that you are the God of Peace for me in every situation. Thank you that you never leave me. Help me to be open with others when I need prayer.

Day 50

Be Honest

Hayley Nock

I have heard all about you, LORD. I am filled with awe by your amazing works. In this time of our deep need, help us again as you did in years gone by. And in your anger, remember your mercy.
Habakkuk 3:2

Habakkuk was a prophet who saw things in the world that troubled him, and he was neither afraid to question God nor afraid to be honest with him. He asked God lots of questions and then said he would wait to hear the answers. God replied, and his answers give Habakkuk a new perspective, which caused the prophet to respond afresh to God in worship and awe.

How often do we struggle with what we see around us, but hold our doubt and questions in? Are we ashamed of what we think or feel?

God is showing us here that we can be honest and bring all our concerns to him. If we listen to him, he will give us a new perspective.

When Habakkuk looked back on all God had done in the past, it gave him faith to ask God to move again in his time.

Pray

Awesome God, come and reveal your perspective on the questions I have. Remind me of your amazing works, so that I can praise you.

Day 51

Be Positive

Fiona Castle

'Can all your worries add a single moment to your life?'
Matthew 6:27

There's a saying, 'Today is the tomorrow you worried about yesterday, and all is well!'

To worry is human. We worry about our jobs, our finances, our children and even our elderly parents. We love them and always want the best for them. Our concern for our loved ones is natural, but worry brings stress, which robs us of our peace and can even cause breakdown. It's much more productive to hand our worries over to the Lord in prayer.

What things are you worried about today? Are you willing to place them in the Lord's hands?

> Don't worry about anything; instead, pray about everything. Tell God what you need, and thank him for all he has done. Then you will experience God's peace, which exceeds anything we can understand. (Philippians 4:6–7)

When you do this, determinedly refuse to allow negative thoughts a place in your mind. Cast them out in the strong name of Jesus.

Pray

Thank you, Lord, that you have given us victory over all the negative thoughts in our lives.

Day 52

Be an Encourager

Fiona Castle

Is there any encouragement from belonging to Christ? . . .
Any fellowship together in the Spirit?
Philippians 2:1

One of the most precious things to me is to receive a letter of encouragement. A little card with a message of love on it means far more to me than the most exotic bouquet of flowers. Often I know God has prompted someone to put pen to paper, to help me in my moment of need.

I have a friend who always makes me feel better for having been with her. She always manages to find something positive to say, and I've often seen her cheer someone up just by commenting on how well they look. We don't have to be super-spiritual to do God's work, we just need to be aware of other people, to send them on their way with a spring in their step.

This is a beautiful ministry of love, and it's open to all of us, even if we're elderly or frail and unable to be as active in the world as we once were.

Can you brighten someone's day today by a letter or word of encouragement or even a silent prayer?

Pray

Dear Lord, nudge me to look for someone to encourage each day.

Day 53

Be Thankful

Fiona Castle

And give thanks for everything to God the Father in the
name of our Lord Jesus Christ.
Ephesians 5:20

Do we take the time to show gratitude for the things people do for us? It's so easy to take other people's efforts for granted.

Do we bother to thank the person at the supermarket checkout, or do we just gather our purchases and rush off? Do we thank the person who cleans the toilets at the motorway service station? There are so many 'invisible' people who rarely get noticed or appreciated.

When I was a child, my mother always made me go to the front of the train after a journey, to thank the engine driver! It doesn't take much effort to seek people out, to have a chat and say thank you.

It isn't always easy to give thanks when things are difficult in your life, but even in tough times, a thankful heart can give us a more positive attitude. We're called to give thanks in everything, not necessarily because life is currently going the way we want or expect, but because we trust Jesus. He is the one who has rescued us, who loves us, and who gives us hope for the future, whatever it holds.

Pray

Give me a thankful heart, Lord, for all you have given me. And help me to show gratitude to others.

Day 54

Be a Wallflower

Rachel Allcock

But the wisdom from above is first of all pure. It is also peace loving, gentle at all times, and willing to yield to others. It is full of mercy and the fruit of good deeds. It shows no favouritism and is always sincere.
James 3:17

I'm not sure many of us would like to be regarded as wallflowers. The term generally describes someone who is shy or reserved. However, I don't think we should view them in such a negative light. In the garden, they are beautiful tall plants with bright, pleasant-smelling flowers. My wallflowers have flowered all year, with no special treatment or pampering.

In this verse, James extols the virtues we associate with being a wallflower. The wisdom that comes from God is not boastful or jealous. Other versions use words such as kind, helpful, genuine and sincere. It is a face without make-up. It is authentic.

I wouldn't choose to go make-up free, but I like the principle. Maybe your role and personality make centre-stage a natural position for you. I have friends who speak to hundreds but never become boastful or look down on the crowd. Whatever our jobs or our natures, we can be humble wallflowers. I want to be that gentle, peacekeeping friend who is 'quick to listen, slow to speak' (James 1:19).

Pray

Lord, help me to seek wisdom, root out jealousy and selfish ambition and plant seeds of peace.

Day 55

Be Trusting

Fiona Castle

'Don't be afraid, for I am with you.'
Isaiah 41:10

I was once interviewed as part of a programme about singleness. There were people who had never married, some who were divorced or separated and some who longed to meet their life partner.

Nowadays I am happy in my single state, but being widowed was a tremendous shock. Not only did I have to do the work of two people initially, I also had to master a whole new set of skills, such as DIY and finance. And I found social events hard at first, when I had to face them alone. That may sound pathetic to those who have always been single, but it was a real hurdle for me.

Others told more painful tales of loss and of shouldering burdens of family sickness and disability, but some stories had a happy ending when new partnerships were formed.

Not all stories have a happy ending. Not all our prayers and longings are answered in the way we hope. Yet prayer is a vital part of our relationship with God, and he invites us to bring him all our needs, and to trust him for the outcome. That way, we grow in faith, and learn to make each day count for the Kingdom.

Pray

Lord, I trust you to answer my prayers, knowing that you are in control of my life, even if the answer isn't the one I would have chosen.

Day 56

Be Teachable

Fiona Castle

Supplement your faith with . . . self-control, and self-control with patient endurance, and patient endurance with godliness, and godliness with brotherly affection, and brotherly affection with love for everyone. The more you grow like this, the more productive and useful you will be in your knowledge of our Lord Jesus Christ.

2 Peter 1:5–8

What an amazing lesson to learn! If I had studied the Bible every day of my life, I believe I would still have much to learn. In fact, even if I had tried to put these verses into practice every day, I still wouldn't have mastered it.

Peter's teaching here is not simply to obey in order to avoid punishment, but that as we give ourselves and our lives to God, we begin to experience his forgiveness and loving acceptance in order for us to live peace-filled lives.

All this is to enable us to be productive and useful wherever God places us. Whether we are at school, at work, or in our homes, we can spread the Good News, not just with words but also with our love for others.

Pray

Dear God, help me to learn daily from your word and to have the determination to put it into practice.

Day 57

Be Flexible

Fiona Castle

And though they worshipped the LORD, they continued to
follow their own gods according to the religious customs of the
nations from which they came. And this is still going on today.
2 Kings 17:33–34

The Old Testament is filled with stories of traditions: some of them remind people of God's promises; others belonged to the nations that did not fear God.

In families, we all develop traditions which bring us together for celebrations such as Christmas and New Year. Often these traditions are passed on through the generations. However, some traditions become rituals which we follow because we've always done things that way, rather than focussing on the purpose.

Sadly, this can happen today in our churches and services, too. Sometimes changes cause confusion and even annoyance.

When a new church leader arrives with fresh ideas for ways to draw in the younger generation, people who are set in their ways find it very difficult. I know of a church which split because of a decision to remove the pews and replace them with chairs!

We must be careful not to get stuck in our traditions, but rather embrace the change that comes with new life in the Holy Spirit, so that our worship is always fresh and honouring to God.

Pray

Lord, help me to embrace change, when it brings honour to your name.

Day 58

Be a Listener

Fiona Castle

Timely advice is lovely, like golden apples in a silver basket.
Proverbs 25:11

If you had a difficult decision to make and needed sound advice, who would you go to? You need someone you can trust, who is a good listener and who wants the best for you.

Teachers have great responsibilities, as they give advice to their pupils and students. Some have the wisdom to impart advice with encouragement and positivity, but others find it all too easy to criticize and produce a sense of failure and inadequacy in response. Which kind of teacher would you prefer?

Sometimes the best way to give advice is to listen and then ask relevant questions, rather than offering solutions.

The book of Proverbs has many verses about advice. 'Spouting off before listening to the facts is both shameful and foolish' (18:13). 'Fools think their own way is right, but the wise listen to others' (12:15).

We mustn't use advice as an excuse to lecture, but if others share their problems, we should listen humbly and prayerfully, and respond with thoughtful reasoning and with the person's best interests at heart.

Pray

Help me, Lord, not to rush to give advice, but to listen prayerfully.

Day 59

Be Unafraid

Fiona Castle

'Don't be afraid . . . I bring you good news that will bring
great joy to all people.'
Luke 2:10

Familiar words at Christmas. But what do they mean for the
rest of the year? It's those first three words which bring the
verse alive for me.

What holds people back from committing their lives to
Christ? The biggest factor must be fear:

- Fear that their comfortable lives will be turned upside down.
- Fear that they'll be laughed at.
- Fear that God will ask too much from them.

Suddenly the angel's words are relevant to everyone: God
is telling his people not to be afraid. He brings good news,
peace and joy.

What wonderful words they are. They don't need to be only
brought out at Christmas: the Good News is for every day of
the year. And not only is it good, but it's available for everyone.

Won't you join me in sharing it with one of your friends, so
they can discover the joy of eternal life which you found
when you received Jesus Christ as your Saviour and Lord?

Pray

Thank you, Lord Jesus, that through you we have good news
to share with others – the assurance of eternal life. We are so
grateful for such a gift.

Day 60

Be an Intercessor

Fiona Castle

Always be joyful. Never stop praying. Be thankful in all circumstances, for this is God's will for you who belong to Christ Jesus.
1 Thessalonians 5:16–18

I have never minded long car journeys. When the family were younger I was always busy, and a long drive was a rare opportunity for uninterrupted prayer!

But one day I had an amazing experience. As I drove, I began to feel warm and cocooned, as if a soft blanket of love surrounded me. I asked the Lord what it meant, and the reply came, 'Someone is praying for you.'

We seldom know who those saints are who support us in prayer. I do know one, though. When I was young, I had an uncle in California. On the few occasions we met, he would try to share the Good News with me, but at that time, I just wasn't able to accept it. He never minded, but just went on quietly praying for me. I was so thankful that years later, after I became a Christian, I was able to thank him and rejoice with him that I had found Jesus as my Saviour.

No prayer we make in intercession for others is ever wasted. It may be the very time they desperately need strength or protection, and it's our privilege to join with the Spirit in linking them to God's grace.

Pray

Father, I thank you for those who faithfully support us in prayer, whatever the circumstances.

Day 61

Be Accepting

Fiona Castle

Just as our bodies have many parts and each part has a special function, so it is with Christ's body. We are many parts of one body, and we all belong to each other.
Romans 12:4–5

One of my favourite autumn activities is picking blackberries. I wander along the hedgerows, peacefully praising God for the bountiful harvest.

I always find the juiciest blackberries are just out of reach, and I topple into the brambles and nettles as I try to stretch just that little bit higher. But often I don't need to try so hard. If I take the trouble to turn over the lower leaves, some of the best clusters are hiding under there, just waiting to be picked!

It reminds me of the gifts of the Spirit. We don't need to strain to reach for the most prominent gifts: they may not be our best fit. God will show us the gifts he has for us, to be used for his glory.

He has a plan for each of us, and like those blackberries, his gifts are richly satisfying – if we will only look, and reach out, and receive what he is longing to give us.

Pray

Lord, I'm willing to use whatever gifts you give me, to serve you.

Day 62

Be Proactive

Rachel Allcock

Philip ran over and heard the man reading from the prophet
Isaiah. Philip asked, 'Do you understand what you are
reading?'
Acts 8:30

An angel tells Philip to go along the desert road, and the
Holy Spirit tells him to walk beside the Ethiopian's carriage.
He hears the man reading, and at this point, Philip must
have understood the Spirit's guiding. He asks the man if he
understands what he's reading, and the Ethiopian urges him
to join him. Philip takes the Scripture and uses it as a starting
point to tell the Good News about Jesus.

Recently, I heard of a Christian woman who answered the
phone to yet another scam caller. Instead of replying with
abuse or putting the phone down, she felt the Holy Spirit
prompt her to speak kindly to the man and offer to pray for
him. The caller opened up about how much he hated the job
but was desperate for the money to feed his family. She wasn't
physically there, running alongside his carriage, but the
same Holy Spirit who worked in Philip's life was prompting
her to reach out over the phone and show compassion.

Pray

Holy Spirit, help us to be proactive in explaining the Good
News when we are led by you.

Day 63

Be Brave

Fiona Castle

So be strong and courageous! Do not be afraid and do not panic before them. For the LORD your God will personally go ahead of you. He will neither fail you nor abandon you.
Deuteronomy 31:6

Courage is determination to do the right thing for the right reason, however difficult it might seem. Courage isn't the absence of fear; courage makes fear ineffective and gives us a confident assurance that we can overcome. There is a saying that courage is fear that has said its prayers. Very true!

What are your fears? Where do you lack courage? Is it starting a new job or attempting a new challenge? I can understand such fears. The first time I was asked to speak at a coffee morning and tell my story of becoming a Christian, I was so nervous I couldn't eat for three days! I had to face those fears, and I still have to do so today.

But how much better to have a try – even if you fail – than not to bother and then wonder, what if? Decide to take up a challenge today, even if it's way out of your comfort zone. Our true courage comes from God, because he is sovereign and we can trust him to help us.

Pray

Thank you, Lord, that we can trust you to help us when our courage fails.

Day 64

Be in the Word

Mandy Catto

All Scripture is inspired by God and is useful to teach us what is true and to make us realize what is wrong in our lives. It corrects us when we are wrong and teaches us to do what is right.

2 Timothy 3:16–17

My friend has a pile of devotional books beside her bed. Each morning she reaches for her Bible and uses the devotionals to inspire her, reading one writer after another until she feels God speaking to her. She laughs as she tells me this, and she knows that maybe she is keeping going until she reads what she wants to hear. But I love that she wrestles with these readings and turns to the Bible to hear from God every morning.

We know that we can trust the Holy Spirit to use these divinely inspired words to talk to us today, and every day. The Bible is there for the positives: for the model of the right way to live, soaked in truth. And it's also there for the negatives: the correction of our mistakes and disobedience. Perhaps we prefer to read about the positives than the negatives. But they all come from God and they guide our walk with him. They enable us to know the Trinity – Father, Son and Holy Spirit – and to live our lives fully engaged and thriving.

Pray

Thank you, God, for the Bible, your living, loving word. Help me to read it and live it every day.

Day 65

Be Gentle

Fiona Castle

A gentle answer deflects anger, but hard words make tempers flare.
Proverbs 15:1

A gentle spirit in a person brings calm into a situation. There is peace in the heart of a gentle person, which can make a positive difference, whether in the home, at school or in the workplace.

When my granddaughter was 5 years old and had just started school, she was staying with me while her parents were away. It was always difficult to get her ready for school, so I indulged her by allowing her to watch television while she ate her breakfast (not recommended!). I asked her twice to hurry or she'd be late for school. She obviously wasn't listening to me, so I raised my voice and spoke sternly. She replied, 'If you ask me nicely, Granny, I might do as you say!'

Jesus said, 'A tree is identified by its fruit . . . A good person produces good things from the treasury of a good heart' (Luke 6:44–45).

Next time you need to get a message across, try being gentle!

Pray

Lord, renew a gentle spirit in me each day, so that I have the right response to everyone.

Day 66

Be an Enabler

Rhiannon Goulding

'Fill in the valleys, and level the mountains and hills.
Straighten the curves, and smooth out the rough places.'
Isaiah 40:4

My legs were getting red and blotchy below my pretty skirt as I forged ahead at the front of the single-file procession. I was getting stung and scratched again and again by the overgrown nettles and brambles. I really did want to get down to the golden sand of the beach and this winding path was the only way. My cool-box was getting heavy, sweat was dripping down my face and I was wondering if it was worth it.

I sat down on the cool-box for a rest and my husband, in his long trousers and appropriate shoes, overtook me, stamping down the nettles and bending back the brambles along the path as he went. When I set off again, suddenly my journey became easier and my legs had a bit of a break.

How often has someone walked in front of us making the path ahead easier? How often does God go before us in our life, removing obstacles, straightening the curves and smoothing out the rough places? And what if we could be that person for the people coming behind us, pushing back the nettles and clearing the way for progress?

Pray

Lord Jesus, show me how to encourage and enable other people, just as your Holy Spirit smooths the way for me.

Day 67

Be Rested

Fiona Castle

'Come to me, all of you who are weary and carry heavy burdens, and I will give you rest. Take my yoke upon you. Let me teach you, because I am humble and gentle at heart, and you will find rest for your souls.'
Matthew 11:28–29

Stress is a big problem in today's society, with demands in the workplace or home and financial concerns as well. Are you weary and carrying heavy burdens today?

Jesus' answer isn't that he'll pop you into bed with a hot water bottle, sing you a lullaby and let you sleep! He asks you to follow his example. When life was busy for him, he would take time to disappear from the crowds to rest and pray. Doing this enables you to find peace for your soul, even in the midst of difficult situations.

Look at the things that are causing you stress. Is every one of them really necessary, and what God has inspired you to do? If not, perhaps today is an opportunity to lay down your heavy burdens, and rest.

'His peace will guard your hearts and minds as you live in Christ Jesus' (Philippians 4:7).

Pray

Lord Jesus, I lay my burdens down before you right now, and ask that you would give me rest as I seek your plans for my future.

Day 68

Be Sensitive

Fiona Castle

Cry out for insight, and ask for understanding. Search
for them as you would for silver; seek them like hidden
treasures. Then you will understand what it means to fear the
LORD, and you will gain knowledge of God.
Proverbs 2:3–5

Sometimes our efforts to be supportive are not as tactful as they might be, and we feel we're saying the wrong thing. We might know the basic facts about a person's life which are causing them trouble, but without understanding their background or circumstances.

When I was going through the grieving process, I found it disconcerting to have people say, 'I understand exactly how you're feeling.' I wanted to say, 'No, you don't!' But I had to accept that they were trying to be helpful and at least hadn't avoided me.

Perhaps it would be more sensitive to suggest that you can only try to imagine how someone might be feeling. In fact, sometimes actions speak louder than words: a hug, a listening ear or just an offer of practical help can be encouraging and consoling.

So it is with God. We can only understand a fraction of who he is and how we can live our lives for him. But he understands us completely!

Pray

Father God, I cry to you for insight and understanding. Help me to live wisely and to be sensitive to the needs of others.

Day 69

Be Together

Hayley Nock

Let us think of ways to motivate one another to acts of love and good works. And let us not neglect our meeting together, as some people do, but encourage one another, especially now that the day of his return is drawing near.
Hebrews 10:24–25

I answered a text message in a hurry without reading it properly, and said, 'Yes'. Later I realized I had agreed and paid to enter the Wolf Run. It's a 10 km run with major obstacles – you can only enter as a team of five or more, and they needed me! There was no letting them down.

But I was not a runner! So we started to train. When I was lazing on the sofa, they would call me and I'd have to go and run. I enjoyed being with them and felt honoured to be part of the team, but it was hard.

It was scary just reading the disclaimer for the race. I was tired after the warm-up. The obstacles were unbelievable. We worked as a team, pushing, pulling, dragging and encouraging each other over each obstacle. But we did it. What an amazing buzz, satisfaction and sense of togetherness!

In life, we are not meant to go it alone. God's plan is for us to be in a community and grow in faith together. Let's join that community, be part of it and invite others to join too. And let's push, pull, believe in, and encourage each other on.

Pray

Dear Lord, thank you that you created us to be part of a real family community. Show me who I can encourage and help today, and bring people alongside me too.

Day 70

Be Willing

Fiona Castle

> Imitate God, therefore, in everything you do, because you are his dear children. Live a life filled with love, following the example of Christ.
> Ephesians 5:1–2

Jesus had many disciples, from whom he chose his twelve apostles to be with him wherever he went. They were a varied bunch, from different backgrounds. They weren't chosen because they were particularly talented, but simply because they were his willing followers and some faced unpleasant and untimely deaths because of their faith.

It should be an encouragement to us that although we may not have the right credentials, degrees or qualifications, we still have the opportunity to follow him if we have a willing heart. The disciples slipped up and made mistakes but, apart from Judas Iscariot, they were faithful in pursuing the purpose Jesus had for them.

We may not feel particularly talented or equipped, but remember – God doesn't call the equipped, he equips the called. And we're *all* called!

Pray

Dear Lord, I thank you that you have called me to follow you. Help me to be faithful to that calling.

Day 71

Be Helpful

Fiona Castle

Two people are better off than one, for they can help each
other succeed. If one person falls, the other can reach out
and help. But someone who falls alone is in real trouble.
Ecclesiastes 4:9–10

My son, who is passionate about doing what he can to save
the planet, has just taught me a lesson about trees that has
amazed me!

He said that, probably, we have all had leisurely walks through
woodlands. Yet perhaps we do not realize that the roots of
the trees deliberately connect with each other to form a
support system, using a variety of fungi to communicate.
One might have access to water, or different nutrients, or
sunlight. No one tree has access to all, but they share what
they have and help one another. That way, they are all able to
grow and thrive and cope with the storms of life.

What a wonderful illustration of how we, as humans, can
share our resources! We can help others in need, so that we
can all thrive effectively, for the purpose of the Kingdom.
Trees need each other and so do we, to complement each
other's strengths and weaknesses.

Pray

Dear God, thank you for helping me understand the intricate
complexities of your world. Help me to use every opportunity
to be generous and helpful to others.

Day 72

Be Positive

Fiona Castle

Instead, be filled with the Holy Spirit, singing psalms and hymns and spiritual songs among yourselves, and making music to the Lord in your hearts. And give thanks for everything to God the Father in the name of our Lord Jesus Christ.

Ephesians 5:18–20

I heard a story of a woman who was always negative about everything, to the extent that people began to avoid her when they saw her. She constantly focussed on the difficulties in her life, which filled her with self-pity and anxiety.

A friend one day suggested she should take up a three-week challenge of being positive and thankful for every daily experience. She agreed to give it a try and discovered that concentrating on all the positive things in her life broke the bonds of her constant negative thinking.

She learned to focus on being thankful, whatever happened each day. It had a transforming effect on her and it eventually became a lifetime strategy for facing problems, which drew her closer to the Lord.

God does not promise a trouble-free life, but he promises never to leave or forsake us.

Pray

Father, help me to focus not on my problems but on the security of knowing that you are always with me, through good times and bad.

Day 73

Be Respectful

Fiona Castle

'There is no greater love than to lay down one's life for
one's friends.'
John 15:13

My brother-in-law was a patient man who never complained.
One day, however, caught up in the rush on a London Tube
station, he was pushed over. 'Get a move on!' came a voice
from behind him.

He limped his way onto the train and confronted his abuser.
'I can't run,' he said. 'I got this injury in the Second World War,
fighting for people like you!' There was silence.

Sometimes I watch people in the street. Why are they
frowning? What's going on in their lives that makes them
look so worried? Of course, we'll never know the answers, but
we can always pray for them.

When we recall the millions who have died, been injured or
bereaved in wars, we remember those sacrifices with thanks –
and resolve to try to make the world a better, less aggressive
place. We may not be called to literally lay down our life for
our friends. But as we think of those who have done so, let's
be reminded to act with kindness and love in every area of
our lives.

Pray

Forgive me, Lord, when I have failed to understand or
appreciate the many people who have made sacrifices for
others, whether through wars or persecution.

Day 74

Be Grateful

Rachel Allcock

> I could have no greater joy than to hear that my children are following the truth.
> 3 John 4

Did you grow up going to Sunday school camps, Bible camps or youth groups? If so, what are your enduring memories of those times? For me, apart from all the chatty bus rides and third helpings of ice cream, one of the most memorable aspects has to be the people who mentored me – the leaders. I used to hang on every word they said. When we take our own children to Christian holiday camps, the leaders generously write messages in birthday cards over the week and these are sent out throughout the year. The smiles and memories that come flooding back make these cards even more treasured than the ones with money floating out!

I imagine that Gaius, the recipient of this letter, also hung on every word his friend and teacher wrote. There must have been a huge smile on his face when he read those first few sentences and learned that his mentor was proud of him. John goes on to thank Gaius for being hospitable to the travelling teachers, and he continues to teach his friend through this short but encouraging letter.

Have you ever thought to write to the leaders who befriended you in your youth?

Pray

Lord, thank you for those who helped me in the early days of my faith. Help me to find a way to thank them, if possible.

Day 75

Be Clear-sighted

Fiona Castle

Yes, everything else is worthless when compared with the infinite value of knowing Christ Jesus my Lord.
Philippians 3:8

Last year I visited a seaside resort towards the end of the holiday season. The amusement arcades drew the eye with flashing signs and glittering lights, inviting people to spend money and enjoy themselves. I pictured the little parade of shops in winter: dark and empty, with rain-streaked windows – not an alluring sight.

But on the other side of the sand dunes, the North Sea would always remain the same – just as majestic, with its rolling waves and churning white horses, while storm clouds raced each other to the horizon.

Generations have looked at those same waters with awe, and wondered at the grandeur of God's handiwork. Its permanence was reassuring, confronting the row of tawdry pleasure palaces. God's creation is there when all man's efforts fade and crumble.

In a similar way, we need to hold onto things that have lasting importance. All earthly human desires will fade. All that will survive in eternity are the things with which Jesus is associated. Everything else is ultimately worthless.

Let's be thankful that Jesus offers us things of eternal value.

Pray

Thank you, Jesus, that the eternal gift you provide makes all human desires fade into oblivion.

Day 76

Be Thankful

Jaz Potter

Give thanks to the LORD, for he is good! His faithful love endures for ever.

Psalm 107:1

We can all identify with the feeling when you get something new and you really enjoy it: it's so exciting. But after you've had that thing for a while, the novelty wears off and you begin to look for the next 'I want'. It's easy to fall into this habit; our culture sets us up to think this way, and it's how advertising works.

However, I once heard a psychologist say that if you *choose* to stay grateful for your new item, the original feelings stay with you. At first, I wasn't sure about this. But then we got a new front door. I had designed the glass myself, so it was particularly special and I loved it. It sounds trivial, but I decided that every time I opened the door I would deliberately choose to be grateful for it. Now, many years later, I can confirm that my little experiment proves the rule. The novelty of having a door I designed has never worn off.

I love how science proves what God taught us from the beginning. We are called to cultivate a grateful heart. This thankfulness is widely recognized as essential to our well-being.

Pray

Dear God, help me to be thankful for all your provision today. Help me to see your hand at work even in the small things. I choose to be grateful.

Day 77

Be Innovative

Fiona Castle

He has created us anew in Christ Jesus, so we can do the
good things he planned for us long ago.
Ephesians 2:10

There is a saying that the greatest mistake a person can make
is to be afraid of making one. It is so important to seek God's
purpose and plans for our lives, so that we can live life to the
full and make the most of the opportunities he gives us.

We are all unique, and express ourselves in different ways,
so we don't need to be jealous of others or feel inferior. We
won't always get it right, but as long as we seek to be God
honouring in our creativity, we don't need to fear. I always
admire people who maximize opportunities and are not
afraid to take risks with new ideas and inspiration.

We need to pray for the leaders who encourage us to move
forward in faith for the future, enabling us to see God's path
for us through the wisdom of the Holy Spirit.

Don't be afraid to try something new. Remember, a lone
amateur built the Ark; a large team of professionals built the
Titanic!

Pray

Dear Lord, give me the courage to face the future, knowing
that you walk ahead of me to show me the way.

Day 78

Be Light-hearted

Rachel Allcock

A cheerful heart is good medicine, but a broken spirit saps a person's strength.
Proverbs 17:22

At my primary school, the headmaster could be found at the end of a long, creaky corridor, in a room full of smoke. From what I remember, he rarely left this office. Considering his aloofness, my headmaster did have a profound impact on my life, purely by giving his pupils a motto to live by: 'If in doubt whether to laugh or cry, laugh every time.'

Since I am always close to both laughter and tears, this motto has helped tip the balance when I'm not sure which way to go! I've found it's been helpful to learn to laugh at myself. Sharing embarrassing stories can help to break the ice. Go out, see friends and bring life to someone else's broken spirit. Choose to laugh, choose to be cheerful.

Just as with exercise, we may not always 'feel like it' but it is restorative and preventative medicine – take every opportunity for cheerfulness you can. Joy or grief of the mind impacts the strength of the body: the NIV version says 'a crushed spirit dries up the bones.' So don't pull out of that party at the last minute! It might be the shot of calcium and vitamin D that your body is crying out for.

Pray

Help me see the value of laughter and joy and share this with others.

Day 79

Be a Believer

Fiona Castle

'I tell you the truth, those who listen to my message and believe in God who sent me have eternal life.'
John 5:24

My sister once made the interesting statement that there is a difference between churchianity and Christianity! Personally, I believed in God from early childhood, but I thought going to church was all I needed. I was 35 when I discovered the real truth about Christianity.

Some people go to church just out of habit. Some think of it like insurance (a way of getting on the right side of God), others like a hospital to heal their wounds. But once you know Jesus, church is so much more; it is a life-changing experience which equips us and gives us strength to face all that happens to us in life, and allows us to pass that love and security on to the next generation.

When the Holy Spirit lives within us, faith is no longer a ritual to observe, but an entirely different way of facing each day. We love to gather as a church, not only to study the truth of the Bible but also to learn to apply it, in order to be effective in the world around us. We are all different, but we are a family in Christ.

Pray

Lord, I believe. Help me to share your message with truth and reality.

Day 80

Be Afflicted

Rhiannon Goulding

Jacob named the place Peniel (which means 'face of God'),
for he said, 'I have seen God face to face, yet my life has been
spared.' The sun was rising as Jacob left Peniel, and he was
limping because of the injury to his hip.
Genesis 32:30–31

I was telling a friend about a difficult situation I had dealt with years ago, and I cried. She said, 'If you still cry about it, you're not healed from the pain.' This stuck with me, but I knew it wasn't right. I was forgiven, I had moved on, but the situation had affected me deeply. It had left me with a limp – a permanent reminder of the battle I'd been through. We bear scars from the fights we've survived.

I hated my limp at the beginning – it caused me pain. But I have come to accept and even appreciate it. It keeps me grounded, keeps me always looking for grace, stops me judging and helps me to realize we don't always understand what other people have been through.

We have to make allowances for other people's injuries. I hope I never forget the lesson I learned and pray I won't feel the pressure to fight the tears when I think of it. I'm conscious of keeping an eye out for other people who have been hurt like me. My injury has become my strength.

Pray

Jesus, teach me to treat people with tenderness and love.

Day 81

Be Thoughtful

Fiona Castle

Do everything without complaining and arguing, so that no one can criticize you. Live clean, innocent lives as children of God, shining like bright lights in a world full of crooked and perverse people.
Philippians 2:14–15

I once read a story about a man who offered a colleague a lift home after a terrible day in which everything had gone wrong. Once home, his friend invited him in to meet his family, and as they approached the house, he saw the man reach out to a small tree and touch it with both hands. When he opened the door there was a tremendous transformation: he stood straighter and he was smiling as he hugged his children.

When asked about this, he replied, 'Oh, that's my trouble tree. My work problems don't belong at home, so I hang them there before I go in. Funny thing is, there always seem fewer the next morning!'

It's such a good illustration of how our attitudes can influence everything around us.

Let's pray that the love and peace of Jesus will shine through us to those we meet, wherever our day takes us. Let's ask him to help us make someone's day better because of our thoughtfulness.

Pray

Dear God, prevent my lips from saying negative words, rather than thoughtful and encouraging ones.

Day 82

Be Trusting

Mandy Catto

Trust in the LORD with all your heart; do not depend on your own understanding. Seek his will in all you do, and he will show you which path to take.
Proverbs 3:5–6

The year 2020 was filled with promise as my son's wedding approached at the beginning of April. Plans were made, dresses were bought and plane tickets were purchased, and we looked forward to the gathering of relatives and friends in a historic church in Washington DC.

The threat of the coronavirus seemed distant until it began to dominate the news. First the grandparents had to cancel, then the British relatives all realized they couldn't fly in. Soon it became obvious that even local friends and family would not be able to attend. Should the wedding be cancelled?

My son and his beautiful fiancée kept moving forward in faith, trying to be safe, wise and positive. The wedding certificate was ready and my husband was the officiant, so it was technically possible. Cake ingredients were borrowed from various friends; flowers were left on the doorstep by the only online florist open. We trusted in God and went ahead with a quiet ceremony with ten of us there. Not what anyone had expected, but we were grateful to be healthy and felt God's presence throughout. He was close to us and blessed us with a joyful day.

Pray

Father, thank you that you are a strong refuge in times of turmoil. Help me to trust in you as I rest in your presence.

Day 83

Be Joyful

Fiona Castle

We were filled with laughter, and we sang for joy. And the other nations said, 'What amazing things the LORD has done for them.'
Psalm 126:2

I woke up feeling grim, and I knew it was going to be 'one of those days'. I knew I had a fever without reaching for the thermometer. I struggled out of bed, knowing that a busy day lay ahead. So, after a quiet time during which I appealed to God for strength, I plunged into the day's activities. I took my mother to visit a friend, but didn't tell either of them how ill I was feeling.

The following day, the friend phoned to say how lovely it had been to see me, and looking so well, too! 'You seemed so happy that it really made my day,' she said. 'You made me feel happy too.' If only she knew!

It made me realize how, as Christians, we can express our joy through our faces as well as with our mouths. No matter what's going on inside us, we can still brighten other people's days by a cheery word or smile. After all, as Christians we have so much to smile about, don't we?

Pray

Lord, help me to brighten someone's day today, knowing that a simple smile or cheery word can make a difference.

Day 84

Be Ready

Fiona Castle

The LORD is my shepherd; I have all that I need.
Psalm 23:1

When my children were young, I found it almost impossible to find time to pray. There was always something that needed attention.

One of the pastors of my church pointed me to Psalm 23: he told me that a shepherd always went ahead of the sheep to make sure that they had a safe place to graze and drink. I gradually began to see the picture of a loving God who led me like that. It wasn't that God didn't offer me opportunities to be quiet and alone with him, but rather that I wasn't spotting them.

The next day, I asked the Lord to show me the time and place he had identified for my moment of peace. And it came. Since then I've often sensed God telling me to stop what I'm doing and turn to him. When I'm obedient – and I can't always say I am – it's always a blessing.

Do take the opportunities God is going to give you today to meet with him. Be ready to identify the moment God speaks to you and says, 'Come and spend a few moments with me.' You'll not regret it.

Pray

Dear loving Father, let me hear your voice telling me when to draw aside to replenish my mind and spirit.

Day 85

Be Honest

Fiona Castle

> About an hour later someone else insisted, 'This must be one of them, because he is a Galilean, too.' But Peter said, 'Man, I don't know what you are talking about.'
> Luke 22:59–60

Peter denied that he knew Jesus for his own safety. He knew the consequences of admitting he was one of the disciples, so he tried to protect himself. However, he eventually and sorrowfully had to admit what he had done.

I don't suppose anyone is exempt from making excuses for one reason or another . . . we're late for a meeting, or forgot to phone or visit someone. We can always blame someone or something that was beyond our control.

Excuses are a cover-up – an attempt to make us look good when we're not. We need to be strong enough to take responsibility for our actions and humble enough to apologize for a made-up story. I remember my mother saying, when I was a child, 'Be sure your sins will find you out!' I might lie, or make an excuse and get away with it, but God knows the truth and a sense of guilt will prevail until I admit it.

Thankfully, God forgives and understands our weaknesses and allows us to make a fresh start.

Pray

Help me to be honest, Lord, and not try to make excuses about my failures.

Day 86

Be Active

Fiona Castle

For we are God's masterpiece. He has created us anew in Christ Jesus, so we can do the good things he planned for us long ago.
Ephesians 2:10

I'm not particularly a fan of football, but occasionally I watch a game on TV. When I do, I'm often shocked by the way the spectators yell criticism from the stands and shout instructions from the comfort of their seats, even though they've probably never played a game in their lives!

When we're active in our work as Christians, we have to be aware that onlookers will be only too ready to criticize what we're doing. We have to stand firm in our faith, assured that, although we won't get everything right, we're doing God's will, and working to further the purposes of God's kingdom.

Constructive criticism may come from people who have genuine concerns and do their best to help us. But we must beware of those who just want things to be done their way, for their benefit, without bothering to become involved themselves.

We have to rely on prayer and trust in the Holy Spirit. God knows our hearts. Let's not allow ourselves to be distracted from being obedient and serving him.

Pray

Help me, Lord, not to shout from the sidelines, but to be active in your purpose for my life.

Day 87

Be Persevering

Fiona Castle

Each time he said, 'My grace is all you need. My power works best in weakness.' So now I am glad to boast about my weaknesses, so that the power of Christ can work through me.

2 Corinthians 12:9

Failure isn't final. We all fail at different times – whether it's school exams, sports or not getting the hoped-for new job at work. Sometimes it's trying to keep our temper, or being considerate!

Most inventors have to experiment many times before succeeding with a new product. Beethoven's music teacher declared him hopeless at composing! Fred Astaire's first audition described him as, 'Can't act. Slightly bald. Can dance a little.' Only when you accept failure as final are you finally a failure.

As Christians, we can have the courage and perseverance to avoid failure or to prevail through it, because we know it's part of God's plan for our lives. Our failures along the way can teach us helpful lessons if we don't admit defeat and give up.

Much later, with hindsight, we can look back on the ways our lives have panned out. That's when we recognize that some failures have led to the best decisions we have made in our lives.

Pray

Thank you, Lord, that you understand my weaknesses, and that you still love me.

Day 88

Be Modest

Rachel Allcock

'You have been deceived by your own pride because you live in a rock fortress and make your home high in the mountains. "Who can ever reach us way up here?" you ask boastfully. But even if you soar as high as eagles and build your nest among the stars, I will bring you crashing down,' says the LORD.

Obadiah 1:3–4

I once knew someone who thought he was invincible. He didn't eat vegetables but prided himself on his physique. He drove way too fast but never got caught. I'd listen to his escapades and extravagances, then lecture him about taking his vitamins and slowing down.

The ancient Edomites in today's verse have been deceived by their own pride. The prophet Obadiah does not hold back in revealing God's rebuke for refusing to help defend Jerusalem (and their cousins) and then rejoicing in Israel's misfortune.

We all have a tendency towards pride and delusion. Convinced by some latest fad or health craze, we think we can outwit death and disease, or protect our family with every type of insurance. God wants us to make wise choices, but obsessing over success or health is arrogant and unwise. God doesn't want us to build a fortress that blocks him out.

Pray

Lord, help me run to your strong tower instead of trying to build my own.

Day 89

Be Adaptable

Esther Tregilgas

Yes, I try to find common ground with everyone, doing everything I can to save some. I do everything to spread the Good News and share in its blessings.

1 Corinthians 9:22–23

I've just dropped my youngest daughter off at pre-school for the first time: she wandered straight in with barely a backward glance and half a wave. All my children reacted differently at this point. One became very quiet, trying to be brave. One was desperate to start and ran in without looking back. And the third had to be handed over kicking and screaming! My four daughters look very similar but each has her own personality, temperament, spirit and desire.

How different God has made each of them, and each of us. We need different things and different styles and approaches suit us.

In the verses preceding this one Paul explains that to the Jews he was a Jew, to the Gentiles a Gentile and to the weak he became weak. Paul didn't change his beliefs or the message of Jesus, but he changed his behaviour and approach.

My neighbour has very different beliefs from my best friend. They have different starting points in their views about Jesus and about the church. They each need a different approach, but they both still need Jesus.

Pray

Father, please teach me to adapt myself to reach the people around me.

Day 90

Be Grateful

Fiona Castle

Be thankful in all circumstances, for this is God's will for you
who belong to Christ Jesus.
1 Thessalonians 5:18

Perhaps you know the old hymn by Johnson Oatman which says, 'Count your blessings, name them one by one, and it will surprise you what the Lord has done.' Do we always count our blessings? Or are we more likely to count and complain about things that are difficult, annoying or tiresome?

Are you a 'glass half full' or a 'glass half empty' person? Do you always focus on the negative side of life and of people and their opinions, or do you look for the positive and good things, in order to encourage people?

I have had the privilege, over the years, of visiting many countries where the poverty is extreme, living quarters are shacks or tents and food supplies are minimal. Yet the people have been among the happiest, most joyful I've ever met, who are grateful for small mercies. It is always a very humbling experience.

As a result, each night when I climb into my warm bed, I thank God for the comforts of central heating, electricity, clean clothes and food in the fridge. How could I not have a grateful heart?

Pray

Lord God, help us to maintain a spirit of constant gratitude through our lives for all you have given us.

Day 91

Be Joyful

Mandy Catto

And Nehemiah continued, 'Go and celebrate with a feast of rich foods and sweet drinks, and share gifts of food with people who have nothing prepared. This is a sacred day before our LORD. Don't be dejected and sad, for the joy of the LORD is your strength!'

Nehemiah 8:10

I love these words from Nehemiah, encouraging us to party! To share the best foods and sweet drinks spontaneously when others are unprepared – on sacred days, too! Perhaps this gives us licence to enjoy our favourite food and fun together on Sundays and holidays?

When Nehemiah issued this declaration, the people had just read together from the Law and were feeling low and dejected. Nehemiah exhorted them to turn their weeping into rejoicing, not because of their circumstances, but because of God. It is the deep joy that comes from the Lord, emanating from his character and his blessings, that leads us to celebrate.

Who can you meet and celebrate with today? What food do you have that you can share with someone who has nothing? How can you display the joy of the Lord and show that it is your strength?

Pray

Lord, thank you that you can turn despair into joy. Show me the people in my life and community that I can share this joy with. Guide me towards opportunities to celebrate.

Day 92

Be Faithful

Fiona Castle

Let's not get tired of doing what is good. At just the right time we will reap a harvest of blessing if we don't give up.
Galatians 6:9

Many years ago, a young man asked John Stott to pray for a friend who was 'going into the ministry'.

'But we're *all* in ministry,' the scholar responded. 'If we belong to Christ, we're all serving him whatever we're doing.'

It's true! Whether we're serving in a shop, sweeping the streets or running a multi-million-pound business, if we belong to Christ, we should aim to work to his glory. Some people feel their work is unimportant, but God doesn't see it that way. He sees the heart.

Recently a pastor met someone he hadn't seen since he was a child. This lady was thrilled to meet him again after so long. 'I knew God's hand was on you,' she said, 'so I prayed for you every day for twenty years.'

What a ministry! An unknown warrior prayed faithfully, without ever knowing if she would discover the outcome.

We may not know until we reach eternity whether our lives helped others, but we need to remain faithful to his calling, wherever that may lead us.

Pray

Dear Lord, because we are all precious to you, help us to seek your purpose for our lives, wherever that might be.

Day 93

Be Humble

Rachel Allcock

All honour and glory to God for ever and ever!
He is the eternal King, the unseen one who never dies; he
alone is God. Amen.
1 Timothy 1:17

A travelling fair comes to my home town every September, thanks to an ancient royal statute. The main street is closed off, and various rides and amusements take the place of the traffic. As teenagers, we would ride the rickety Ferris wheel. Each year, we felt a strange need to call out to any friends we spotted way below us. I'm not really sure why we couldn't just sit back and enjoy the ride. I guess that it's similar to our need to be seen on social media today. Did that day trip really happen if we didn't showcase it to our friends?

Teenagers (in fact any-agers) notoriously lack humility. Our need to be seen is in stark contrast with the humility of God, who chose to be unseen. He is worthy of all honour and praise, yet he is an invisible God. Through Jesus, he entrusted us to be his image-bearers!

In our desire to be seen, to take the credit for that new idea, that act of kindness, or that quality many admire in us, we very often forget to acknowledge that we are God's workmanship and that it is through him we can do all things.

Pray

Dear Lord, thank you that you entrusted me to bear your image. Please help me to acknowledge you in all that I do.

Day 94

Be Comforted

Fiona Castle

A time to cry and a time to laugh.
A time to grieve and a time to dance.
Ecclesiastes 3:4

There is no way out of grief but through it. There is no magic formula, no spiritual or emotional trick which can let us off the hook. The passage of time will enable us to get used to the feeling of the loved one not being around any more, but even that won't change the fact of our bereavement.

The Holy Spirit brings us comfort and peace, but God does not protect us from the reality of human emotions. He wants our eyes to be open to the reality of suffering and death, and fixed on Jesus, who knew the greatest pain of all. He shares our grief and enables us to face it with love and gentleness.

I have always said that there is no blueprint to coping with bereavement. Everyone comes to it from a different background and in different circumstances, so we must allow people to deal with it in their own way. I know, though, that I should not give in to self-pity, but rather have a heart of gratitude, with a determination to laugh and dance!

Pray

Thank you, Lord, that your everlasting arms are under me to hold me up when I am low.

Day 95

Be Useful

Fiona Castle

Make the most of every opportunity in these evil days.
Don't act thoughtlessly, but understand what the Lord wants
you to do.
Ephesians 5:16–17

When Peter stepped out of the boat to walk on water towards Jesus, he was brave and impulsive, until he recognized his human limitations and began to sink. Jesus berated him for his lack of faith, but at least he had the courage to try something he never imagined he could do. All the other disciples stayed in the boat and watched him, but did nothing.

We all have limitations. I recognize that nowadays I don't have the opportunities I had when I was younger, when life was very different. Still, I dread the thought of being useless, so I want to be as active as possible, using my time wisely so that I don't waste it and end up with regrets.

Opportunities in my life might not be as compelling as they used to be, but I know I still have a purpose.

As the saying goes, 'You might as well be useful where you are, as you certainly can be of no use where you're not!'

Pray

Dear Lord, help me always to be seeking ways in which I can serve you in this world.

Day 96

Be at Peace

Fiona Castle

You will keep in perfect peace all who trust in you, all whose thoughts are fixed on you!
Isaiah 26:3

To be at peace with someone means to be in a harmonious relationship with them – and so it is with our relationship with God. If we trust him to be with us through all our problems and difficulties, we can know his peace.

It's easy to be peaceful when we stroll through the country-side, listening to the birds singing and without a care in the world! It's a different thing to know God's peace when your world is falling apart. But that is the peace that God supplies – when we know our future is assured and that he knows and understands all we are going through.

For years, I was terrified of the dark. My husband worked away from home most of the time, and I was responsible alone for the safety of the children. I found it hard to sleep!

But when I gave my life to Jesus all that changed. 'In peace I will lie down and sleep, for you alone, O LORD, will keep me safe' (Psalm 4:8).

What are you fearful of today? Give it to the Lord and he will give you peace.

Pray

Thank you, Lord, that you continue to give me your peace, even in difficult circumstances.

Day 97

Be Diligent

Mandy Catto

'I correct and discipline everyone I love. So be diligent and turn from your indifference.'
Revelation 3:19

A good parent knows the issues, challenges and rebellions that their child is presenting. They do the right thing by actively engaging with the problematic behaviour and addressing the situation because they love their child. They do not want to ignore issues and they speak up, waiting for the 'I'm sorry' and a change of heart and behaviour.

When I was 7 years old, I wanted to have more friends at school, so I snuck into the treat cupboard at home and helped myself to a dozen Breakaway chocolate biscuits, which I handed out in the playground. When the loss was discovered, I had to own up and apologize. I remember the feeling of embarrassment to this day. That was the last time I took a dozen biscuits, and a valuable and positive conversation followed about the right way to make friends.

God shows his love for us by not leaving us in our sin. He helps us to repent and move forward by pointing issues out through prayer, or his word, or teaching us through consequences. He asks us to repent, but also to be zealous. To be fervent, enthusiastic, deliberate and devoted as we grow in our faith.

Pray

Lord, thank you for loving me so much that you know me and discipline me. Help me to repent, to turn around and be zealous for you.

Day 98

Be Wise

Fiona Castle

> If you listen to constructive criticism, you will be at home among the wise. If you reject discipline, you only harm yourself; but if you listen to correction, you grow in understanding.
> Proverbs 15:31–32

My husband, who was an entertainer, used to read all the newspaper reviews of his performances. There might be half a dozen positive write-ups, but if there was one negative one, he used to say, 'I'll wear that bad one on my sleeve all week!' It's so easy to focus on the negative and forget the positive.

If we feel we're being criticized, we need to evaluate where the criticism comes from and why. If it's constructive and given by someone we trust, then we should be grateful and learn from it. Sometimes it can be painful, but very worthwhile, and much more useful than carrying on in life without improvement.

Of course, we can be criticized for our faith as Christians, but usually it takes the form of ridicule or dismissive remarks. Consider instead the Christians in other countries who face real persecution and perhaps even death for their faith. Let's pray for them, and may they be an example to us for standing firm in such circumstances.

Pray

Make me strong in your love, Lord, to face criticism and use it wisely.

Be Courageous

Fiona Castle

And we know that God causes everything to work together
for the good of those who love God and are called according
to his purpose for them.

Romans 8:28

When my four children were tiny, I often wished I could have their illnesses for them. At least I'd understand what was happening, and that I'd soon be better! I think most parents feel that way, throughout the childhood years. We'd love to protect our children from pain and sadness.

Of course, that's impossible – and we would be denying them the opportunity to learn and mature. In their teenage years, we watch them plunge headlong towards pitfalls we'd rather they avoided, and suffer the pain of broken relationships. We try to guide and advise but we have to let them make their own mistakes.

I think God must feel the pain of our mistakes just as keenly as parents do for their children. But, like them, he stands ready to comfort us, and goes on loving in spite of the mess we often make of things.

Although I often don't understand why things happen as they do, I find God is always able to use them in some way. Then I can turn round and say, 'Thank you, Lord, for the lesson you taught me.'

Pray

Dear God, help me to face every challenge with courage and the assurance that you will be by my side.

Be Content

Fiona Castle

> Yet true godliness with contentment is itself great wealth.
> After all, we brought nothing with us when we came into the
> world, and we can't take anything with us when we leave it.
> 1 Timothy 6:6–7

If you read any newspaper or magazine, the articles and advertisements seem to suggest that happiness lies in earning lots of money and buying more and more things. Yet we all know people who have very little and still seem contented.

A religious leader commented that in all the memorial and funeral services he had taken, no one giving a eulogy had ever mentioned the size of house or car or bank account of the deceased, but only what they had done for others.

Money can buy . . .

· A present, not a future
· A house, not a home
· Amusement, but not happiness
· Entertainment, but not fulfilment
· Insurance, but not assurance
· Medicine, but not health
· Religion, but not salvation
· A passport to everywhere but heaven

Pray

Lord, help me to know the true worth of what I have, and to value your gifts to me.

Day 101

Be Genuine

Fiona Castle

Let your conversation be gracious and attractive so that you
will have the right response for everyone.
Colossians 4:6

Does your life demonstrate the truth of what your lips say?
That is a challenging question! Most people come to faith
through friendship and conversations with friends who
share their faith with gentleness.

When people are going through difficult times of illness,
stress or bereavement, they turn to someone they trust. If
we're always busy, preoccupied with many tasks (perhaps
lots of church work), they won't feel comfortable enough
to share their concerns. We need to show genuine interest,
patience and compassion.

I had a friend I had known since school. She worked at a local
supermarket. It was noticeable that there was always a queue
at her checkout, even though other desks were available. The
reason was that she always had time for the customers, she
chatted and asked questions, she got to know the regulars
and people knew she genuinely cared about them.

At her funeral, the church was filled with customers as well
as all the other workers from the supermarket who knew her.

Her life lived out the faith she professed.

Pray

Lord, let my life show what my lips say.

Day 102

Be Willing

Fiona Castle

Just as our bodies have many parts and each part has a
special function, so it is with Christ's body. We are many parts
of one body, and we all belong to each other.
Romans 12:4–5

I love this illustration of how we should all work together, all
differently, to function successfully for Christ. I am filled with
awe at the intricate details of the human body, enabling it to
work properly! Likewise, as Christians, we all have different
work to do, to bring the love of Christ to the world.

There are obvious leaders who preach and teach, but then
there are 'enablers', like the secretaries, fundraisers, DIY
experts, cleaners of the buildings, and those who pray.
There are those who give their time to teach the children
and young people, to encourage the next generation. They
are all important to keep the church, as the body of Christ,
functioning successfully.

Don't underestimate your value as you take the opportunities
God has given you.

Pray

Father, make clear to me the work you have chosen for me to
do, so that I can faithfully work as part of your church today.

Day 103

Be Thoughtful

Fiona Castle

'And Solomon, my son, learn to know the God of your ancestors intimately. Worship and serve him with your whole heart and a willing mind. For the LORD sees every heart and knows every plan and thought.'
1 Chronicles 28:9

Whatever we're doing, we need to check our motives. What does God see in our hearts? Are we acting out of compassion or for what we can gain from it? Are we putting others first when we're driving, or waiting in a queue in the supermarket?

God alone knows our hearts. Ask him to show us today if our motives are pure. In our own homes, are we thoughtful towards others who are going through stressful situations – work, exams or job seeking? Are we prepared to think through the best way to help, support and encourage them, rather than just dismissing their moods and reactions?

They say you have to walk a mile in someone's shoes to understand what they're going through and how they feel. If we care for other people imaginatively, we can work out what they need. Remember, our example is Jesus, who came to live and die as one of us to bring us eternal life.

Pray

Dear God, help me understand how others might be feeling today, so that I don't make thoughtless assumptions.

Day 104

Be Unremarkable

Sarah McKerney

'There's a young boy here with five barley loaves and two fish.
But what good is that with this huge crowd?'
John 6:9

Jesus is speaking to the large crowd and it's getting late. The people don't want to leave because they are captivated by Jesus. The disciples come to Jesus with the issue of a hungry crowd and Jesus' response is simple: feed the people. You can imagine the disciples' indignation. 'You expect us to feed this crowd? We need more notice than an hour to cater for over 5,000 people! We need a budget! This is a bit of a stretch!'

However, the disciples discover a boy with some food, and Jesus feeds the multitude from that single packed lunch.

I was responsible for packed lunches in my home when my children were at school. It was a job I loathed. But just imagine a parent that morning lovingly (or perhaps, like me, begrudgingly) preparing that packed lunch. That mundane, ordinary task was central to one of the greatest miracles. Whatever we have, whatever we give, God takes it and multiplies it.

Pray

Lord, there are times when my life feels unremarkable and mundane. Open my eyes to see that you take what we have and multiply it. Use what I have for your will, to feed others.

Day 105

Be Enthusiastic

Mandy Catto

So I have reason to be enthusiastic about all Christ Jesus has done through me in my service to God.
Romans 15:17

In an age of cynicism and negativity, it is hard to be enthusiastic. Sometimes people think it's naive, overly positive or odd. Or maybe it just requires too much energy in an exhausting world.

But through Jesus, we can be enthusiastic. We have the best positive news in the universe: Jesus saves! So whatever our feelings on any one day, and whatever our personality type, we have the best message. And the Holy Spirit gives us the passion and dynamism to be an enthusiast.

I was once walking in London and came across a team of smiley young adults giving out free samples of a new ice cream. I caught their enthusiasm as they extolled the flavours and benefits of their product. I did more than just take a sample – I ate a pint tub right there, and I don't normally like ice cream! If they could be so zealous about frozen milk, eggs and sugar, then maybe I can be brave about my faith. After all, it has fewer calories, better benefits and a promise of eternal life!

Pray

Lord, give me the enthusiasm and courage to be a messenger of the Good News to someone I meet today. Don't let lack of energy or confidence hold me back. Holy Spirit, give me the gift of enthusiasm to convey the life-giving message of hope in Jesus.

Day 106

Be Spirit-led

Hayley Nock

'For the Holy Spirit will teach you at that time what needs to be said.'
Luke 12:12

I remember taking a holiday in a country that is, in general, hostile to the Christian faith. I was with a group of other Christians who had been invited to the home of a family that did not yet know Jesus. We were all packed into a small room for a meal. Suddenly someone asked me to speak to them from the Bible, and my heart was in my mouth. I threw up a quick, silent prayer: 'God, help me!' I started to speak, and as the interpreter translated my words, the next line would pop into my head. I was left in awe of God as he worked among this household.

I had never experienced this before: there have been many times where I haven't stepped out like this. However, that experience brought this verse to mind. God will give us the words to say if we ask him. It is all done through his Holy Spirit.

Are there areas where I can step out in faith?

Pray

Thank you, God, that you promised to give us all that we need. Lord, please fill me more with your Holy Spirit, and help me rely on you in both small and large situations.

Day 107

Be Adventurous

Rachel Allcock

'Let's go across to the outpost of those pagans,' Jonathan
said to his armour bearer. 'Perhaps the LORD will help us, for
nothing can hinder the LORD. He can win a battle whether
he has many warriors or only a few!'
1 Samuel 14:6

We once drove past the beach at Southport when the tide
was – unusually – lapping up at the sea wall. I always kick
myself that I didn't stop and look, but we were on our way
to the cinema. Recently, I rushed there to see another 'high
tide', but it turned out to be just an expanse of puddles on
wet sand! I've never seen that proper high tide again. It
makes me think of all the great new projects that we don't
have time to join. Years later, we realize we missed out.

Today's verse comes from a chapter entitled 'Jonathan's
Daring Plan'. Jonathan and his armour-bearer sneak down
between two rocky cliffs to spy on a Philistine outpost,
confident that the Lord will send a sign if they should go
ahead and fight them. He does, and they experience an
exhilarating victory!

In our first year of marriage, we joined a mission trip to
Romania. In our fourth year, we went to live in Canada. I
wouldn't have done any of these things without my own
Jonathan! If (like me) you lack a spirit of adventure, tag along
with someone who has it.

Pray

Help me, Lord, to seize the opportunities you send.

Day 108

Be Changed

Fiona Castle

'Now repent of your sins and turn to God, so that your sins may be wiped away. Then times of refreshment will come from the presence of the Lord, and he will again send you Jesus, your appointed Messiah.'
Acts 3:19–20

There's a house in my street that has been there for as long as I can remember. It always looks tidy and well kept, but when I passed it recently I realized it must be undergoing a great deal of refurbishment. There was a large skip outside, laden with old windows and kitchen equipment. It would take a while to complete the renovation.

Strangely, I saw this as an illustration of the time I became a Christian. On the outside, my life appeared to be successful and acceptable, but on the inside, there was chaos! So much rubbish had to be dealt with, in order to complete the change Jesus had made in my life, but it was such a worthwhile project. Of course, it is an ongoing process, but the initial transformation was amazing and had a positive impact on every part of my life.

An inner change of heart and mind, which comes through repentance, brings great joy.

Pray

Thank you, Jesus, that you have given me new life, through finding and trusting you at all times.

Day 109

Be Secure

Fiona Castle

God is our refuge and strength, always ready to help in times
of trouble. So we will not fear when earthquakes come and
the mountains crumble into the sea.
Psalm 46:1–2

Often we read in the news about natural disasters in other parts of the world, such as earthquakes, fires and floods. It must be terrifying to be caught up in something like that, and I wonder how I'd cope.

However, we all go through difficulties which cause us fear. It is a natural reaction. But we're not meant to live in fear: God has promised to be with us at all times. We can know his peace and strength in all adversities. If we give our lives to him, we know that he goes ahead of us and he will give us courage to face whatever the future brings.

What are your fears today? Are they causing you to lose peace of mind and heart? Put your hand in the hand of the Lord and give him whatever is causing you fear.

'Such love has no fear, because perfect love expels all fear' (1 John 4:18).

Pray

Thank you, Father, that you are my refuge in times of trouble, so that I know I am secure in your love.

Day 110

Be Thoughtful

Fiona Castle

Work willingly at whatever you do, as though you were
working for the Lord rather than for people.
Colossians 3:23

Whenever I'm planning parties, Christmas celebrations, Easter egg hunts, or decorating the house, I get to the point of thinking everything has become too commercial. As a Christian, I'm also torn by my plenty compared with the poverty of the Third World. One day, I poured my feelings out to God. I felt I was giving our children more than they really needed, but I didn't want them to be deprived just because of my conscience.

But then I sensed that God understood my dilemma – torn between giving gifts and giving to the needy. He showed me that if I bought my presents lovingly and prayerfully, he was pleased. If I decorated the house and prepared food to make the family happy, it pleased him. In fact, if I did all my work 'as unto the Lord', it would please him. And there would be time and money left for the poor.

So, when you're faced with a similar dilemma, relax and allow God to guide you in all the preparations for the festivities. You'll find that however much glitter, icing, tinsel, chocolate or flowers surround your celebration, Christ will still be the centre of everything you do.

Pray

Father, help me to trust in your guidance, and show me how to please you.

Day 111

Be Trusting

Fiona Castle

> But Jesus didn't trust them, because he knew all about
> people. No one needed to tell him about human nature, for
> he knew what was in each person's heart.
> John 2:24–25

Jesus came into the world to save sinners. He knew what we humans were like. He was discerning, right from the start – aware that his purpose was to show us a different way to live. He loved us enough to die for us, in order that we could receive new life in him – amazing grace.

Even though we have discovered that transformation through him, we are not perfect and, as the verse says, he knows what we are really like! Oswald Chambers points out that Jesus was never bitter or disappointed because he did not put his trust in any person but only in God. If we trust in people more than we trust God, we will end up despairing because no human can be perfect. Chambers advises us never to trust anything but the grace of God.

Pray

Dear Lord Jesus, help me always to put my trust in you before any human being. Remind me that you are the only one in whom I can totally trust.

Day 112

Be Infectious

Fiona Castle

What good is it, dear brothers and sisters, if you say you have faith but don't show it by your actions? Can that kind of faith save anyone?
James 2:14

We naturally try to avoid infections wherever possible, by vaccinations or simply by keeping away from people who are ill. But what about being infected by something good?

There is a saying: 'Faith is infectious – is yours worth catching?' How does that make you feel? We are so blessed to live with the knowledge that our future is assured and that God has promised he will never leave or forsake us. But do we live it out? Do we live in such a way that those who don't know Jesus wonder how we can live with such assurance? Or, on the contrary, do we make people shy away and avoid us at all costs? A challenging thought!

People are naturally attracted to those who are always kind, loving and generous so, as Christ-followers our lives should display those qualities. That will provide the opportunity to tell others of his love and salvation.

Pray

Dear Lord Jesus, help me to live my life in a way that will attract others, not to me, but to you. You changed my life, and only you can change the lives of those with whom I come in contact, in the power of your Holy Spirit.

Be Guided

Fiona Castle

Show me the right path, O LORD; point out the road for me
to follow.
Psalm 25:4

There's a well-known poem by Robert Frost, called 'The Road Not Taken'. At the end, the poet recalls that he chose the road less travelled, which 'has made all the difference'. The poem doesn't say whether the road he chose was the right one, because he would never know where the other one would have taken him.

In reality, it is often impossible to see where a life-altering decision will lead. It is natural, though, to contemplate the 'what ifs' when an important choice has to be made. Perhaps we don't know anyone who can give us advice, who has had to make a similar decision. But when we turn to the Lord and ask for direction from him, he will give us a sense of peace if the choice we make is part of his plan and purpose for us.

We can make mistakes, but he also shows us that we can learn from those mistakes and seek his way to guide us back onto the right road.

Pray

Teach me your ways, O Lord my God, and I will walk in your truth.

Day 114

Be Enduring

Fiona Castle

God blesses those who patiently endure testing and
temptation. Afterward they will receive the crown of life that
God has promised to those who love him.
James 1:12

Do you know anyone who has never had any adversity in life?
I doubt it! We have all had to face difficulties, disappointment
and struggles of one kind or another.

There is a saying that whatever doesn't kill you will make you
stronger. Is that true of you? Some adversities are temporarily
afflicting, while others can be permanently disabling. It's
how we handle these adversities that matters.

I remember when my husband was dying of cancer, a lovely
but unknown person wrote to me saying that 'problems are
growth activators'. I found that so empowering at a very difficult
time and I've never forgotten it. We can learn so much through
tough times that we never would if life were always easy.

Jesus didn't come into the world to stop suffering, to explain it or
take it away, but to fill it with his presence. How can we understand
the road we travel? It is the Lord who directs our steps.

Pray

Thank you, Lord that you direct our steps, even when the
road ahead is rough.

Day 115

Be Ready

Mandy Catto

Instead, you must worship Christ as Lord of your life. And if someone asks about your hope as a believer, always be ready to explain it. But do this in a gentle and respectful way.
1 Peter 3:15–16

Do you ever find that a thought from the Bible gets stuck in your head, and keeps popping up at random times during the day? I love the phrase 'always be ready to explain'. There was a period when I felt God asking me to be ready, to look for opportunities and questions from friends who are intrigued by faith. My job in all this was to be rooted in Christ.

During that time, I had to face a difficult gynaecological procedure. I was gowned up and facing my worst fears as the anaesthetist entered the theatre and began a conversation about my job. I mentioned that I worked in a Bible college. In a room full of masked nursing staff, he asked about faith in Jesus and whether he was really the only way to heaven. At that moment I found myself thinking, 'Really, Lord? You want me to talk about Jesus now?' It was a unique opportunity for a conversation that I could hold only with God's help. Always be ready!

Pray

Jesus, help me to truly hold you as the Lord of my life. Lord, help me to always be ready to explain at any moment and in any situation.

Day 116

Be Fun

Rhiannon Goulding

'The thief's purpose is to steal and kill and destroy. My purpose is to give them a rich and satisfying life.'
John 10:10

When I was in China a few years ago, I found myself in a small gathering comprising a handful of missionary families. I got talking to a lady who had moved to China in her fifties – to a remote little village, miles from anywhere, the only foreigner for some distance. Her journey had been a fascinating one. It would take a journey of hours on a train for her to meet anyone who spoke even a little English. My children and I asked her question after question, finding each answer as exciting and intriguing as the last.

As we got ready to leave, I happened to ask what advice she'd offer for living such a full life. She answered in five simple words: 'Just have fun, fun, fun!' Then she prayed for us, that as we moved into the next stage of our life, we would have fun.

What a prayer! What a way to live! Our lives are often over-crowded with routines, demands, obligations and must-dos, to such a degree that we squeeze out whatever fun there might be. This wonderful lady was a powerful example to me of making space for fun.

Pray

Lord Jesus, help me to remember that you came to give us a rich and satisfying life.

Day 117

Be a Witness

Fiona Castle

'Therefore, go and make disciples of all the nations, baptizing
them in the name of the Father and the Son and the Holy
Spirit.'
Matthew 28:19

Before he died, Jesus had prayed for the disciples in the
words which are known as the High Priestly prayer, but then
he went on to say, 'I am praying, not only for these disciples,
but also for all who will ever believe in me because of their
testimony.'

It came as such a shock when I realized that at that point
Jesus was praying for you and me! Had the disciples not
been obedient to their task, we wouldn't have the privilege
of knowing the love of Jesus and the assurance of eternal life
through him.

Well, now it's our responsibility to take up that challenge to
share the Gospel. What opportunities do we have today to
make his name known? Many of the people we meet won't
ever go through a church door to find out about him for
themselves, if we don't invite them. We are called to be light-
bearers in our dark world, to give our friends the best news
they could ever hear.

Pray

Lord, help me to make your name known, especially to the
next generation.

Day 118

Be Trusting

Mandy Catto

The LORD is good, a strong refuge when trouble comes. He is
close to those who trust in him.
Nahum 1:7

Good – one of the simplest, yet most powerful words. The
concept of a good God is one that we teach to children and
they get it! Yet it continues to intrigue and challenge us as
adults.

Because of God's utter holiness, perfection and complete
lack of evil and sin, we know that we can trust him. He is
for ever good; he will always be our refuge. Times of trouble
and distress will come upon us. In this broken world, we
face sickness, financial problems, broken relationships and
hardships. Sometimes, when we feel overwhelmed, it is
difficult to trust, yet he asks us to trust in him, in his eternal
goodness and all-encompassing care. And if we truly trust in
his care, everything looks different. All is calm.

Move away from the regrets of the past; stop stressing over
worries about the future; focus on the present, where God
promises to be right with us. Take a moment to be aware of
his presence in your life today, and spend time dwelling on
his goodness. He asks you, right now, to trust in him.

Pray

Lord, you are so good. May your Holy Spirit fill me with the
knowledge of your goodness and presence. Help me to trust
in you completely and know how deeply you care.

Day 119

Be Generous

Rachel Allcock

Two people are better off than one, for they can help each other succeed. If one person falls, the other can reach out and help. But someone who falls alone is in real trouble.
Ecclesiastes 4:9–10

One of my favourite films, Disney's *Cars*, sees super-competitive Chick Hicks crash into retiring racing car The King in his over-zealous efforts to win the Piston Cup. Our hero, Lightning McQueen, sacrifices his chance of a win, choosing instead to push the old car to help him finish his last race. The rookie lays aside his ambition and honours the veteran racer. After all, as McQueen learned earlier in the film, the trophy is 'just an empty cup'.

What is the point in winning when we leave others limping? Why celebrate a hollow victory?

We are not created to go it alone. Those of us who race through our weeks, eager to tick off our to-do lists and clock up our eight hours in freshly laundered bedding are missing something! All around us, there are individuals who need someone to help them up today. It might mean you don't empty your dishwasher until 2.53 p.m. It might mean you have to stay up late to catch up on paperwork. But you can flop into your unmade bed satisfied that you are not the individualistic recipient of an empty cup.

Pray

Lord, help me to be generous with my time and look out for others today.

Day 120

Be a Fighter

Sarah McKerney

'Don't worry about this Philistine,' David told Saul.
'I'll go and fight him!'
1 Samuel 17:32

A young boy is instructed by his father to take a basket of food to his three older brothers, who are on the front line of a war. The opposing Philistine army has a war-winning hero, a giant named Goliath. The Israelites are terrified of Goliath; no one wants to fight this mighty man. But the shepherd boy David steps forward, toppling Goliath with nothing more than a simple sling and a stone.

What is interesting is that David had fought and won a battle once before, using the same weapon. He was alone with his flock when he came face to face with a lion. His first battle was a very personal one: he was seeking victory for himself. This personal victory was his training ground for the slaying of Goliath. This time he was seeking victory for others. He was fighting for the people of Israel.

The personal battles we fight and win train us to battle on behalf of others. Who are you going into battle for today?

Pray

Lord, thank you for the battles I have won with your strength. Show me how I can use those personal victories to fight on behalf of others in need.

Day 121

Be Exceptional

Fiona Castle

Instead, give yourselves completely to God, for you were
dead, but now you have new life. So use your whole body as
an instrument to do what is right for the glory of God.
Romans 6:13

When we give our lives to Jesus, many of us have no idea
what that means, or where it will take us, or what he will
expect of us. I often think of the words of Isaiah, who heard
the Lord asking whom he should send as a messenger to his
people. Isaiah replied, 'Lord, I'll go! Send me.'

Sadly, my response is more often, 'Lord, I'll go, but why don't
you send someone else, who would be far better at it than I
am?' Is it a female response, that we tend to think of others
as better equipped than we are, and more able?

Oswald Chambers wrote that it is easy to assume that we
have to do amazing acts for God, but we don't. What we
have to do is learn to be exceptional in the ordinary things
of day-to-day life, to remain holy 'in mean streets' when the
people around us are mean and unkind. That is a hard thing
to learn, and it takes time.

Whatever God is calling you to do today – however menial,
however simple – do it with great love.

Pray

Dear God, please help me to be exceptional in my love for
your world and those in it that I meet today. Pour your love
through me to others.

Day 122

Be Curse-averse

Rachel Allcock

But most of all, my brothers and sisters, never take an oath,
by heaven or earth or anything else. Just say a simple yes or
no, so that you will not sin and be condemned.
James 5:12

The 'most of all' in this verse is unsettling and it seems oddly
placed coming at the end of a section about patience and
endurance. James 5:7–12 starts with a warning against
grumbling about each other, 'For look – the Judge is standing
at the door!' (James 5:9). James then gives examples of
patience in suffering, referring to the prophets. They continued
to speak the truth in spite of persecution, mistreatment and
abuse. Next, he honours Job for his endurance: throughout
his suffering, Job resisted everyone's exasperated pleas to
give up, curse God and die (Job 2:9).

Yes, this section is about endurance but, above all, it is about
how we behave and communicate. That is the reason for the
severity of this verse. When someone 'swears on their life',
or on some other person or object, it's a serious thing. Why
be so dramatic and invite condemnation by doing this? If
you are full of integrity, a simple 'yes' or 'no' is enough. By all
means, shout out to God and tell him how you feel. But hold
your tongue when you are tempted to use God's name to
curse or swear an oath.

Pray

Lord God, help me to consider how and when I might need
to tame my tongue.

Day 123

Be You

Rhiannon Goulding

Thank you for making me so wonderfully complex! Your workmanship is marvellous – how well I know it.
Psalm 139:14

Sometimes it can take a long time, a lifetime, to become comfortable in one's own skin. I spent the first forty years of my life in discomfort, wishing I was quieter, thinner, more reserved, less forthright, more sensitive, less evasive. It's taken some time for me to recognize that apart from the things I can change or alter, there is a huge part of me that is . . . well . . . just me! And I have been created and fashioned that way. God has intricately wired me to be the way I am, and for a purpose. The people I meet and know need my type of person, as I need the type of people they are.

I'm a mixed bag, a variety of qualities. I'm celebrating some of those, working on others and leaving still others to grace. In the meantime, I am coming to appreciate that despite there being many aspects of me that I might struggle with, God seems to be using those very same things to encourage, bless and strengthen those around me. Perhaps the greatest gift we can give to those in our world, is not the person we're trying to be, but the person we genuinely, authentically are!

Pray

Dear God, help me to always be the person you created me to be, to fulfil your purposes and help others.

Day 124

Be a Sharer

Fiona Castle

'You didn't choose me. I chose you. I appointed you to go
and produce lasting fruit, so that the Father will give you
whatever you ask for, using my name.'
John 15:16

Our fruit-bearing opportunities come as we befriend others.
The Lord enables us to become aware of a need or a problem
in someone's life, and to seek his guidance as we allow him
to work through us to bring peace and healing in the power
of the Holy Spirit.

Jesus is the friend of sinners, who are lonely, troubled and
insecure. He is the only one who can transform lives, and he
calls us to be agents of that change through our friendship.
When we listen to our friends with empathy and sensitivity,
we earn the right to share with them what Jesus has done in
our lives and is longing to do for them.

If Christ is your greatest friend, how could you help but
introduce him to others as the best and most trustworthy
friend they could ever imagine?

Pray

Lord Jesus, I use your name to bring new life to those who
don't yet know you, because you are the only answer to their
needs.

Day 125

Be Focussed

Fiona Castle

'Seek the Kingdom of God above all else, and live righteously,
and he will give you everything you need.'
Matthew 6:33

Modern life is busy. Those of us with families and jobs try to do everything, rushing from one task to the next, and modern media and communications add to the pressure. You can be online and reachable 24 hours a day.

Is this the way God wants us to live our lives?

If you knew that this would be your last year on earth, what would you decide to change? What would your priorities be? Would you ask God to show you where you had trodden the wrong path? What is really important? It's good to be focussed and to make the most of our time, but sometimes we overdo it.

At my advanced age, I recognize the importance of spending quality time with family and friends, to try to understand, support and encourage them. Time is short. No one knows what tomorrow may bring. I want to leave some happy memories, rather than being too busy to bother!

Make time count!

Pray

Help me, Lord, to make my time count, so that I don't waste it but rejoice in every moment.

Day 126

Be a Messenger

Fiona Castle

And how can they believe in him if they have never heard about him? And how can they hear about him unless someone tells them?

Romans 10:14

Early one morning, when I was walking the dog, I passed the sorting office. An army of postmen issued forth, carrying their bags of mail. What was in all those letters, I wondered? Exciting news, love letters or depressing bills? The post can make or mar your day – what a responsibility!

Christians are a bit like postmen: we gather together as God's people to receive the word, then scatter to our separate lives to share God's love. But while the postman doesn't know whether he carries good news or bad, we can be sure we have Good News to share, if only people are willing to accept it. But we have to live out the gospel first, to show people that it's a message worth receiving.

There are so many lonely, disillusioned people in the world, who are desperate to find new meaning in their lives. Are we willing to share the promise of new life in Jesus?

Pray

Thank you, Lord, that you have given me good news – the greatest news to share with others. Give me opportunities, I pray.

Day 127

Be Comforted

Rachel Allcock

'I will comfort you there in Jerusalem as a mother comforts her child.'
Isaiah 66:13

One night, when I was maybe 9 or 10 years old, I had stomach pains and my mum called for the doctor. He had to feel my tummy and I was embarrassed because I had big belly-warmers on (this was our junior-school name for big knickers)! Although my mum must have been worried, she did a great job of hiding it. I remember having such a good time that night: spare-room bed, sleepover with my mum, and a midnight read of the 'Stocking Fillers' catalogue!

Isn't it strange how we often have fond memories attached to childhood illness? For me, the pain and sickness are not what first come to mind. Maybe you benefitted from grandparents spoiling you, days on the sofa, or lots of individual attention when usually it was shared between many siblings.

As adults, there are plenty of times when we feel like children – we need a grown-up, then look around and realize that we're the grown-ups! In Isaiah 66, God promises comfort to Jerusalem, as a mother comforts her child. However old or young we are, we can claim that promise and turn to him when we're floundering.

Pray

I pray, Lord, that in times of loneliness, upset, and desperate need, you will be the source of my comfort.

Day 128

Be Loved

Fiona Castle

Indeed, nothing in all creation will ever be able to separate us from the love of God that is revealed in Christ Jesus our Lord.
Romans 8:39

Do you feel accepted? Do you know you are loved? From early childhood, we long to be accepted by our peers so that we feel secure. As adults, we want to be accepted in our work, to receive approval – and often our self-worth is bound up in our need to be valued, when we feel we don't match up.

There is a story of a young man at university who, because of financial constraints, was having to cram two years' study into one. However hard he worked, he never felt he was doing well enough.

One day, feeling very low, he noticed his professor walking towards him. The professor stopped and grabbed him by the collar, looked him in the eye and said, 'Young man, you are loved *now*!'

His acceptance was not dependent on his exam results! Jesus' love for us is the same yesterday, today and for ever. And whether we succeed or fail in life, his grace is sufficient.

Pray

Thank you, Lord, that whatever I do and wherever I go, I will never be separated from your love.

Be Friends

Jaz Potter

> Four men arrived carrying a paralysed man on a mat. They couldn't bring him to Jesus because of the crowd, so they dug a hole through the roof above his head. Then they lowered the man on his mat, right down in front of Jesus.
>
> Mark 2:3–4

This is the story of a paralysed man who is forgiven and healed by Jesus. However, I want to highlight the four men that carried the mat.

We don't know what the relationship was between them all, but there was love enough and compassion enough for them to join forces to carry him to Jesus. They were so sure that Jesus could heal him. And when they realized they weren't able to get in, they were crazy enough to take the roof off Simon's house.

These men had such love for their friend that they went to extraordinary lengths to help him encounter Jesus. I also love that there were four of them: each took a corner, each took a share of the weight, they worked together.

We are called to be disciple makers and I believe this is best done through genuine, authentic friendships. Which means we sometimes have to go out of our way to develop friendships and support one another as we befriend those who don't yet know the love Jesus offers.

Pray

Dear God, help me to become a mat-carrying Christian. Use me to help carry people to Jesus.

Day 130

Be Watchful

Sarah McKerney

'Then a despised Samaritan came along, and when he saw
the man, he felt compassion for him.'
Luke 10:33

I wonder where they were going – the priest, the Levite and
the Samaritan? Perhaps they had an important meeting to
attend and were running late. Perhaps they wanted to get
home to watch *Bake Off*. Perhaps it wasn't that they didn't
care, but they didn't have time, or simply didn't think it was
their responsibility.

It's unlikely that the Samaritan woke up that day expecting
to be a hero. He didn't go out looking for someone to rescue
or to help. The Bible doesn't tell us that God 'called him' to
go to that place, to find that man, to help him. The Bible tells
us that the Samaritan man was simply on a journey and he
came across a man who had been attacked. He was just
going about his ordinary business and literally bumped into
someone who needed help.

I'm challenged. Do I live my life with my eyes open to see
those in need, who I just happen to come across? I rush to
work, dash round the supermarket, multi-tasking, juggling
all the balls of my professional, family and church life. But do
I actually see those around me? Because that's our calling.

Pray

Lord, help me to pay attention to those I come across on my
journey, and be ready to notice what they need.

Day 131

Be Encouraged

Mandy Catto

I felt encouraged because the gracious hand of the LORD my God was on me.
Ezra 7:28

Ezra was a leader during difficult times, trying to rebuild the Temple and the faith of the Israelite people returning from tyranny and exile. He faced political and personal opposition as he gathered the people and encouraged them to rebuild the walls and turn to God. Seven times in this short book, he is grateful for the 'gracious hand' of the Lord which he knows is upon him. This little phrase is used more here than anywhere else in the Bible. God was protecting, strengthening and building up the people because of his grace and mercy. And Ezra was encouraged! Throughout this difficult process, he looked out for signs of God's presence and blessing and pointed it out! His constant positivity led others to renew their faith. He was encouraged by remembering God's mercy and he encouraged others.

Do we look out for signs of God's presence? Can we point out his mercy when we see it? Being ready to notice the hand of God is a sure step in building up your faith, which then shines out to others.

Pray

O Lord my God, may I see your gracious hand working in my life. Help me to look up and see you everywhere. May I be encouraged by being aware of your love and presence. Help me to speak about you and encourage others.

Day 132

Be Connected

Fiona Castle

'For I will pour out water to quench your thirst and to irrigate your parched fields. And I will pour out my Spirit on your descendants, and my blessing on your children.'
Isaiah 44:3

Have you ever tramped through the highlands of Scotland and suddenly come across a bubbling stream bursting out of the rocks? I did as a child – and I still remember cupping my hands to take a long, refreshing drink. There's no sweeter water than that of a fresh mountain stream.

But if I wanted that water on tap at home, I'd have to plumb directly into the source. Once it's been through a reservoir and treated with chemicals, it isn't the same.

Jesus told us that he is able to give us water from the river of life which will totally satisfy us, and if we drink of it, we will never thirst again. But first, we have to be plumbed into the source – which is Jesus.

If we want living water flowing through our lives, we must first experience a personal relationship with Jesus. We have to acknowledge him as Lord and Saviour; then make sure we allow his life and love to flow through us and out to others.

Pray

Lord, I pray that your rivers of living water will flow through our nation, so that people will understand the truth of your word and follow you.

Day 133

Be an Encourager

Rhiannon Goulding

So encourage each other and build each other up, just as you are already doing.
1 Thessalonians 5:11

As a non-runner, I decided to join a running club, and on my first week they gave me a welcome we could all learn from. Although I didn't look much like a runner or particularly feel like one (a phoney who didn't belong), the welcome and encouragement from the whole group made me feel like a valued part of the team.

On my maiden run, I was greeted by smiles, cheers and waves from people I'd never met! One lovely lady asked, 'Is it your first time?' When I nodded she said, 'Good on you for making that big move.' She offered gentle advice about the course in front of me. As I struggled up the first hill, one of the faster runners slowed down to give me some encouragement. On each change of direction, someone with a smiling face pointed the way, shouting encouragement to keep going: 'You've got this! Strong girls!'

Wow! What if we could learn from this in our church groups? What if we became encouragers, building people up at every step, pointing the way forward with a smile and a cheer? By the end of my first run I wasn't a spectator any more, I was part of the group.

Pray

Lord Jesus, as your Holy Spirit comforts and encourages us, teach us to nurture others.

Be Receptive

Fiona Castle

> In his grace, God has given us different gifts for doing certain things well.
> Romans 12:6

Our talents and abilities are gifts from God. The important thing is that we recognize them and use them for his glory. Not all gifts are recognized or will make us famous. It doesn't mean they are less important because they are unseen. Some of the greatest of God's servants are those who enable others to do great works.

What about the people who teach the children of missionaries in far-flung countries, so that they can share the Good News of Jesus? What about those who do the washing and cleaning in places of healing or learning?

Romans 12:5 tells us, 'so it is with Christ's body. We are many parts of one body, and we all belong to each other.' We need to receive our gifts with joy and willingness, whatever they are.

I love the suggestion that God is the composer, Jesus is the conductor and we are the musicians, all playing different instruments, which, if played well, make a beautiful sound together!

Pray

Help me, Lord God, to make a beautiful sound with the opportunities you have given me.

Day 135

Be Persevering

Fiona Castle

For you know that when your faith is tested, your endurance has a chance to grow. So let it grow, for when your endurance is fully developed, you will be perfect and complete, needing nothing.

James 1:3–4

We can start a new project with great enthusiasm and creativity, but as the days go on and problems mount up, it's often difficult to continue without being sidetracked by people who tell us we should never have started it in the first place! But in the letter to the Philippians Paul says that when trouble comes, we should let it be an opportunity for joy!

I have always tried to encourage my children that it is far better to have a go and fail, than not to bother and then later wonder, 'What if?' How many of us have won trophies or medals as top runners or athletes? Not many – but that shouldn't stop us doing our very best in the circumstances in which we live. Our ultimate goal, anyway, is not worldly but eternal, through our hope in our Lord Jesus Christ, who has already paid the price for us. We have no need to fear, but to rejoice.

Don't give up!

Pray

Lord, help me not to give up when I go through difficulties. Help me to trust that my faith will grow as a result of them.

Day 136

Be a Believer

Mandy Catto

'For this is how God loved the world: He gave his one and only Son, so that everyone who believes in him will not perish but have eternal life.'
John 3:16

This verse is the most famous in the Bible. Jesus spoke these words to Nicodemus, a Pharisee and religious leader. He came to Jesus with questions, genuinely wanting to know more, but also speaking to Jesus at night, showing perhaps that he was scared of speaking to this rebel rabbi when the other Pharisees were around. And because of this clandestine conversation, we hear Jesus set out the Gospel – the clearest explanation of who the Son of God is, why he came, who sent him and the promise of eternal life to all who believe.

Nicodemus moves on in his faith and is the only Pharisee to stand up for Jesus in John 7. When the Pharisees ask rhetorically, 'Is there a single one of us who believes?' Nicodemus is the one to speak up and ask for a fair trial. He believes and he has the courage to declare it. After the death of Jesus, Nicodemus steps in with expensive perfumed ointment to anoint his body. He believes and he shows his love for his Saviour.

Pray

Father God, thank you for loving me so much. Jesus, thank you for dying for me and giving me eternal life. I believe in you. Help me to speak up for you and find ways to show my love.

Day 137

Be Perceptive

Fiona Castle

'God blesses those whose hearts are pure,
for they shall see God.'
Matthew 5:8

There are so many ways in which we use the words 'I see'. We naturally say we can see something with our eyes, but we also say, 'Oh, I see,' when we suddenly understand something that has previously perplexed us. We also have the gift of insight when we make a discovery. 'Now I see the answer to the situation that has been troubling me.'

In a similar way, when we receive the gift of faith and God's love and forgiveness towards us, it is as if a bright light has been switched on inside us. As John Newton put it in his famous hymn 'Amazing Grace': 'I once was lost but now am found, was blind but now I see.' When we see with the eyes of our hearts, we grow in compassion for others, as we seek to care for them and try to understand the background to their needs.

So, as we go about our day, with its usual stresses and pressures, let us seek God's purpose as we see the world through his eyes, not just our own.

Pray

Dear God, I thank you that I can see not only with my eyes, but also with the eyes of my heart, to recognize the needs of others. Help me to be sensitive to those needs today.

Day 138

Be Disciplined

Fiona Castle

'Don't make light of the LORD's discipline, and don't give up when he corrects you' . . . Who ever heard of a child who is never disciplined by its father?
Hebrews 12:5,7

During a recent visit to the dentist, I saw an impression of a very decayed set of teeth. I was shocked to learn that they belonged to a 20-year-old. As a boy, he refused to brush his teeth because he didn't like the taste of toothpaste, and his mother had given in to avoid battles. Maybe that made life easier when he was a child – but how awful to see the result when he grew up.

In these verses we learn that God is doing the loving thing when he disciplines us: he knows what's best for us. Later, verse 11 says, 'afterwards there will be a peaceful harvest of right living for those who are trained in this way.'

I often thought of these verses when I disciplined my own children. Being strict sometimes made me feel miserable, but I knew it was necessary. God's word is always true, and we find peace in obeying it.

Take time today to read the whole of Hebrews chapter 12 and ask God to show you what you need to learn from it – and enjoy the encouragement it brings!

Pray

Dear God, I appreciate that you discipline me to keep me on track, because you know what is best for me.

Be Transformed

Mandy Catto

Don't copy the behaviour and customs of this world, but let God transform you into a new person by changing the way you think. Then you will learn to know God's will for you, which is good and pleasing and perfect.

Romans 12:2

When we think of transformation, we often think about behaviour and habits. At New Year we make resolutions – to go to the gym more often, to eat less chocolate or to make fewer online purchases. By the end of January, we have usually forgotten or given up these resolutions and our habits remain unchanged. When Paul writes to the Romans, he has a different starting point: be a new person by changing the way you think. Our actions flow out of our thoughts, beliefs and motivation. Our heart leads the way, transforming our thoughts, and then our actions flow from there.

Lasting change comes from altered core beliefs – not about the sugar content of chocolate, but a deeper understanding of who God is. If we truly understand how much he loves us and wants the best for us, then following his instructions and suggestions makes perfect sense.

Pray

Lord, help me to be transformed by my beliefs. May I forgive others because I have been forgiven; love others because I am deeply loved by you, and share Jesus because he died for me.

Day 140

Be Rooted

Fiona Castle

Your roots will grow down into God's love and keep
you strong.
Ephesians 3:17

'There are just two things we can give our children,' said the
mother of one of my son's school friends, 'roots and wings.'

I've no idea whether she was a Christian, but she certainly
reflected what God asks of us as parents.

A clingy toddler is showing he's nervous – only when he feels
safe can he start to explore. Older children are the same. If they
feel secure in the love and trust of their parents, and if that love
is founded on the love of Jesus, then they'll have confidence.

I remember when our 16-year-old daughter announced that
she couldn't wait to leave home and get a flat of her own. For
a moment, I felt like a failure – but then I realized that she
was showing how secure she felt. She was ready to spread
her wings and become independent. We had done our job.

There's something in this for all of us. We all need our roots
securely grounded in God's love, to enable us to face any
situation that life brings. We need not fear being let down,
because God has promised never to fail us or forsake us.

Pray

Father God, thank you for the love that feeds us and helps us
to grow into the life you give us.

Day 141

Be in Awe

Mandy Catto

The LORD merely spoke, and the heavens were created. He
breathed the word, and all the stars were born. He assigned
the sea its boundaries and locked the oceans in vast reservoirs.
Let the whole world fear the LORD, and let everyone stand in
awe of him. For when he spoke, the world began!

Psalm 33:6–9

This week I met up with a friend from youth-group days,
who shared her adventures over the last five years. She
works hard as a nurse in A & E for nine months, saving up
enough money to go travelling for three months every year.
She has travelled to Australia, New Zealand, South America,
India and Africa.

She summed up the wonders of the lakes, mountains,
plains, valleys and oceans she has seen in two words: 'Wow!'
and 'How?' Wowed by the incredible beauty and diversity
of God's incredible creation. And constantly asking 'How?'
when faced with new and unexpected phenomena. Her
favourite place was South Island in New Zealand, with the
Salt Plains of Bolivia a close second. Her world-view had
certainly expanded, along with her faith, as she stood in awe
of God through it all.

Pray

Creator God, thank you for the gift of your beautiful world.
Give me time today to pause and look around. May I stand
in awe of you. Help me to acknowledge you as the Creator in
conversations with others.

Day 142

Be a Beneficiary

Rachel Allcock

And they will see his face, and his name will be written on their foreheads.
Revelation 22:4

When one of my favourite high-street shops launched a range of science-themed stationery, I hurried to pick up a journal for my science-teacher husband. It features an image of a glass, with water and the air above it, both labelled. The caption reads, 'Technically, the glass is full.'

This really inspired me. We don't have to choose to be optimistic 'glass half-full' or pessimistic 'glass half-empty' people. We can be 'glass full'. It's not great to be labelled pessimistic or optimistic, and I for one can't decide which I am.

If we embrace who we are in Christ, we can be 'glass full'. This will only happen if we allow the invisible element in our glasses to be filled by the Holy Spirit. It's like the difference between happiness and joy: something in your life may make you happy, but happiness is shallow and will not last. The great news is that there is a deep joy that can only come from a hope in Christ, and this priceless element will fill your glass. Ultimately, there will be no optimist or pessimist, no A-type personality, no mental health struggles. We'll all have the same name written on our foreheads: Jesus.

Pray

Jesus, thank you for giving joy. Help us to accept that gift, and recognize that our glasses are full, whether we are happy or not.

Day 143

Be Original

Rachel Allcock

Thank you for making me so wonderfully complex! Your workmanship is marvellous – how well I know it.
Psalm 139:14

Zebras are stripy. However, thanks to a genetic mutation, it is possible to find a spotty zebra in the wild. And what colour is a robin? They're not all red and brown: there are a few pure white ones! The natural world is full of surprises.

I have plenty of simple, darker-coloured outfits for unconfident or trying-to-be-sophisticated days. But the clothes that make me happiest are covered in patterns and are hopefully unique to me! It's not great to find your dress matches someone else's, is it?

Thankfully, confidence and originality are celebrated now more than ever. There's no such thing as 'quite unique' – something is either unique or it's not. And God has designed each one of us to be unique! For that spotty zebra, it can't always be easy. Plenty of children's stories narrate the difficulties faced by creatures who feel they stand out. But we are made to stand out! Each aspect of your face, your body, your personality and your temperament are unique to you. When struggling with your appearance, remember: even if we all ate the same food and did the same amount of exercise, we wouldn't look the same. We're not meant to be clones. Don't waste another day waiting to become a better version of yourself.

Pray

Lord, help me to honour you by loving my uniqueness and appreciating my complexity.

Day 144

Be Concerned

Fiona Castle

'I have seen your hard work and your patient endurance.
I know you don't tolerate evil people.'
Revelation 2:2

The word 'endurance' is sometimes thought of as the same as 'tolerance'. We are called to be patient and tolerant when things don't go the way we want. But the next sentence shows the difference: 'You don't tolerate evil people.' There is a saying which illustrates this: 'Whatever you tolerate you will never change.'

We are called to be a 'voice for the voiceless', to stand up against injustice in the world. By closing our eyes to injustice, we are neglecting the opportunities God gives us to stand against the persecution, poverty, slavery and sex trafficking which cause suffering to millions.

Proverbs 31:8–9 says, 'Speak up for those who cannot speak for themselves; ensure justice for those being crushed. Yes, speak up for the poor and helpless, and see that they get justice.'

As long as we fail to do anything positive to alleviate the suffering of others, we are merely continuing to contribute to it. The greatest threat to the world today is not terrorism or war, but indifference.

Pray

Lord, give me a constant concern for your suffering people around the world, and show me where I can help.

Be a Giant-killer

Rhiannon Goulding

> As Goliath moved closer to attack, David quickly ran out to meet him.
>
> 1 Samuel 17:48

Do you have family traits you don't like? Maybe you always see the bad in situations and the worst in people. Were you brought up to look away when it gets difficult, or be passive-aggressive? Do you tend to look after yourself first, or gossip about people or church? Have you unquestioningly accepted the statement, 'We've never got on with that side of the family'?

In every family, ungodly opinions and behaviours develop and take root. We inherit so many good things, but we also adopt many nasty habits. We brush these off, defending ourselves with phrases like, 'It's just the way we do it, it's how we talk.'

In our family we call these Goliaths. If we don't confront these attitudes and behaviours, if we don't fight them and kill them, then our children will have to do it, or our children's children. We don't want them to inherit these Goliaths. They are big, dangerous and hard to destroy. So, how do we change ingrained behaviour?

Recognize when you do it, say what it is, say sorry, speak truth, make new bridges, forgive and build a family free from giants.

Pray

Lord Jesus, sometimes our habits seem stronger than we are. Help us to face up to the truth about ourselves, and give us strength to overcome them.

Day 146

Be an Example

Fiona Castle

Don't let anyone think less of you because you are young. Be an example to all believers in what you say, in the way you live, in your love, your faith, and your purity.
1 Timothy 4:12

Paul wrote these words to Timothy from prison, teaching and mentoring this young man so that he in turn could teach others.

As we grow, we need to follow others who set us a good example of how to behave. And in our turn, we need to consider what sort of example our lives set to others, whether those others are colleagues in our workplace, fellow students or our own children.

Billy Graham put it like this:

- We are the Bible the world is reading.
- We are the creeds the world is needing.
- We are the sermons the world is heeding.

That is some responsibility!

If people were asked to write a definition of Christianity from what they see in you, what do you think they would write? How can you live in love, faith and purity?

Having a servant heart might be a good beginning!

Pray

Heavenly Father, enable me to be an example of your love and joy to all I meet today.

Day 147

Be Significant

Rachel Allcock

> May the LORD our God be with us as he was with our
> ancestors; may he never leave us or abandon us.
> 1 Kings 8:57

Have you ever helped clear a house after a relative has passed away? I vividly remember going with my mum to clear my Great Grandma's house. I'd never been upstairs there, so it was exciting for me to look through all the mementos of a life I hadn't really considered. To me, Great Grandma had been a tiny old lady with a lovely smile, who toasted bread over the fire, kept hair in a brown paper bag to help the birds make their nests and used the scary toilet at the end of the garden.

Upstairs we found her old Bible. Inside, she had written the date on which she had given her life to Jesus. It was wonderful to see this and think about my Great Grandma as a teenage girl who knew friendships, heartbreak and joy, just like me. She had experienced forgiveness and grace, just like me.

My other Great Grandma was born in 1899 and died in 2001; her life touched three centuries! How many generations back can you trace your family tree? Our ancestors are not as distant as we might think.

Pray

Father God, help me to walk with you throughout my life, so future generations may do so too.

Day 148

Be Free

Fiona Castle

'But not a single sparrow can fall to the ground without your Father knowing it. And the very hairs on your head are all numbered. So don't be afraid; you are more valuable to God than a whole flock of sparrows.'
Matthew 10:29–31

It's very common for women to suffer from low self-esteem. So often people are defined by their job description, but whether we work full-time or part-time, stay at home or volunteer, we can lack a positive identity and undervalue ourselves. Our self-image affects us all our lives. It could be called a psychological disease.

Our consumer society markets beauty, image, wealth and success with pictures of glamorous women, making us feel inadequate. We need to let go of our fear of rejection and our fear of what others think of us – if indeed they *are* thinking of us!

Jesus encourages us by illustrating our amazing value to God, which is not fleeting but eternal. When our self-esteem is grounded in our Creator rather than ourselves, we are set free to be the person he created us to be – loved with an everlasting love.

Pray

Jesus, thank you that you set me free to become the person you created me to be, and that I am precious to you.

Day 149

Be Vulnerable

Rachel Allcock

I pray that God, the source of hope, will fill you completely with joy and peace because you trust in him. Then you will overflow with confident hope through the power of the Holy Spirit.
Romans 15:13

A few hours after my over-40 health check, the doctor called. My iron levels were dangerously low, and he told me to make an urgent appointment. One symptom of anaemia is hair loss, and sure enough, over the next year, my hair just seemed to stop growing, thin out and then sprout again in curly clumps. After growing up being told that my hair was my crowning glory, I lost a lot of confidence. People who hadn't seen me for months would remark, 'Oh, you've cut your hair.'

Opening up about my anaemia and my health worries has brought so many opportunities to connect on a deeper level with the women around me. I've also been forced to find value in myself beyond what I look like, how people define me, or my health. My issues were minuscule compared to what many suffer every day, but through them, God reminded me to be open with those around me. Yes, sometimes I over-shared (sorry to those who had to listen to my colonoscopy story), but I hope that my over-sharing gave others the confidence to speak up.

Pray

Loving Father God, thank you for the blessing of empathetic conversations. Help us to validate our friends' experiences by opening up about our own struggles.

Day 150

Be a Follower

Fiona Castle

You must have the same attitude that Christ Jesus had.
Philippians 2:5

I was recently challenged by this verse when I was asked, 'What would your life be like, even for one day, if you were to think or act like Jesus?'

Think about it! What have you already thought, said or done, that wouldn't have happened if you had thought first, 'How would Jesus have handled this?' How could your life be different if Jesus' priorities governed all you do? Does Jesus' love for you govern your behaviour?

We can alter our lives by altering our attitudes – it's our thought-life, not our circumstances, that determines our happiness and peace. It's not so much what happens, but how we handle what happens that's important.

A medical study observed that our bodies relax when we speak positive words and the blood-flow increases to our brain, which helps us to handle situations more effectively. All the more reason why we need to guard our attitudes!

Pray

Give me the right attitude, Lord Jesus. Help me to follow your example.

Day 151

Be Grateful

Fiona Castle

Be thankful in all circumstances, for this is God's will for you
who belong to Christ Jesus.
1 Thessalonians 5:18

Recently I travelled to the Isle of Wight to speak at an evening event. It was a bitterly cold day and once we landed at Cowes, gale-force winds added to the chill. I was feeling very sorry for myself by the time I reached the venue, but was able to thaw out in a quiet corner with a cup of coffee and a magazine.

The first article I read described the appalling conditions in a detention centre for African immigrants in Italy. Survival is all they can hope for, in a fly-ridden place with no sanitation, no food and little hope of work.

I read the article with shame in my heart. How could I complain, when I had a warm home to go back to? I had food in the fridge and clean clothes in the wardrobe. These poor people had fled from violence and famine and I was complaining about feeling cold! It was a salutary lesson.

It reminded me to exchange self-pity for gratitude . . . to thank God for the innumerable blessings in my life, rather than focussing on the negatives.

Pray

Father, I thank you for all the blessings you have bestowed on me. Show me today what I can do to bless others.

Day 152

Be Mindful

Fiona Castle

Even when I walk through the darkest valley, I will not be afraid, for you are close beside me. Your rod and your staff protect and comfort me.
Psalm 23:4

To actively choose to go through dark times would demonstrate a strangely negative attitude to life. To choose God's will, even though it might mean going through dark times, is very different. It's a positive attitude because he has promised to be close beside us in our difficulties.

I remember a preacher once saying, 'Don't forget in the darkness what God has shown you in the light.' It was sound advice. But after going through my own times of darkness, I have learned that I can turn that saying on its head, and say, 'Don't forget, in the light, what God has shown you in the darkness.' I have learned so much in my dark times that I never would have discovered if life had always been easy. Those experiences develop trust, stability and an important balance that stands me in good stead in times of uncertainty.

Christ's peace is experienced not only in the absence of darkness, but in the midst of it. Character is what you are in the dark!

Pray

Dear God, I thank you for all you have taught me in the dark times, enabling me to rejoice in your love and security.

Be Generous

Fiona Castle

And don't forget to do good and to share with those in need.
These are the sacrifices that please God.
Hebrews 13:16

Generosity is not simply sharing or giving away possessions and money, but more importantly giving of ourselves in our time, our energy and our talents.

We live in a materialistic society where money and possessions are very important, and where people take pride in the size of their houses, high earnings and exotic holidays. How very different from some people in the poorest countries, who share what little they have to bless others.

There are so many people in the world today who are in need in different ways. The problems are so enormous, it's hard to think that anything we do could make any difference. The charity, Global Care, has a strap line which says, 'Can't do everything. Mustn't do nothing. Can do something.' Generosity in that case is not only giving money, but may be time, energy, encouragement, help and prayers.

In the words of King David in 1 Chronicles 29:14, 'Everything we have has come from you, and we give you only what you first gave us!'

Pray

Lord, remind me that everything we have belongs to you, and help me to share all I have with others.

Day 154

Be Present

Becky Burr

For everything there is a season, a time for every activity under heaven.
Ecclesiastes 3:1

Have you ever wished you could control time? That you could stop the clock to savour a special moment, or fast-forward a tough day at work?

When I read this verse and the beautiful poem that follows, I sense God telling me to release my attempts to control time (which are futile anyway!), to take a deep breath, accept that there is time for everything and be present in each moment rather than rushing onto the next thing.

There is a time for washing and ironing and there's a time to spend joyous, spontaneous moments with the kids. There is a time to work-work-work and there is a time to rest. There is a time to cook and clean and there's a time to enjoy your husband's company. There is a time for DIY and there is a time for a glass of wine with friends.

In order to be women who embrace the present, we need to accept there is a time for everything. Even when our plans don't work out, the most important thing is that we seek God in that moment and take any opportunities that God is giving us.

Pray

Lord, I am sorry that I try to control time. I accept that there is a time for everything; give me wisdom to know how to spend my time.

Be Joyful

Fiona Castle

Always be full of joy in the Lord. I say it again – rejoice!
Philippians 4:4

There's a big difference between joy and happiness. Happiness is dependent on things in life going the way you want – life without problems. But joy can be present even in the midst of sorrow and disaster. I don't think I understood this until I experienced it myself.

When my husband died, I was heartbroken, knowing that the person I loved most in the world was no longer with me. Life would never be the same again. However, through the tears, I experienced a joy that was inexpressible. It brought peace in my heart that gave me the courage to keep going and move forward in a way I never would have thought possible. Then I understood that when we keep our eyes on Jesus, in the knowledge of his love for us, we can know joy even in the hardest of times.

When we gave our lives to Jesus, he never promised that everything would be fine as a result. He told us that in the world we will have trouble, but to take heart, because he has overcome the world.

Pray

Lord, I choose to be filled with your joy, today and every day.

Day 156

Be Appreciative

Rhiannon Goulding

Love each other with genuine affection, and take delight in
honouring each other.
Romans 12:10

Across the road from my house, there's the most beautiful
garden. Every day I glance across as I turn left into my drive,
and I get so much enjoyment from seeing what's in flower
in every season. The new couple who live there spend hours
tending it, pruning the shrubs and weeding the beds, and
I get the pleasure of seeing it. I keep thinking that one day,
when life's quieter, I'll have a driveway like that.

One sunny day I got out of my car and thought, 'I must stop
and tell them what joy it brings me.' So I went across and
said, 'Thank you for your garden, I really enjoy seeing it.' The
woman there was so pleased that someone had noticed and
appreciated it. She was lovely – she even gave me some tips
on easy ways to improve my own dilapidated drive!

I wonder how many people we pass every day, who feel
as if no one notices their hard work. Why not take time to
stop and say thank you to someone in your community or
church? Let them know that they are seen and that their
contribution has an impact on your life. Helping people to
feel valued is a gift you can give them.

Pray

Lord, please help me to see the places where a kind word
can make a difference to someone today.

Be Light

Fiona Castle

'You are the light of the world – like a city on a hilltop that cannot be hidden. No one lights a lamp and then puts it under a basket. Instead, a lamp is placed on a stand, where it gives light to everyone in the house.'
Matthew 5:14–15

There are certain people who seem to light up a room by their presence, not because they monopolize the conversation, or by how they are dressed, but simply by being there. Have you ever been to a theatre where one particular actress seems to light up the stage by her presence and voice?

In this passage, Jesus has called his disciples aside to teach them to be salt and light in the world. As his followers, how can we be that salt and light in the dark world in which we are living today? Are we able to bring encouragement and positivity to those who are downhearted? Can we be an example of resilience as we go through trials and difficulties? Paul reminds us that, 'We now have this light shining in our hearts, but we ourselves are like fragile clay jars containing this great treasure. This makes it clear that our great power is from God, not from ourselves' (2 Corinthians 4:7).

Pray

Dear Lord, help me to show your love to those I meet today, through your light shining within me.

Day 158

Be Hopeful

Sarah McKerney

And he felt the hand of the LORD upon him.
Ezekiel 1:3

We've all had that moment in life when everything changes: the death of a loved one; the loss of an unborn child; leaving the job we loved or betrayed by that friend we trusted. These are times which leave us wondering what the future holds and how we will navigate our new circumstances. In those moments, we often wonder where God is.

Ezekiel lived during such a time. He faced probably the most significant crisis in the history of the nation of Israel. Jerusalem was invaded and the tribe of Judah was exiled in Babylon. Priesthood was supposed to be Ezekiel's destiny, but he was torn from the Promised Land and exiled, and the Temple had been destroyed. Residing now in a place of despair and helpless confusion, Ezekiel must have questioned where God was in all this.

Yet verse 3 tells us that 'he felt the hand of the Lord take hold of him', even though he must have felt that God was far away. The book of Ezekiel is ultimately a message of hope in despair. For Ezekiel life might not have been the same as it was before, but the Temple would be rebuilt. And in that moment of disappointment, Ezekiel found a new calling. His new mission and new purpose were born out of that wretched place.

Pray

Lord God, help me to feel your hand upon me, and to know my hope is in you.

Day 159

Be Enough

Rachel Allcock

'For the Lord your God is living among you. He is a mighty saviour. He will take delight in you with gladness. With his love, he will calm all your fears. He will rejoice over you with joyful songs.'
Zephaniah 3:17

Lockdown proved that one of my children had become dependent on teacher feedback (otherwise, what's the point in doing the work, he wrongly wondered). It also proved that I had become dependent on people saying nice things – about something I was wearing, something I had written or a problem I had solved.

I was reminded of a harsh truth: if I depend on what others comment or don't, or reply or don't, I will be disappointed many times. I learned to look up to my Father in heaven, instead of looking down waiting for notifications on my phone.

It's hard, though. I think that's one of the reasons we were designed to live in community. We can encourage each other, worship together and laugh with each other. Once taken for granted, these joys became things I craved during that time of isolation. If you don't find yourself in a kind group, I encourage you to seek one out. If you find yourself in a sarcastic, harsh work environment, I pray you are able to embrace God's delight over you, and that this is enough.

Pray

Lord Jesus, I'm sorry I often forget that you are more than enough for me.

Day 160

Be Cleansed

Fiona Castle

For I fully expect and hope that I will never be ashamed, but that I will continue to be bold for Christ, as I have been in the past. And I trust that my life will bring honour to Christ, whether I live or die.

Philippians 1:20

We all know the expression about something being fit for purpose – or not – whether it's an electrical gadget or a pair of walking boots! But perhaps at the beginning of the year, or a new season, it is a good time to take stock of our lives, our work and our attitudes. Are we fit for purpose? More importantly, are we being faithful to God's plan and purpose for our lives? If not, what needs to change?

If my body, as Paul says, is the temple of the Holy Spirit, perhaps the Temple needs a spring clean from time to time. Do I bring glory to God by the way I behave? It's easy to get into a routine, without allowing the Holy Spirit to discipline and inspire us each day.

Today, let's ask the Holy Spirit to cleanse us and to help us stay focussed and on target towards his purpose being fulfilled in our lives.

Pray

Father, I pray for the cleansing of your Holy Spirit today, that I might be inspired to begin afresh to take your love wherever you choose to send me.

Day 161

Be Transformed

Jaz Potter

For God is working in you, giving you the desire and the
power to do what pleases him.
Philippians 2:13

I remember working with a group of young people who found themselves on the wrong side of the law. As we got to know one another, it became apparent they didn't feel any guilt or remorse for stealing items or damaging property. In fact, their universal response was, 'Well, all those people are insured.'

In turn, I'm aware how easy it is for the victims of such crimes to exaggerate when making a claim: 'I've been paying premiums for years and never made a claim till now,' they say or, 'They'll put my premiums up anyway.' And so it goes round in circles.

This kind of behaviour is called rationalization. It's easy to make excuses for our actions. Sometimes it's so subtle we don't even realize we are doing it.

This verse reminds us of our high calling, and it reassures us that we can't live the Christian life in our own strength. We so easily run out of steam when we try to do it all ourselves. It is God himself who gives us the ability to work out our faith each day, by filling us with his wonderful Holy Spirit who counsels and directs us.

Pray

Dear God, fill me today and grow my desire to do what pleases you.

Be Constant

Rhiannon Goulding

So prepare your minds for action and exercise self-control.
Put all your hope in the gracious salvation that will come to
you when Jesus Christ is revealed to the world.

1 Peter 1:13

A woman was speaking to me about someone who had messed up and was in a bad way. Her tone was harsh. 'Well, if she carries on,' she declared, 'she'll harden her heart towards God, and then she won't ever come back.'

My heart broke as I found myself asking, where is our grace? The grace we so freely and wholeheartedly hold on to in our darkest moments. May my heart always be searching for a way back for people, as opposed to creating more hurdles for them to climb over. I want to be the one removing the barriers for their return to God. I want grace to be in my every word.

So in your dealings with people, keep the route home clear and inviting. Show love in your texts, calls, letters, likes and comments, and never ever give up doing so. Prepare your mind for action, seek the fallen and draw them back to the loving God, who is always full of grace and forgiveness.

Pray

Lord Jesus, it's so tempting to be judgemental. Help me always to be loving and pointing the way to you.

Day 163

Be Determined

Fiona Castle

'I am with you always, even to the end of the age.'
Matthew 28:20

Does anyone remember Eddie 'the Eagle' Edwards? In 1988 he was the first ever competitor to represent Great Britain at ski jumping at the Winter Olympics. You might have seen the sports comedy film made about him, 30 years afterwards! He didn't win any medals, but he was eventually embraced as a national treasure, and a byword for determination.

He reminds me of the story of the disciples when they see Jesus walking on the water. Peter says boldly, 'Lord, if it's really you, tell me to come to you.' Jesus encourages him, and Peter gets out of the boat and starts walking. It's only when he looks down at the churning water beneath him that he panics and starts to sink, but Jesus holds him and helps him back on board.

At least Peter had the courage to try. The other disciples were still sitting comfortably in the boat!

This challenges me. Am I prepared to step out of my comfort zone and get my feet wet? Am I ready to follow where the Lord leads me and try something new? Am I willing to persevere, even when I fail?

As Jesus said afterwards: 'Why did you doubt me?'

Pray

Lord, I am willing to step out of my comfort zone in order to follow you, today and every day.

Be a Messenger

Fiona Castle

'There is salvation in no one else! God has given no other
name under heaven by which we must be saved.'
Acts 4:12

Christmas is probably the biggest universal celebration. We send cards and parcels across the world, often spending more than we can afford. Decorations and sparkling lights shine in streets and homes. Easter doesn't have such an impact. Hot cross buns, Easter eggs and the occasional Easter bunny is as far as it goes. Yet without the resurrection of Jesus, Christmas would mean nothing. Christianity would not have emerged as the greatest, most liberating, life-saving faith in the world.

Sadly, many people go along with both celebrations without any idea of the real meaning of them.

Selwyn Hughes said that in all other religions, man is reaching up to God, trying to gain his approval. The Christian faith is different: God is reaching down to man. Jesus gave his life so that we could be forgiven and accepted.

We are saved, not because we're good enough, but because of Jesus' willingness to pay the price. That is the wonderful message we have to share. So let's celebrate Easter all year round, and continue to be God's messengers wherever he sends us.

Pray

Dear God, send me out as your messenger to declare the sacrificial gift you have given us, through the life, death and resurrection of our Lord Jesus Christ.

Day 165

Be Trusting

Fiona Castle

You love him even though you have never seen him. Though you do not see him now, you trust him; and you rejoice with a glorious, inexpressible joy. The reward for trusting him will be the salvation of your souls.

1 Peter 1:8–9

As Christians, we are called to live a life of trust. There are many things in the Bible I don't understand but, because my life changed so positively when I became a Christian, I trust the Lord in all my circumstances.

Sometimes our lives enter very dark places, when it's harder to trust: illness, disappointment, bereavement, heartbreak. Yet the act of holding on to our faith in God gives us strength to endure and to pass through that valley.

Jesus trusted his Father. He did not want to suffer death on the cross, yet he said, 'Not my will but yours.' We know that the cross led to the resurrection and opened the way to heaven for all of us. Sometimes our faith is tested when things don't go the way we would like, but only God sees the bigger picture and knows the purposes he has for us and for the world.

Pray

Thank you, Lord, for bringing your purposes to pass, even through a broken heart.

Day 166

Be a Witness

Fiona Castle

Be careful to live properly among your unbelieving
neighbours.
1 Peter 2:12

It is challenging to realize that we can be assessed far more objectively by the way we behave than by what we say. Simple acts of kindness and thoughtfulness can speak more than a thousand words.

As Christians, we all have the responsibility and opportunity to show the love of Jesus by the way we treat people and care for them. In our busy lives, it is often easier to keep ourselves to ourselves and to avoid interacting with others, but we have a daily opportunity to share his love by looking around for those who might be in need of help or an encouraging word.

We can build friendships with those people by showing compassion in their afflictions and by aiming to understand their problems. If we do this with tenderness, being good listeners, we can eventually share our own stories of overcoming difficulties or bereavements or failures. Then we can tell them how, by discovering the love of Jesus, we are assured of his presence at all times, and that even though he never promises us a perfect life, he will never leave us or forsake us.

We are all ambassadors for Christ.

Pray

Lord Jesus, help me to be aware of those around me each day, and to care for their needs with the love and compassion you have shown me.

Be Uncluttered

Rachel Allcock

As a dog returns to its vomit, so a fool repeats his foolishness.
Proverbs 26:11

I have no problem clearing clothes from the kids' cupboards, but I hate the job of sorting mine out, and it's our bedroom that tends to get left out when we have a big tidy up. Over the past few years, decluttering has once again become 'the answer' to a simpler, more fulfilled life (though I'm sure that, by now, another fad has taken its place). All these solutions to a better life come down to habits.

A read through a few chapters of Proverbs is a good way to shake ourselves out of a great many lazy habits. Once we've had a good clear-out of our mind, our hang-ups, our 'stuff', we need to establish some kind of routine to keep things tidy. What freedom can we experience when we can access our gifts, delight in the treasure of our hearts, enjoy spending time with God and think in an uncluttered way?

I love the directness of this pithy proverb. Let's strive not to return to our old ways, like the dog. It's hard to do this on our own, but do you know what the wild dogs do? They run with a pack.

Pray

Lord, help me build accountability with someone so we can pray together and build good habits.

Day 168

Be Good

Fiona Castle

And I am certain that God, who began the good work within you, will continue his work until it is finally finished on the day that Christ Jesus returns.

Philippians 1:6

As I approached middle age, I remember noticing the change of pace. The children were growing up and didn't need me as much. After spending so many years rushing around struggling to find time for everything, it was easy to feel a little redundant.

That feels a long time ago now! There have been much more dramatic changes over the years. Yet each stage of life brings its blessings and new opportunities and we should look for those – not by struggling to stay young, but by waiting on God to show us his purpose for the next stage in our lives.

As Christians, we have a wonderful bonus, too. We have the assurance that God loves us, knows us and understands us just as we are at this moment.

We don't need to pretend to be something we're not. I'm encouraged by Paul's letter to Titus, which says, 'Similarly, teach the older women to live in a way that honours God . . . they should teach others what is good' (Titus 2:3).

I'd like to be a teacher of goodness!

Pray

Lord, help us to trust in your will for us, whatever stage of life we're at.

Day 169

Be a Friend

Fiona Castle

> Do not despise these small beginnings, for the LORD rejoices to see the work begin.
> Zechariah 4:10

Let's think about small beginnings.

Sometimes we don't have faith to believe we could lead a neighbour to Christ. We don't even have the courage to raise the subject. But do we have faith to believe she might come round for coffee? Yes, that might be easy.

So do we have the faith to believe we could offer to babysit? She might be delighted. Maybe we could ask her over for dinner.

If we gradually build up a trusting relationship, she might start to wonder how we cope with problems, how we view the world. Other conversations might spring from that.

There are many situations which seem impossible from a human perspective. But if we start praying and believing, one step at a time, it's amazing how obstacles are removed and the way becomes clearer. We mustn't allow ourselves to make excuses for our lack of faith, but we should make the effort to build up our faith by exercising it. By taking it little by little, we can gradually build up faith to believe for more.

Pray

I pray, Lord, that you would give me wisdom as I build friendships with people, in a way that will draw them towards you, rather than put them off.

Day 170

Be Calm

Jaz Potter

'The thief's purpose is to steal and kill and destroy. My purpose is to give them a rich and satisfying life.'
John 10:10

During lockdown, I was placed on furlough. As is customary, I set up an auto-reply to work emails, giving alternative contact details for someone who could help with enquiries.

One Saturday evening, I received a mail-shot email. My system auto-replied to the sender – to which their email auto-replied, explaining that there was no one in the office and they would get back to me soon. As soon as that reply arrived, my system auto-replied . . . this went on and on. Every few seconds another email arrived, and by the 404th email, I was overwhelmed. It was as though my computer had been taken over and for a moment I felt helpless – until I realized I knew the organizer, and they could sort it out for me.

We know it's God who is the author or 'organizer' of our lives. He knows us: he can stop us feeling overwhelmed and bring about the breakthrough we need. He doesn't steal our joy, but promises us a rich and satisfying life.

Pray

Dear God, help me to stay in contact with you today, the ultimate organizer of my life. Help me to sense your closeness as I go about my daily work, and when I feel overwhelmed, help me know you are near.

Be Confident

Fiona Castle

I pray that your hearts will be flooded with light so that you can understand the confident hope he has given to those he called – his holy people who are his rich and glorious inheritance.

Ephesians 1:18

Do you feel that your heart is flooded with light as you worship the one who saved you and has given you new life in him? God's overwhelming love for us takes us beyond our daily chores and struggles, so that we may place our trust in him.

He calls us to rise to the occasion, whatever our circumstances, even through trials and difficulties and grief, in order that we can be used for his glory.

God has given me so much, and in return I long to be used by him to draw others to faith. The wonderful fact is that he allows us to play a part in his plan for the world and the coming of his kingdom. What a privilege it is! Let's be willing to submit to his will, confident that he is working through us.

Pray

Lord, may all you have generously given me be used to feed and nourish others.

Day 172

Be Patient

Rhiannon Goulding

'The young man became so hungry that even the pods he
was feeding the pigs looked good to him.'
Luke 15:16

One of our teenagers was going through a difficult stage
and making some wrong decisions. We had an argument
and he went to stay with friends. My heart was in pieces. I
couldn't sleep for worry.

Then the story of the prodigal son came to mind. I thought
about the dad in the story. If he'd had the technology, would
he have called, or waited? Would he have looked for clues
on social media so he could go and 'save him' and bring him
home, or would he have just waited for his return when he
was ready? As I read the passage again, I felt a strong urge
to pray for pigs in my teenager's life. I prayed that the pigs
would come quickly and not cause lasting damage. The
verse says that while he was sitting with the pigs, he 'came to
his senses'. When he found himself in a bad place, he finally
came to his senses and went home.

For the next few weeks, I prayed harder than I ever had before.
I prayed that the pigs would come, that those situations
would make him look at things differently and come home.
After some time, my prodigal returned safely.

Pray

Father, give me wisdom to know when to act, and when to
trust you to keep my loved ones safe.

Be Fearless

Fiona Castle

God is our refuge and strength, always ready to help in times
of trouble. So we will not fear when earthquakes come and
the mountains crumble into the sea.
Psalm 46:1–2

Can we honestly say that we live without fear, whatever our circumstances? Are we able to stand firm, trusting God, whatever troubles we are facing? It's natural to be fearful when we're waiting for exam results, wondering whether an application for a new job is successful or awaiting the results of serious medical tests. Our human nature causes us to be fearful in so many circumstances. Yet in 1 John 4:16 and 18 we read: 'God is love, and all who live in love live in God, and God lives in them . . . Such love has no fear, because perfect love expels all fear.'

Many of us feel inadequate and live in fear of what others might think of us, but we don't need to be afraid when God is living within us. We need to face our fears, retrace them to their roots and cast them out, knowing that his love for us is sufficient to meet all our needs. Aim to live this day without allowing any fears to diminish God's love for you.

Pray

Lord, with your help, today I banish all fears from my mind and my life, and allow your love to flow through me to enable me to face all that happens.

Day 174

Be Blooming

Fiona Castle

And so, dear brothers and sisters, I plead with you to give
your bodies to God because of all he has done for you.
Let them be a living and holy sacrifice – the kind he will
find acceptable.
Romans 12:1

We have all heard wonderful stories of missionaries who have sacrificed everything for the gospel. And often we compare ourselves and feel useless. Or perhaps we live under the cloud of having been told as children that we won't amount to much.

But in Hebrews it says, 'Let us run with perseverance the race that is marked out for us.' That's us as individuals, created and loved by God. We all have different gifts and different areas of influence, and we can't see the whole picture or foresee all that may grow from the small seeds we sow. God uses us where we are.

It's so tempting to focus on the strengths of others and compare them with our weaknesses, but we need to feel comfortable in our own skins and seek out the opportunities God has given us. Let's remind ourselves that we are God's masterpiece and that we are 'fearfully and wonderfully made'.

Bloom where you're planted!

Pray

Lord, help me to be the best that I can be, in the situation where you have placed me to do your will.

Be Loved

Mandy Catto

'I have always loved you,' says the LORD.
Malachi 1:2

God is the only one who knew you before you were born. He knew all about you – your character, name, features, talents and weaknesses – before you were conceived. From before the beginning of time, God knew you. And for all that time of knowing you, he loved you. The truth of an eternity of knowledge and love that is uniquely yours is comforting, and yet overwhelming too.

If you are having a moment of feeling that no one understands you, then look up and remember that God understands you. If you ever feel that no one notices you, realize that God always notices and is looking on with love for you. If no one has told you recently that they love you, then read these beautiful words from the prophet Malachi: the God of love has always loved you.

When God's people first heard these words, they immediately replied, 'Really, but how?' Eternal love is a lot to take in and they questioned it. Maybe we question it too? 'I don't feel lovable today.' 'Last year was so hard; I felt abandonment, not love.' Be assured – God promises that he loves you right now and he always has.

Pray

Loving Father God, thank you that you have known me and loved me since before time began. Help me to know and receive your love for me today.

Day 176

Be Loving

Fiona Castle

And may the Lord make your love for one another and for all people grow and overflow, just as our love for you overflows.
1 Thessalonians 3:12

I grew up during the Second World War, and my doctor father was always busy – but his parenting was firm and loving. I know I was blessed.

In today's society, the pressures on family life are enormous. In his book, *The Sixty-Minute Father*, Rob Parsons tells a modern-day parable of a father who nearly drops his newborn son when he reaches into his pocket for his mobile phone. He catches the baby, but the mobile determines never to be thwarted again. It rings in the middle of a bedtime story, or a board game, or during a serious conversation with a teenager. The father fails to spot the mobile's strategy. Once the son leaves home, the phone stops ringing!

We can be sure that our tasks and work responsibilities will never be as dear to us as those we love. If we neglect the people close to us, one day we'll regret missed opportunities and the weakening of relationships.

Pray

Lord, help me to live my life in a way that won't cause me to end up with regrets. Help me to be a loving person, with your love overflowing to others.

Be Merciful

Fiona Castle

So let us come boldly to the throne of our gracious God.
There we will receive his mercy, and we will find grace to help
us when we need it most.
Hebrews 4:16

The Bible teaches us to seek forgiveness when we have wronged others and to forgive others when they have wronged us. It sounds simple and straightforward, but not so easy to put into practice. But God is our example, because he extends to us the ultimate pardon.

The whole basis of the Christian faith is receiving God's mercy through Jesus' act of sacrificial love towards us. He was willing to pay the price for all the wrong we have done, through his death on the cross. Once we acknowledge this and repent, we are forgiven. What a gift!

Surely such mercy towards us should cause us to extend mercy to others; but it is easy to forget this when we have been unfairly treated or maligned. However, when we allow resentments to build up in us, we are the losers, because holding on to bitterness and anger destroys our peace and joy.

Who needs your mercy and forgiveness today? Show it, and you too will experience healing.

Pray

Dear God, please help me to show mercy today and to let go of any resentments I hold towards anyone who has hurt me. Thank you that you are a merciful God.

Day 178

Be a Servant

Fiona Castle

'And since I, your Lord and Teacher, have washed your feet,
you ought to wash each other's feet.'
John 13:14

Recently I was told about a church in Cologne which has a huge poster above the exit, saying 'Servants' Entrance'. This has really challenged me! We are God's servants, called to go where he directs and to spread the gospel, not just with our words but with our lives.

How do others see us? Are we caring, loving, patient, faithful friends and colleagues? Does the way we act make other people want to find what we have found?

The way we behave is seen by the world as a kind of advertisement for faith – what a responsibility! If we are trustworthy, peace-loving and humble, people will notice. If we're not, that will be noticed too.

We need to build up trust with our neighbours, so that when trouble comes along, we can be the ones to help and support them. I've met very few people who have rejected my offer to pray for them.

So let's remember, we go into the world through the servants' entrance, to be God's messengers of his love for his world.

Pray

Challenge me, Lord, to be the messenger of your love for the world wherever I go.

Day 179

Be Tactile

Rachel Allcock

'May he restore your youth and care for you in your old age. For he is the son of your daughter-in-law who loves you and has been better to you than seven sons!' Naomi took the baby and cuddled him to her breast. And she cared for him as if he were her own.
Ruth 4:15–16

It must have been awful for grandparents in lockdown not to be able to visit their new grandchildren. Back when my children were babies, I sometimes resented them being passed around after church – they came back hot and rumpled and smelling of several different perfumes. However, I could see from the joy on people's faces that by sharing my baby, I was blessing others. We all learned in lockdown that a deficit of hugs was detrimental to our wellbeing.

I love the tender, tactile relationship portrayed by Naomi and Ruth. It was Ruth's baby, but she was happy to share him with her mother-in-law. The neighbours rejoiced with Naomi that she now had a son again! There must still have been some differences of opinion about baby-led weaning, first shoes, manners at the table, and so on! However, this happy ending illustrates how, with a lot of understanding and generosity, we can bless our relatives and friends – and even restore their health – by sharing out the baby-cuddles.

Pray

Father God, thank you for the healing power of hugs.

Day 180

Be a Teacher

Fiona Castle

And you must commit yourselves wholeheartedly to these commands that I am giving you today. Repeat them again and again to your children.
Deuteronomy 6:6–7

A while ago, I noticed that Rainbows, Brownies, Guides and Rangers had changed their membership promise to omit any mention of God. I understand that this change was made so the groups could include those of all faiths or none, but it saddened me.

At the same time, young people face increasing pressures through social media and the celebrity culture. They measure themselves against unrealistic standards of physical appearance or wealth, but not the values of integrity, compassion or faith.

In an age of online bullying and abuse, it seems unfashionable to stand up for the Christian values which can improve life for the next generation. In a largely secular society, we need to find gentle ways of talking about Jesus, and telling our young people that they are loved, just as they are.

Many of those uniformed organizations meet on church premises and are staffed by Christian volunteers. Let's pray that they will find imaginative ways to reach the young people in their care with the Good News of Jesus.

Pray

Lord, your values are the only ones that matter, now and for eternity. Give all who belong to you the courage to share them.

Be Humble

Fiona Castle

Be humble, thinking of others as better than yourselves.
Philippians 2:3

This verse can give the wrong impression. When I was a child my mother read it to me, and as a result, I thought I should always assume everyone else was better than me.

However, humility is not about effacing ourselves, or destroying our own self-worth. On the contrary, it's about having an honest recognition of our worth as God sees us. He knows and loves us just as we are. We don't need to try to gain his approval by being cleverer than people around us or getting high-powered jobs!

There's a beautiful saying, 'Under the cross no one is above another. All are equal.' So many people feel unworthy or not good enough, as if they're always failing, but God doesn't see us like that. Yes, he gives us different gifts and opportunities, but he doesn't love us any less than a Prime Minister or a Princess!

We are all children of God, and we have an example of humility in Jesus, who 'humbled himself in obedience to God and died a criminal's death on a cross'. Alleluia, what a Saviour!

Pray

Thank you, Lord, that through your death on the cross you showed us what true humility is. Help me to learn from it.

Day 182

Be Adaptable

Sarah Jones

> An angel of the Lord appeared to him in a dream. 'Joseph, son of David,' the angel said, 'do not be afraid to take Mary as your wife. For the child within her was conceived by the Holy Spirit.'
> Matthew 1:20

A single mum friend of mine once said to me, 'Sarah, I don't think I'm going to find anyone again. What man wants to take on a child who isn't his own?'

'Joseph did,' I replied. This encouraged her and gave her hope.

We don't know what the future will bring, and our best-laid plans can be changed in an instant. Joseph must have been full of trepidation when he woke from his dream and took Mary as his wife. He embraced the privilege and responsibility of bringing up a child who wasn't his own. He was vital to the family's safety and direction: God told him where to live and how to escape danger. Joseph brought Jesus up in the Jewish traditions and took him to the Temple.

As the years went on, I'm sure he wondered, 'What can I offer the Son of God? How can I teach him anything?' But I believe Joseph faced his insecurities and got on with it, teaching Jesus not only carpentry but also faith by his example.

Joseph was obedient and adaptable, and he learned to love and protect his new family.

Pray

Father God, help me to protect and guide those you place in my path.

Day 183

Be Loving

Mandy Catto

Love means doing what God has commanded us, and he has commanded us to love one another, just as you heard from the beginning.

2 John 1:6

What is love? Scientists say it is a powerful and permanent neurological condition. Shakespeare writes, 'Love is an ever-fixed mark.' The *Peanuts* characters said, 'Love is walking hand in hand.' The band Wet Wet Wet sang, 'Love is all around'. Wikipedia defines love as a mix of feelings and actions that shows a deep liking for someone or something.

Rarely do we hear that love is walking in obedience to God. John's first letter states that God is love six times; in his second letter he expands this concept as he defines what love means: to be obedient to God and to love others. Love them, even when it is hard to like them. Love when it is not reciprocated.

John reminds us that right from the beginning we have been asked by God to love. In Leviticus 19:18 Moses set out the commandment to love your neighbour as yourself, and Jesus reinforced the importance of this in Matthew 22:39, calling it the second commandment, equal to loving God.

Who will you choose to love today? Will you take the first step in showing love to someone who needs it?

Pray

Father God, help me to love as you do. Give me strength to follow your commands and love others, showing your love to them through my actions and affirming words.

Day 184

Be Observant

Sarah McKerney

> There the angel of the LORD appeared to him in a blazing
> fire from the middle of a bush. Moses stared in amazement.
> Though the bush was engulfed in flames, it didn't burn up.
> Exodus 3:2

I grew up in Christian family and this story is very familiar to me. I remember reading it as a child and thinking, 'Wow, a burning bush!' But when I read it again as an adult, I realized that there is nothing remarkable about a burning bush in the middle of a desert. Think about it: that mixture of hot sun, arid land and a bush so parched that it was probably tinder. A bush catching fire in the desert was a common daily sight, like a cow in the Lancashire countryside. It was an ordinary thing.

And yet God came to Moses in that ordinary burning bush. I began to wonder, where do I expect to see God? Do I expect to see God in the extraordinary, the spectacular, the supernatural? What if I am so busy looking for God in the extraordinary that I miss God at work in the ordinary?

God is at work all around us, in the seemingly small and insignificant, and if we pay attention to the ordinary things, we can find God there.

Pray

Thank you, Lord, that you work in and through the ordinary. Help me today to see you at work in the small things.

Day 185

Be Released

Fiona Castle

So Christ has truly set us free. Now make sure that you stay
free, and don't get tied up again in slavery to the law.
Galatians 5:1

When we find new life in Christ, we are set free from our former
lives, our sins, our traditions and our conduct. The Holy Spirit
now lives within us to lead us; to provide us with his wisdom
and to guide us to live the life God has called us to live.

How can we explain that wonderful freedom to those whose
religion is simply a ritual? Just going to church can be a
comfortable habit, especially if it doesn't affect us for the rest
of the week! But once we know Jesus as our Saviour, all that
changes. We are freed from rules, but instead we really want
to do his will.

So even though our circumstances might constrict us, through
the power of the Holy Spirit we can know true freedom.

'Because the Spirit who lives in you is greater than the spirit
who lives in the world' (1 John 4:4).

We can go on our way rejoicing, knowing we have been set
free!

Pray

Thank you, Jesus, that you set me free when I found new life
in you. Help me always to live in that freedom.

Day 186

Be Present

Fiona Castle

Work willingly at whatever you do, as though you were working for the Lord rather than for people.
Colossians 3:23

I'm not good at multi-tasking, and I need peace and quiet to discipline myself to write. That was never easy to come by when our children were growing up. One of them would appear as soon as I sat down to work. So I'd stop and make a cup of tea, provide a snack to prevent imminent starvation, and listen to the day's events – and by then it wasn't worth starting my own project.

I knew they were capable of looking after themselves, but I wanted them to feel happy about coming home. I don't suppose they ever noticed, but I didn't want them to feel that I was too busy for them. I wanted them to feel valued. Parents make these little loving sacrifices, copying the greater sacrifice of Jesus.

God knows our needs and promises to take care of them, so long as we are prepared to put him first. My problem is not in the faithfulness of God's word to me, but in my obedience to it!

Pray

Father God, remind me each day not to do what I think is important, but to seek your wisdom for making my time count.

Day 187

Be Free

Rhiannon Goulding

They are like trees planted along the riverbank, bearing fruit each season.
Psalm 1:3

Whenever I return home to Wales, I'm always amazed to meet people I knew 20 years ago, who still assume I'm passionate about the things I liked back in those days. Then there are those who know me now: they're aware of some of the things I care deeply about but, at times, they can speak of me as if those are the *only* things I care about.

In both cases, the temptation is to feel labelled, contained, bottled!

The reality is that like a tree, constantly producing fresh leaves and fresh fruit in season, so we see our passions and commitments grow, change, mature and shift. Our friends may feel more comfortable placing a label or a definition on us – they can do it about what we love to do as much as about the person we are. But God is a God of creativity and originality. His desire is for each of us to live as an original and not as a copy. God never packs, boxes and labels us. Instead, he stirs us to be constantly renewing our focus and commitment.

Pray

Lord, I pray that each day you stir me to be focussed on you and your purpose for my life.

Day 188

Be Encouraging

Fiona Castle

And I am certain that God, who began the good work within you, will continue his work until it is finally finished on the day when Christ Jesus returns.

Philippians 1:6

We all need encouragers! When strength fails, we're weary and discouraged, we need someone to come alongside us, to build us up and inspire us to move forward. They fill us with renewed courage. The best teachers are those who encourage their pupils, looking for the good points rather than putting them down and telling them they are no good. I am sure we've all had experiences of both!

When we're alongside other Christians, we need to encourage and affirm them in the work they are doing for God. This doesn't mean they're doing everything perfectly, or that they couldn't do things differently, but it's important to be supportive – in our actions as well as words.

I know of children who have crumbled under continual negative comments, and other children who, in contrast, have thought, 'I'll show you!' and succeeded in spite of criticism.

Who can you encourage today? Is there a friend or a child or someone in your church who needs building up? Be that encourager and you might be surprised at the difference it makes.

Pray

Lord, continue to work through me day by day, to encourage others.

Day 189

Be Secure

Fiona Castle

'Anyone who listens to my teaching and follows it is wise, like
a person who builds a house on solid rock.'
Matthew 7:24

We all want security, whether it's through house or car insurance, burglar alarms, or a good salary. We feel safe if we're surrounded by such back-ups, against a world that is able to wreck all our comforts in a moment. Our plans can be ruined instantly, whether it's through floods, or earthquakes or other events.

So where does your security lie, in this ever-changing world? The Bible teaches us that we can trust God through all these crises, as he is the only lasting source of security, which will never change.

Sometimes the problem can be within ourselves, because we feel we don't measure up to other people's expectations, which gives us a sense of insecurity. This can be especially true of women, because we often judge ourselves when we look at others and feel that they are far more competent than we are, whether at work, or homemaking or child-rearing.

Our greatest security lies in knowing that nothing can separate us from God's love and assurance.

Pray

Thank you, Father, that I am secure in the knowledge of your love, and that nothing can separate me from it.

Day 190

Be Guided

Fiona Castle

'Seek the Kingdom of God above all else, and live righteously,
and he will give you everything you need. So don't worry
about tomorrow, for tomorrow will bring its own worries.
Today's trouble is enough for today.'
Matthew 6:33–34

Many of us lament our lack of free time, but whenever we have a break, we fail to use it well, because we think of all the things we should be doing, and feel guilty if we sit and relax. Urgency is addictive.

We get hooked on reacting to outside demands, because in our society, busyness often equals status. Yet we need to stop and be still – for our own health, as well as to take stock and assess what really needs doing. Not every problem is a call for us to solve it.

It's only when we place our lives in God's hands that we learn to let go and let God guide us. You have never lived this moment before and you'll never be able to live it again, so listen to what he tells you!

Pray

Loving Heavenly Father, help me to make the most of every moment, so that I don't look back with regrets.

Day 191

Be Fruitful

Fiona Castle

So I say, let the Holy Spirit guide your lives.
Galatians 5:16

This year our church was challenged to do forty acts of kindness – one each day during Lent. I found it quite a task to see if I could do just that!

However, I realized that kindness is only one flavour of the fruit of the Spirit, which includes love, joy, peace, patience, kindness, goodness, faithfulness, gentleness and self-control. If I was struggling to focus on just one of the results of the Holy Spirit in my life, what about all the others? Does the nourishment of the Spirit produce patience and goodness in me from day to day?

Jesus calls us to be salt and light to those around us. We are all missionaries to those who do not yet know his love. We may be successful in doing kindnesses for forty days, just as we can abstain from eating chocolate for Lent. But the fruit of the Spirit is for life. Maybe we can start today to apply Paul's advice and see if it can change our attitude to our circumstances every day.

Pray

Father, please give me the Holy Spirit's wisdom to live my life to serve others.

Day 192

Be Calm

Mandy Catto

'For the LORD your God is living among you. He is a mighty saviour. He will take delight in you with gladness. With his love, he will calm all your fears. He will rejoice over you with joyful songs.'
Zephaniah 3:17

These words in Zephaniah bring amazing promises of God's near presence for those who turn to him. The Trinity is displayed here with the Lord living among us today in the Holy Spirit. Jesus is your mighty saviour. God delights in you, he loves to watch you as you go about your day.

He promises to calm your fears, all your fears, with his love. Telling someone to be calm, especially in the midst of a time of fear or anxiety, is not often helpful. But God promises to calm fears with his overwhelming, never changing, all-consuming love. He is trustworthy and always fulfils his promises.

Finally, God brims with joy as he covers you with songs. What would the sound of God's singing be like? Creation began with just his spoken word, so how incredible is his singing? C.S. Lewis gives a powerful picture of God singing, through Aslan in *The Magician's Nephew*: a beautiful, rippling, triumphant, tingling sound beyond comparison.

Pray

Lord God, thank you that I know your presence. You saved me and you delight in me. Because of your love, I can be calm today as you rejoice over me with song.

Day 193

Be Faithful

Fiona Castle

He makes the whole body fit together perfectly. As each part does its own special work, it helps the other parts grow, so that the whole body is healthy and growing and full of love.
Ephesians 4:16

If you think of your life as a tapestry, how colourful would your picture be? Would the stitches be eye-catching or mostly the edges and background? Of course, it is not completed yet, so what can you do to make it more colourful and more thoughtfully stitched? As the verse suggests, we all have different work to do and so long as we are using our time wisely, our lives will be carefully interwoven with others, so that God's purpose will be fulfilled in this world.

The back of the tapestry is not a pretty sight, but if the problems of our lives can't be sorted, they need to be left behind – no one sees the knots or tangles at the back! God knows them, understands our frailties and gives us freedom to stitch different colours.

Let us complete the tapestries of our lives with the unique colours God has given each of us.

Pray

Lord, help me to be faithful to the particular work you have given me to do, till my tapestry is complete.

Day 194

Be an Example

Fiona Castle

And you yourself must be an example to them by doing good works of every kind.
Titus 2:7

We are all unique, so we should not feel that we must follow the examples of others. However, we can follow the exemplary values of people we admire and respect. She is so kind . . . he is so thoughtful . . . she always laughs at her troubles! It's easy to admire other people's achievements and deplore our own failures, but we must remember that we all have different strengths and weaknesses.

Our ultimate role model, of course, is Jesus. How can we possibly be Christlike? If people look at us, do they understand more about Christ because of our behaviour? I find it difficult to even think about that!

Jesus said in Matthew 5:13, 'You are the salt of the earth. But what good is salt if it has lost its flavour?' Don't hide your light under a basket, but don't be puffed up with self-righteousness! Being a good role model means having a servant heart of humility and love.

Ask the Holy Spirit to work through you as you face everything that will come your way today, and give you wisdom in all you do.

Pray

Heavenly Father, show me how I can be an example for good in your world today.

Day 195

Be Grateful

Fiona Castle

Don't love money; be satisfied with what you have. For God has said, 'I will never fail you. I will never abandon you.'
Hebrews 13:5

I was brought up during the war, when everyone learned to make do and mend, so I've always been thrifty where clothes were concerned. But I enjoy window-shopping, and thinking what I'll save up for!

One day I found myself in a West End store when the new season's fashions had just arrived, and the bright colours and fresh designs caught my eye. I found myself thinking how lovely it would be to have unlimited credit and buy just what I pleased! As soon as I realized what my mind was up to, I came to my senses and repented of my greed. I thought of each outfit in my wardrobe and thanked God for blessing me so abundantly with everything I need.

That small incident taught me how many times we take for granted what we have and become dissatisfied and full of self-pity; we have to be constantly on our guard against such attitudes, which turn us aside from remembering God's goodness.

Pray

Remind me, Lord, each day, to be grateful for your provision for me, and never to take your goodness for granted.

Day 196

Be God's Child

Rhiannon Goulding

So you have not received a spirit that makes you fearful slaves. Instead, you received God's Spirit when he adopted you as his own children. Now we call him, 'Abba, Father.'
Romans 8:15

When my husband and I adopted our boys some years ago, it took some time to get used to being addressed by our first names. I'd been so accustomed to my girls calling me Mum, it felt strange not being called the same by my two boys!

I can still remember the day my eldest boy came skating into the kitchen, paper plates on his feet, dressed as a superhero, stopping just short of me and asking, 'Can I call you Mum now?'

Although he was already legally mine, it was that moment that he truly felt like my son. I knew it was a huge statement of the acceptance and comfort he'd found in our home to be able to call me 'Mum'.

So often, we find ourselves in the family of God feeling a bit of an outsider, detached, even a fraud. But just like me, I know God feels differently. He longs for you and me to call him 'Dad'! Even when we hide behind costumes and escape behind disguises, God sees beyond it. He offers us a welcome, acceptance and love. It's is a wonderful moment when, like my son, we realize that we're accepted, we're loved and we belong.

Pray

Dear heavenly Father, thank you that whatever our back-grounds, you accept, welcome and love us as your children.

Day 197

Be Loving

Fiona Castle

> Don't let the sun go down while you are still angry.
> Ephesians 4:26

I remember, with great embarrassment, my husband quoting this verse in public and adding, 'Well we did, and in the morning I would wake up and think: are we still arguing or are we not? And I'd take one look at her face and I'd know – we're arguing!'

It was true, but I'm glad to say that life became very different when I invited Jesus into my life and heart! I had been quite a moody person, but Jesus changed my attitude completely. I certainly learned the truth of the saying, 'The greater part of our happiness or misery depends on our dispositions and not on our circumstances' (Martha Washington).

Once I had given my life to Jesus, I trusted him to teach me how to respond to life's circumstances, rather than to get in a strop because things were not going my way.

It is so important to discuss issues and differences in a rational way, in order not to damage relationships, but rather to deepen them with a greater understanding of the person involved.

Speaking the truth in love is the most powerful way to overcome anger.

Pray

Lord Jesus, help me always to speak the truth, in a loving and caring way, in order to keep the atmosphere calm and clear.

Day 198

Be Still

Fiona Castle

He lets me rest in green pastures; he leads me beside
peaceful streams. He renews my strength.
Psalm 23:2–3

We live in an age of stress and pressure, because of the pace
of life as we hurry from one activity to another. There can
even be a sense of pride in being known as someone who is
always busy and a great achiever.

Of course, it's important to take opportunities and to make
the most of our time, but that doesn't mean we shouldn't
take a break occasionally! God designed the seventh day of
his creation as a time to relax physically and be refreshed
spiritually. That is why, traditionally, Sunday was a day of rest.

As women, we tend to constantly make 'To Do' lists, but I
also think it's important to make a 'Not To Do' list, in order
to slow down and take a break! We don't need to respond
to everything immediately. It is only as we rest that we can
allow ourselves to be still and listen to God, and allow him to
restore our strength, both physically and spiritually.

Pray

Thank you Lord, for reminding me that resting is part of your
plan for my life.

Day 199

Be Persistent

Mandy Catto

'May the LORD, the God of Israel, under whose wings you have come to take refuge, reward you fully for what you have done.'
Ruth 2:12

Ruth was a young widow who stayed loyal to her mother-in-law and moved country to help and protect her, sticking by her even when she was bitterly rejected. In difficult circumstances, she undertook hard physical labour in farm fields to stave off starvation. She was not afraid to seek out help from an older relative and eventually brought redemption and new life to the family, becoming the great-grandmother of David, the most famous of Israel's kings. She was born a Moabite, and embraced the God of Israel as an adult. She was loyal and hardworking, overcoming bereavement, starvation and loneliness to find security and happiness.

What is God calling you to persist with at this time in your life? Is there a difficult person who continues to need your love, although they may appear to be rejecting you? Is there a work situation that requires your commitment and loyalty? God honours those who honour him.

Pray

Lord God, give me the strength to be loyal in difficult relationships. Help me to work hard in all circumstances and be persistent in what you are calling me to do. Thank you that you will give me refuge under your wings.

Day 200

Be Slow to Speak

Hayley Nock

> You must all be quick to listen, slow to speak, and slow to get angry.
> James 1:19

When my husband and I first got married, money was very tight. We had joint bank accounts and everything was shared, but each month we didn't know how we would get by and pay the bills.

One morning, the post came as usual, and I noticed it was my husband's name on all the bills: there was no 'Mr and Mrs'. I was angry and let him know it. After I'd finished complaining, he explained his reasoning. He was concerned that if ever we couldn't pay, I would be safe because it was his name on the bill. He would have to face the consequences!

I was mortified. I'd jumped to the wrong conclusion and got angry before giving him a chance to explain his point of view.

How many times do we speak too quickly, jump to conclusions and live with the result without knowing the full picture?

Pray

Dear Father, please show me if there are situations that I need to put right. Help me by your Spirit to be slow to speak.

Day 201

Be Brave

Fiona Castle

'Therefore, go and make disciples of all the nations, baptizing
them in the name of the Father and the Son and the
Holy Spirit.'
Matthew 28:19

A while ago, I watched the brilliant film *Les Misérables*. I
loved the acting, the singing, the production – but most of
all the description of the amazing generosity of God's grace.

The film depicts the forgiveness of God and the change of
life that results. It also shows the tragic consequence of that
grace being rejected, as one character will not be moved
from his belief in judgement and punishment. There are
revolutionaries fighting for change, and the military who
obey orders to control them, with disastrous results.

As we look around the world today, we realize very little has
changed. There is conflict in so many countries. But the
message of God's love still prevails.

At a time when Christianity is ignored or ridiculed, are we
willing to stand up for what we believe, that Jesus is the way,
the truth and the life, and that no one comes to the Father
except through him?

Let's thank God for all those who work to share God's love
with those who don't yet know him.

Pray

Father, give me the courage to stand up for what I believe,
no matter what the consequences.

Day 202

Be Resilient

Fiona Castle

> We are pressed on every side by troubles, but we are not crushed. We are perplexed, but not driven to despair. We are hunted down, but never abandoned by God. We get knocked down, but we are not destroyed.
> 2 Corinthians 4:8–9

I remember when our whole family went down with a bout of gastric flu, one after another. I caught it from my son and handed it on to my daughter – just before a school exam. I was so upset that I'd passed on the bug at the worst possible time. And especially because I had been praying for good health for her at exam time.

'Why did God let that happen?' I asked a friend. 'Why didn't he answer my prayer for protection?'

She pointed me to this verse.

There are many things we don't understand. When things don't go according to our plans, God wants us to trust him, and not allow Satan to plant seeds of doubt in our minds. God doesn't protect us from every trouble, just as a parent allows a child to learn from mistakes, to develop resilience as an adult.

It's a trivial example, but every experience can help us to grow, and learn to put our trust in God for everything.

Pray

Help me, Lord, to develop resilience through the difficulties I face in life.

Be Ready

Fiona Castle

I will hurry, without delay, to obey your commands.
Psalm 119:60

There's an old saying that 'the road to hell is paved with good intentions'. How many of our intentions actually turn into actions, and if they do, how long does it take?

I might see something that needs repairing and decide to do something about it, but three weeks later I still haven't got round to it! If we wait until we feel ready, we might not do anything.

However, far more importantly, we need to act promptly if we realize people need us. It could be a family in trouble, or an elderly person who needs help with shopping or housework, or a charity that needs a donation. There are so many ways in which we fail to see the urgency of our actions. How devastating if we discover one day that it's too late.

What have you been intending to do lately? Can you make the effort today to put it into practice? It might take courage, but it's worth it. Actions speak louder than words.

Pray

Dear Lord, give me your wisdom, today and every day, to be obedient and not to put off what you want me to do.

Be Brave

Rachel Allcock

Then Esther sent this reply to Mordecai: 'Go and gather together all the Jews of Susa and fast for me. Do not eat or drink for three days, night or day. My maids and I will do the same. And then, though it is against the law, I will go in to see the king. If I must die, I must die.' So Mordecai went away and did everything as Esther had ordered him.

Esther 4:15–17

Esther was chosen to be in a pagan king's harem. This job wouldn't have been top of her career choices, not least for moral and ethical reasons, but it became apparent that she had been placed there 'for just such a time as this' (Esther 4:14). She was obedient and trusting when her uncle told her not to tell anyone about their Jewish heritage.

After a period 'undercover', it was up to Esther to reveal her ethnicity and step in to save her people from a holocaust. She risked death by approaching the king when he had not called for her. But as we read in these verses, her approach to a big, brave decision follows a pattern many of us know to be godly and sensible today: 1. Ask others to pray and fast. 2. Do the same yourself. 3. Be brave and step into your calling.

Pray

Father, help me to be brave and stand up for justice and liberty for people who don't have a voice.

Day 205

Be Accountable

Fiona Castle

> So be careful how you live. Don't live as fools, but like those who are wise. Make the most of every opportunity in these evil days. Don't act thoughtlessly, but understand what the Lord wants you to do.
> Ephesians 5:15–17

I confess that I used to be good at making plans for the future and working to organize an event. But when the time came, I was so busy trying to make the event successful, I didn't take time to enjoy it. Instead, by then, I was looking forward to it being over! In other words, I failed to live in the moment and enjoy the present.

It's an important lesson to learn to make today count, because we have no idea what will happen tomorrow. I have learned that lesson now that I'm a grandmother, enjoying the privilege of being able to spend time with grandchildren, family and friends. Memories are so valuable and we need to be aware that we are creating memories that will either be happy and joy-filled – or otherwise!

Are there relationships or situations you need to put right? Do it today before it's too late!

Pray

Dear God, help me to live today in the present, making the most of every opportunity to spend it effectively.

Day 206

Be Amazed

Fiona Castle

You made all the delicate, inner parts of my body and knit me together in my mother's womb. Thank you for making me so wonderfully complex! Your workmanship is marvellous – how well I know it.
Psalm 139:13–14

When you woke up this morning and looked in the mirror, what did you see? Was it the beautiful you – or the spots and blemishes, wrinkles and puffy eyes? We tend to look at the negatives, rather than the fact that we can actually *walk* to the bathroom and *see* our faces!

I am not a doctor and I never studied science at school, but it doesn't take much intelligence to recognize the complexity of the creation of the human body. We might be able to change our proportions through exercise and improving our diet, but we can't change the way we have been made. We can, however, change our attitude, by refusing to compare ourselves with others, or letting fashion magazines make us feel inadequate. Instead, we can recognize that we are unique and loved by God the way he created us.

Take a moment today to rediscover the joys of breathing, touching, tasting, hearing, eating and speaking! Stand in awe of God's greatness! Be amazed!

Pray

Thank you, Lord, for all the wonders of creation. Help me not to take for granted all you have given me from day to day, but to appreciate every detail of your goodness to me.

Day 207

Be Generous

Fiona Castle

And when we take your gifts to those who need them, they
will thank God.

2 Corinthians 9:11

I help with a children's choir by making their refreshments.
Recently I had to go to Uganda to visit a project that cares
for disabled children in a very deprived area. Before I went, I
asked the children in the choir if they had any soft toys they
no longer needed, and which they were happy to give away.
They generously gave me enough toys to completely fill
my suitcase, which I was able to hand out to all the needy
children.

A short video was made of the children receiving their gifts,
so that I could show it to the choir when I returned home.
They were all so surprised to see their toys being put into
the arms of these disadvantaged children in such poverty-
stricken circumstances.

After they'd watched the video, one little girl came up to me
and said, 'Thank you for giving my toy to that little boy. I loved
that toy so much and I didn't really want to give it away, but
now I see that he needed it so much more than I did.' Such
generosity!

Pray

Dear God, help me to be generous today, and every day.

Day 208

Be a Worshipper

Rhiannon Goulding

Because of your unfailing love, I can enter your house; I will
worship at your Temple with deepest awe.
Psalm 5:7

I recently took one of those 'discover your gift' tests at my local church. The results were largely unsurprising, except for one, which upset me. I'd scored low in the area of worship. I was somewhat disappointed. I love to worship, even though I've not been gifted with a voice for others to enjoy. But singing in the car or dancing as I clean around the house is where I come into my own.

The thought then occurred to me, 'Isn't that worship?' Isn't worship about celebrating the King in your own way, through your own life, be it through prayer or dance or singing – even if your voice leaves a lot to be desired? The truth is that worship, when it springs from a heart full of thankfulness and praise to your God, is always a beautiful, precious, sacred thing.

Pray

Father, thank you for accepting my praise, however I express it. And keep me worshipping you every day.

Be Obedient

Sarah Jones

> Mary responded, 'I am the Lord's servant. May everything you have said about me come true.' And then the angel left her.
> Luke 1:38

If I'm honest, I'm not sure this would be my reaction. Mary was called to carry God's Son, and without hesitation, she was up for it. I can't believe what I'm hearing. This teenage girl, pledged to be married to the lovely Joseph, agrees to get pregnant by the Holy Spirit and go through the trauma and questioning of people staring and not believing her. I'd have been having a panic attack! But not Mary. She doesn't get lured into mind games, confusion or despair at the situation. Instead, she travels two days alone to visit her aunt who is also miraculously pregnant. Wow!

She was obedient straight away. She didn't talk herself out of it, didn't procrastinate, wasn't instantly full of worry and 'what ifs'. What is God asking us to do at the moment? Can we take the same stance and move forward?

I'm sure she was afraid, but we don't hear about it. We hear of her faith. She focussed on God's truth and promises. Don't let fear rob you of your destiny or of the excitement life can hold when we fully yield to him. It is a privilege to be called a child of God.

Pray

Lord God, help me to be inspired by Mary's obedience and faith. I'm ready for a life of adventure with you.

Be Good

Fiona Castle

A good person produces good things from the treasury of a
good heart.
Matthew 12:35

In today's society, a common answer to asking someone how they are, is, 'I'm good, thank you!' Really? The real meaning of goodness is godliness – doing something positive that would aim to exhibit our likeness to God. Goodness is not merely being healthy, or good at doing something, or about nutritious content in food.

I once heard a preacher say, 'If you're holding a cup and someone nudges you, what spills out?' Obviously, whatever is inside the cup! And so it is with us. We may look fine on the outside until someone nudges us, irritates us or causes us pain, then whatever emotions are lurking within us will come tumbling out!

What would spill out of you today, if someone nudged you? Perhaps you are tolerating something that needs changing. Are you willing to face up to attitudes that are not Christlike, and ask for help to change them?

Goodness is one of the fruits of the Holy Spirit and in order even to attempt to achieve such a quality, we have to follow the Holy Spirit's leading in our lives.

Pray

Dear Lord, forgive me if I haven't reacted in a way that honours you when I'm confronted. Change my heart, Lord.

Day 211

Be Trusting

Rhiannon Goulding

The LORD is good, a strong refuge when trouble comes. He is
close to those who trust in him.

Nahum 1:7

It was my first child's first day at school and I couldn't be a part
of it. I was sitting on the bottom stair crying, as I watched her
father do what I'd been looking forward to doing. Afflicted
with ulcerative colitis, I was having another one of those
mornings, semi-immobilized through pain as once again it
had flared up.

For more than 19 years, I've prayed for healing on numerous
occasions. I can't begin to count the important events I've
missed. I've sat in the waiting rooms of hospitals, and spent
untold mornings in bed waiting for the pain to subside so I
could begin my day.

Despite praying with great fervour, healing has eluded me.
'The Lord is good,' Nahum declared, but there are times
when that conviction gets stretched to its limits. He hasn't
given me the answers I've wanted or expected, but despite
this God has remained a refuge, a presence and my source
of comfort. For God doesn't become good only when good
things happen: he is good, whatever happens!

Pray

Dear God, even when my prayers aren't answered in the way
I hope, thank you for remaining my refuge in time of trouble.

Day 212

Be Flexible

Fiona Castle

And we know that God causes everything to work together
for the good of those who love God and are called according
to his purpose for them.
Romans 8:28

Most of us enjoy daily routines in our lives: they make us feel secure and, to an extent, in control. However, change can come at the most unexpected times, and change can evoke fear and anxiety. We are suddenly out of our comfort zone.

We live in a world that is constantly changing, whether through conflict, war, pandemic, climate change or economic catastrophe. No one is exempt.

Change also happens in our church lives: we enjoy fellowship with one another and the routine of our familiar services and activities, and then suddenly a new leader is on the scene. What was wrong with the way things were? Why do we have to change?

This is why we need to learn to be flexible in our thinking and in our lifestyle. Whatever the change might be, we as Christians need to remember that God enables it to work for our good, even when the consequences might be painful. We learn to trust him as we serve him.

Pray

Lord, remind me to trust you and your purpose for my life, even when I see change all around.

Day 213

Be in Awe

Jaz Potter

The heavens proclaim the glory of God. The skies display his craftsmanship.

Psalm 19:1

Have you heard of the archerfish? It's found in much warmer climates than the UK, and it's quite remarkable. It catches its food by forcing spit from its mouth to hit an insect flying above the water: once the insect is knocked out, the fish swims up to the surface and eats it. What's even more remarkable is that, like most fish, its eyes are on the sides of its head. Yet it can still see its prey, and allows for the angle of view and the refraction of light, and compensates for the density of the water the spit must travel through, before hitting the target.

God's creation is beautiful and a mystery. To design a fish to hunt like this must have been a fun moment in creation. This attention to detail reveals how awesome God actually is. He gives us all his attention all of the time, and not only that: he holds all things, the whole of creation, all of the time. He is indeed worthy of our adoration. Look up, look out and see what he is doing. It prompts praise from our lips.

Pray

Dear God, I am in awe of you. Your ways are wonderful, your thoughts are more than I can comprehend. Help me to enjoy you more and more.

Day 214

Be Confident

Mandy Catto

'Now go! I will be with you as you speak, and I will instruct you in what to say.'
Exodus 4:12

Do you look forward to opportunities to speak about your faith with friends? Perhaps you long to share the hope that you have in Jesus. Or maybe, like Moses, you are fearful and dread saying the wrong thing. Do you feel that you don't even know how to start?

When God asked Moses to stand up for his people against Pharaoh, Moses argued back with God six times with different excuses: that he was the wrong person, he wasn't qualified and that no one would listen to him. Finally, he declared that he was not a good speaker and his words would get tangled. God gently but firmly reassured him that he is the giver of words and the one who decides what people hear.

Moses eventually led the people out of slavery and into the Promised Land with confidence and poise, emerging as a leader who spoke the right words at the right moments. He sought the Lord and prayed for help at every turn.

Pray

Lord, be with me today. May I be aware of your presence in every conversation. Give me the right words and the sensitivity to know how to speak up for you.

Day 215

Be Guided

Fiona Castle

When the Spirit of truth comes, he will guide you into all truth.
John 16:13

Lots of people really enjoy doing crossword puzzles. Their day isn't complete till they've filled in all the clues. I'm afraid I have no such talent.

The other day, I started to think about the Christian faith as a crossword puzzle. So many people dismiss it without considering it, saying it's irrelevant, it doesn't make sense, it doesn't mean anything – just how I feel about crossword puzzles.

But if I took the trouble to sit down with the answers and work out the clues, I'm sure light would dawn. And if people took the trouble to read the Bible with the real intention of finding out what it's about, they'd get an insight into the mind of the Creator.

We have to allow the Holy Spirit to sweep away all our preconceived ideas, to reveal what God is saying to us through his word.

The Bible has an answer for every problem we will ever face. It's not always an easy answer, or the one we'd like to hear, but it will be the right one, because it will fit the pattern of life God has worked out for each of us.

Pray

Thank you, Father, that all Scripture is inspired by you, to teach us to live the way you want. Guide me each day and keep me on the right pathway.

Day 216

Be Productive

Fiona Castle

And yet, O LORD, you are our Father. We are the clay, and you
are the potter. We are all formed by your hand.
Isaiah 64:8

We are all created by God uniquely, with different talents
and opportunities. When we look at God's creation, we
discover that even the trees are all different – in shape, size
and purpose. Why does the oak tree produce thousands of
acorns, when only a few will germinate and grow? The rest
are useful to feed birds, squirrels and insects, so in different
ways they all have a purpose.

In a similar way, we might not have the talent at entrepre-
neurial level to become rich and famous, but we must be creative with the opportunities God has given us, to be shaped
for his purpose to make a difference for good in our world.

Are you ambitious, filled with creative ideas of what you will
do and become? You may work hard to bring these ideas to
fruition, yet they may not necessarily be successful. But you
mustn't give up.

We are in the Potter's hands, to be shaped the way he wants.
We can trust him with the future he has for us, so keep
having ideas!

Pray

Lord, help me to keep my eyes on you, in order to continue
to be productive, creative and to make the most of the
opportunities you give me.

Be Aware

Fiona Castle

'The thief's purpose is to steal and kill and destroy. My purpose is to give them a rich and satisfying life.'
John 10:10

This verse is a powerful warning to us from Jesus, teaching us to stand firm against temptation. We need to be constantly aware of Satan's determination to cause us to give in to temptations of one sort or another.

When we become Christians, we might be naive enough to imagine that all will be well – and that because we are following Jesus we will do the right things all the time. However, we soon realize that life is a constant battle against the wiles of the evil one.

Often, temptation begins with what we might call harmless pleasure, but before we know it, it has deteriorated into total disobedience to God's will for our lives. Satan is always on the warpath, and only when we are totally grounded in God's word and truth can we recognize the necessity to stand against him.

In his letter to the Ephesians, Paul teaches us to put on the whole armour of God, in order to be strong in the Lord's mighty power, which overcomes all the powers of darkness and gives us life in all its fullness.

Pray

Father, help me always to stand against temptations in my life in order to be true to your word.

Day 218

Be Just

Esther Tregilgas

> No, O people, the LORD has told you what is good, and this is what he requires of you: to do what is right, to love mercy, and to walk humbly with your God.
>
> Micah 6:8

I love this verse so much – what a challenge that these three things are what God wants: justice, mercy and humility.

My driving instructor was a Christian. He was renowned amongst our family and friends for regularly stopping the car to intervene in the goings-on of inner-city Liverpool life, stopping youths from vandalizing a telephone box and breaking up fights. I was 17 and just trying to have a driving lesson: it was incredibly embarrassing. But looking back now, I see he was acting as a seeker of truth and justice – trying to do what was right.

As I write, it's been a couple of months since the murder of George Floyd. For many people life is unjust. The colour of your skin puts you at a disadvantage. There have recently been fires in a massively overcrowded and under-resourced refugee camp in Greece. These are just two injustices that are happening in the world right now.

Whether you sign a petition, join a protest or speak up about an injustice you see while driving your car, each of us has a part to play in doing what is right, in showing God's incredible mercy and in walking humbly in the footprints of Jesus.

Pray

Father, show me how to walk in your ways.

Day 219

Be Present

Rhiannon Goulding

Love is patient and kind . . . Love never gives up.
1 Corinthians 13:4,7

I was 15, and very cross and very upset. Things were not going well, and I was crying on my bed. I'd broken up with my boyfriend. My room was a mess. I had homework to do and I had got myself into an angry, hormonal mess. Then my dad walked into the room and said, 'I've been trying to teach you how to change a plug for years. Today you're going to learn.' With tears running down my face, I got up and my dad taught me how to change a plug!

I never really understood why this happened. When things were tough, he would teach me how to change the oil, or put water in the car, or other things that seemed irrelevant to my teenage mind.

When I became a parent of teenagers, I finally understood his parenting. He taught me above everything else to stay close, to stay connected. We can't always fix the problems in other people's lives. We can't always understand what they're going through, but we can always stay close beside them, stay connected and be present.

Pray

Lord Jesus, thank you that your love never gives up on us. Teach us to live in your love and show it in our lives and relationships.

Day 220

Be Radiant

Mandy Catto

> I prayed to the LORD, and he answered me. He freed me
> from all my fears. Those who look to him for help will be
> radiant with joy.
> Psalm 34:4–5

All of us have fears and need help sometimes, wherever we are on our faith journey. In this Psalm David recalls a time when he feared for his life and had to run from King Saul and hide who he truly was. Yet he declares that God answered him in the midst of this and freed him, not just from some of his fear, but all his fears. His mood was transformed from extreme anxiety into radiance and joy. The key to this dramatic change was prayer and calling to God for help. Sometimes we are reluctant to acknowledge that we need help.

Is there some anxiety or difficult situation that is dominating your thoughts today? What can you bring to the Lord in prayer? How different will your day be if you are free from fear, filled with joy and radiant? Knowing that God has your back and has freed you will lift your face from a mask of fear to one looking up and out with confidence.

Pray

Lord, thank you that you promise to answer when I call out to you. Please deliver me from my fears as I look to you. May others see you shining through my radiant witness today.

Be Peaceful

Fiona Castle

Search for peace, and work to maintain it.
1 Peter 3:11

One day I was in a very bad mood when I took our youngest son to school, and came home to read these words in the Bible. Although I had hugged him before he left me, I knew things were not right, and I spent the rest of the day praying about him.

1 Peter 5:8 says, 'Stay alert! Watch out for your great enemy, the devil. He prowls round like a roaring lion, looking for someone to devour.' Well, I wasn't exactly torn apart, but I knew then that Satan had tried to rob me of my peace that day. Once I had recognized him, I was able to find a way to make peace with my little boy.

I used to hate to admit that I was wrong, but I have learned there is great peace in being willing to say sorry. If a situation is tense, we must do all we can to bring peace as quickly as possible, whatever the cost to our pride and dignity, to stop Satan from getting a foothold. Let's not feed that hungry lion!

Pray

Lord, give me the humility to admit when I am wrong, and help me to strive for peace in all my relationships.

Day 222

Be Forward-looking

Fiona Castle

But Jesus told him, 'Anyone who puts a hand to the plough
and then looks back is not fit for the Kingdom of God.'
Luke 9:62

Some years ago, I was moving house and I was really sad about it. There were so many happy memories relating to that home, and I couldn't bear the thought that those lovely times would be coming to an end.

On the day of the move, I went for an early-morning walk before the family had woken and I was in tears about the prospect of never seeing the place again. I prayed and suddenly the Lord brought this verse to mind. It was a real challenge and it immediately gave me the courage to leave the past behind and move on. I marched home and told the family what had happened. They, too, became positive. 'Right, let's get going,' they said as they packed their final few belongings before the removal men arrived.

It was a salutary lesson for us all, not to dwell in the past but to take up the challenge of moving forward, with the assurance of knowing the one who holds the future.

Pray

Thank you, Father, that as we move forward in our lives, we are not in the dark, because you light the way.

Day 223

Be Powerful

Mandy Catto

'But may those who love you rise like the sun in all its power!'
Judges 5:31

The book of Judges tells the history of Israel's leader, Deborah. She was a Prophet and Judge who dispensed wisdom and called up an army of 10,000 as the Lord had asked. The army commander Barak asked that she go with them into battle, so she did – exhorting them, 'Get ready! This is the day the LORD will give you victory' (Judges 4:14).

Deborah was counter-cultural; she led the people and won a major national battle at a time when women usually did not have any power. She listened to the Lord and rose up with courage when others were fearful, leading the people of Israel faithfully for forty years.

Her victory song at the end of chapter five exhorts those of us who love God to rise up as powerful as the sun. The temperature of the sun is 10,000° Fahrenheit on its surface and it emits 1,300 watts per square metre; it is the most powerful force in our galaxy. And we are called by this woman of God to rise up and shine like the sun.

Pray

Lord, thank you for the example of Deborah. May I love you, listen to you and be prepared to lead when you call. Help me to rise like the sun in all its power.

Day 224

Be Unique

Fiona Castle

Pay careful attention to your own work, for then you will get the satisfaction of a job well done, and you won't need to compare yourself to anyone else. For we are each responsible for our own conduct.
Galatians 6:4–5

We women are prone to comparing ourselves with others – whether it's in our jobs, our culinary abilities, or our flair for interior design. It's easy to admire people who appear to be far more talented than we are, and to feel we're of little worth – to the extent, sometimes, of seeming to apologize for our own existence!

However, we must remember that we are all unique: no one shares exactly the same abilities. God has created each one of us to fulfil different roles, whether high-powered, or behind the scenes and unnoticed. The important thing is that this is the role God intends for us. We can then be at peace with ourselves, being comfortable in our own skin, in the knowledge that we are each uniquely loved by God and are called to fulfil his purposes.

Remember, we are meant to be here!

Pray

Thank you, Father God, that you created me with a unique purpose. Remind me of that each day, even when I don't feel successful.

Be Yourself

Rhiannon Goulding

There are different kinds of service, but we serve the same Lord. God works in different ways, but it is the same God who does the work in all of us.
1 Corinthians 12:5–6

My friend's house is really calm: all her children talk quietly and listen to what other people are saying. 'Oh, well,' she said when I mentioned it, 'we're a quiet family.'

'That's it,' I thought, 'I want us to be a quiet family too.' Whenever voices were raised at home, I started saying gently, 'We're a quiet family.' I thought it was going well until one day there was a heated argument over a game of Monopoly. Raising my voice over the shouting I banged the table and screamed, 'We are a quiet family!' There was a moment's silence and all the children burst out laughing. 'Mum, we're really not,' one of them said.

How much energy and time we can waste trying to copy just one aspect of someone else's life! We're not quiet: our family is loud and fun, and I wouldn't change it. Each family is different, and we have our own strengths. Instead of focussing on something I couldn't change, I should have been encouraging our family's lively, outgoing friendliness, and accepting the children for who they were.

Pray

Father God, thank you for loving me and accepting me just as I am. Show me how I can serve you best today.

Day 226

Be Fruitful

Fiona Castle

Jesus said: 'I am the true grapevine, and my Father is the gardener. He cuts off every branch of mine that doesn't produce fruit, and he prunes the branches that do bear fruit so they will produce even more. You have already been pruned and purified by the message I have given you.'

John 15:1–3

While gardening recently, I couldn't help being reminded of an old joke. A vicar passes a lovely garden and comments patronizingly, 'Isn't it wonderful what the Lord can do?' The gardener replies, 'Yes, vicar, but you should have seen it when he had it to himself!'

There's a deep truth in that: God can make a garden beautiful, but he needs our co-operation. Unless we're willing to prepare the ground, plant the seeds and hoe the weeds, we can't expect to see much beauty.

Our lives, too, can be beautiful, but we must be willing to be pruned and trained by our reading of God's word.

If we live to please ourselves, the cares of the world can grow until there's no evidence of God's purpose in our lives. We need to submit to him entirely, so he can train us to produce good fruit.

Pray

Heavenly Father, I submit to your will today, in order to take my part in the work for your world and to be fruitful for the Kingdom.

Be Discerning

Fiona Castle

Then Jesus said, 'Let's go off by ourselves to a quiet place and rest awhile.' He said this because there were so many people coming and going that Jesus and his apostles didn't even have time to eat.

Mark 6:31

We live in an age of speed and busyness and feel guilty if we relax. When work piles up and demands continue to be made upon us, we find it very difficult to say 'no'. Why is that?

Is it because we are afraid people will lose respect for us, or we won't feel valued? Or maybe we feel guilty if we don't respond immediately to try to help others?

If we respond to too many outside demands, who loses out? Maybe it is the family whose needs should be our priority, or perhaps our husband, or friends who hope for a little time to talk and relax. We are called to serve others, but we all need some 'down time' to restore our spirits. We don't have to say 'yes' to every request.

Jesus recognized his need to draw aside from the constant demands made on him and to take a rest, so we should follow his example. Learn to say no!

Pray

Dear God, help me to be discerning about the work that I am called to do. Remind me to seek your will and purpose each day, because it is you that I am serving.

Be Admiring

Rachel Allcock

His mouth is sweetness itself; he is desirable in every way.
Such, O women of Jerusalem, is my lover, my friend.
Song of Songs 5:16

Have you ever heard a woman speak of her lover like this? Unfortunately, it's more common to hear derisive comments, criticism or sarcasm. When we get together with other women, it's easy to fall into the habit of criticizing our men and laughing at their faults. I'm not suggesting we go into the physical detail expressed in the Song of Songs, but if we talk about our husbands in an admiring way, it honours and respects them, and builds firm foundations for our families.

It seems boastful and sickly to publicly praise our partners for being amazing, but in the right company, it's essential. Children notice when their parents are loving and affectionate, and it makes them feel safe.

After the initial whirlwind of romance dies down, the kind of love that lasts for years needs to be personal, persistent and seen by the community. The intense vision of love and desire that we read about in the Song of Songs is also a picture of God's love for us. We are his beloved and he seeks an intimate relationship with us – personal, persistent and obvious to all.

Pray

Loving God, thank you for pursuing me with an unquenchable love. Make me unashamed of praising you in public. Show me the right way to build up and admire those I love.

Day 229

Be Guided

Fiona Castle

Your word is a lamp to guide my feet and a light for my path.
Psalm 119:105

When I go for a walk on a lovely summer's day, I like to gaze up at the sky and look around at the view. But if I take the same walk in the winter, I find myself watching the ground, treading gingerly around the ice and snow to avoid falling flat on my face! I can't look ahead because I have to concentrate on the next tentative step.

I think this often happens in our Christian life.

When the going's easy, we drift along, enjoying life and not focussing too much on what God might require of us. Then a crisis comes and life takes on an entirely different perspective. That's when we realize we have to trust God to lead us step by step along the path ahead.

It's in the tough times, when we're continually seeking God's strength and guidance, that we grow and learn.

That's why Peter tells us to rejoice: 'For these trials make you partners with Christ in his suffering, so that you will have the wonderful joy of seeing his glory' (1 Peter 4:13).

Pray

Dear Lord, thank you that I can trust you with every tentative step I take, because you light my way.

Be in Harmony

Mandy Catto

> So then, let us aim for harmony in the church and try to build each other up.
> Romans 14:19

In our relationships and conversations we have two choices: we can build others up or put them down. We can use our body language and words to echo and affirm what others are saying, asking great open questions and listening intently as we focus on harmony.

Harmony in musical terms is the simultaneous sounding of different notes that create chords with a pleasing effect. The notes are not jarring, but spaced with just the right distance to create a perfectly balanced sound. In harmony, we join together and create something more complete and beautiful than any single voice.

By living in harmony, we create more than we could alone. We build others up and encourage them to live life in all its fullness, as Jesus intended. And we thrive personally as we live the way God intended us to – in community.

It takes strength of character and humility to live in harmony because people are flawed, insensitive and sometimes hurtful. In order to create and maintain harmony we often have to be the ones that move and adapt our voices to match others with flexibility and creativity!

Pray

Father God, give me opportunities today to build others up through my words and actions. Show me how I can create harmony in your name.

Day 231

Be Active

Fiona Castle

How do you know what your life will be like tomorrow?
Your life is like the morning fog – it's here a little while, then it's gone.

James 4:14

We all make decisions in life and occasionally we make mistakes. There's a saying that, 'The trouble with life is that you have to live it forwards, but you only understand it backwards!'

None of us knows what will happen tomorrow, however much we try to plan ahead, but as Christians, we can trust the Lord in all circumstances. Our faith doesn't exempt us from life's trials and difficulties, but we mustn't give up. We shall be in eternity far longer than we shall be on earth, which should make us realize how precious each moment is, even when life is tough.

It's not God's role to give us what we want and when we want it. Instead, he calls us to do his will and work for the coming of the kingdom. He calls us to offer ourselves to him as living sacrifices that are holy and pleasing to him (Romans 12:1).

What can we do today to make a difference in this world, if tomorrow would be too late? Don't count your days. Make your days count.

Pray

Father, give me the peace of mind to trust you every day in all circumstances.

Be Transformed

Fiona Castle

This means that anyone who belongs to Christ has become a new person. The old life is gone; a new life has begun!

2 Corinthians 5:17

I gazed with admiration at the wedding cake on display in the shop window. Those delicate icing patterns must have taken a master cake decorator hours to pipe. Yet there was one thing wrong: it was a cardboard display model! The icing was real, but inside it was hollow!

As I looked, I realized what a good picture of myself it was – certainly, before I became a Christian. I'd been so concerned with outward appearances, for myself, my family, my home. Yet everything was hollow, and I was always restless and unfulfilled.

It wasn't until I found Jesus and asked him to take over my life that the emptiness was filled. And just as the inside of a real wedding cake is rich, dark fruit cake, which takes time to prepare and bake, so I found something similar happening in my life. I began to develop and mature. Life was no longer empty. Instead, I longed to be filled with all God had to teach me from his word.

Pray

I am so grateful, Jesus, that you came into my life in the power of your Holy Spirit and filled me with joy.

Day 233

Be Humble

Fiona Castle

'For all those who exalt themselves will be humbled, and those who humble themselves will be exalted.'
Luke 14:11

At a recent communion service, our pastor pointed out that Jesus taught his disciples to be servants, prepared to wash the feet of others. He asked if we were prepared to be like that. I thought I was – I'm not too proud to scrub floors and work unnoticed in the background.

'Of course,' he went on, 'we don't mind being servants until we're treated like one!'

The truth of that really hit me! It's one thing to help when people are appreciative. But if they were to order me around without a 'please' or 'thank you', I know it would bring out the very worst in me – I'd resent it.

Jesus tells us to take up our cross daily and follow him. Can we give up our rights, be obedient to God and abandon our plans for what we want to do, and what we think God should be doing in our lives? Can we be available to others, even when we're busy? And can we do it without counting the cost of what we could have been doing instead?

Sin is my claim to my right to myself – the opposite of humility.

Pray

Lord, give me a humble attitude, ready to do your will without counting the cost.

Be Happy

Rachel Allcock

So go ahead. Eat your food with joy, and drink your wine with
a happy heart, for God approves of this! Wear fine clothes,
with a splash of cologne!
Ecclesiastes 9:7–8

When Wimbledon 2020 was cancelled, we were all urged to
buy and eat strawberries – lots of strawberries. What an invitation to happiness and deliciousness! I spent a lot of money
on berries that month, and when the punnets of strawberries in my disinfected trolley seemed extravagant, I reminded
myself that I was helping the economy, helping in the national effort to stop the glut of summer fruit going to waste.

I read articles urging us to buy the new style summer trousers –
not because we needed them for our holidays (we weren't
going on any), but because we needed to help the fashion
industry get back on track.

I don't need much encouragement to spend money. But this
plea to spend and enjoy life's pleasures got me thinking. What
if we took God's direct instructions seriously? We are to enjoy
life! Like the short shelf life of strawberries, today's potential
for joy won't last. We need to step into it today. What can you
do to bring bright, fresh happiness into your home today?

Pray

Thank you, Lord, for all your good gifts. Help me to cultivate
a joyful heart.

Be Connected

Mandy Catto

'Yes, I am the vine; you are the branches. Those who remain in me, and I in them, will produce much fruit. For apart from me you can do nothing . . . But if you remain in me and my words remain in you, you may ask for anything you want, and it will be granted!'
John 15:5,7

These are some of the last words that Jesus speaks to his disciples. He asks them to remain in him, to be connected as a branch to a vine. The thick, curly trunk of a vine has all the strength of the core. The branches are regularly trimmed and then stretch out – they produce the leaves to catch the sunshine and rain, and provide the nutrition that creates sweet grapes.

Jesus gives us the privilege of being the branches and fruit creators, whether that is in the ministry we do for his kingdom, in the shaping and maturing of our character, or in bringing others to faith. We can do this if his words are in us: read his words, pray them, sing them, share them, live them! There is nothing sweeter than leading someone to know and believe in Jesus for the first time.

Pray

Jesus, thank you for being the true vine. Help me to stay connected closely to you so that your words remain in me. Give me opportunities today to be fruitful for you and to bring you glory.

Be Peaceful

Fiona Castle

'I am leaving you with a gift – peace of mind and heart. And the peace I give is a gift the world cannot give. So don't be troubled or afraid.'
John 14:27

If someone offered you whatever gift you wanted, no matter what the price, what would you choose? A multi-million-pound villa in the Mediterranean with its own swimming pool? A Rolls Royce? A diamond tiara? Would any gift like that bring a lifetime of happiness?

But Jesus is offering this gift to anyone who loves him! What better and more lasting gift could you receive than peace of mind and heart? As Jesus says, it is not the kind of peace the world expects, such as a lazy lie-in, or a day at the beach. It is a unique gift of peace, which is so much more.

Even if we do allow ourselves a lazy day, we probably feel guilty, thinking of all we should be doing. But Jesus releases our minds and hearts, so that whatever is going on in our lives, however difficult, we can reside in his lasting peace.

Pray

Thank you, Jesus, that you have provided my mind and heart with the precious gift of your peace. I praise you, Lord.

Be Obedient

Fiona Castle

'If you love me, obey my commandments . . . Those who accept my commandments and obey them are the ones who love me. And because they love me, my Father will love them. And I will love them and reveal myself to each of them.'

John 14:15,21

As a child, I was brought up with strict discipline. Obedience was paramount! The consequences of my disobedience were punishment and misery. But my parents had my best interests at heart and my obedience always had positive results.

Like a loving parent, God sets standards for our good and to protect us from evil and harm. When we read the Ten Commandments, we understand his motives, because they are designed to keep us from becoming embroiled in situations that will only cause us trouble and heartache.

Jesus summarized the Law in two commandments: love God and love your neighbour. Even if others around us are not familiar with the principles of our faith, we can be examples to them of God's enduring love for us.

Pray

Father, I do love you and want to obey you. Forgive me when I fail.

Be Humble

Fiona Castle

And so, brothers, select seven men who are well respected
and are full of the Spirit and wisdom. We will give them
this responsibility.
Acts 6:3

The apostles were so busy with practical issues, they were unable to fulfil their God-ordained purpose of prayer and teaching. Wisely, they realized they needed to let go of some of their responsibilities and delegate them to others.

I remember many years ago listening to Clive Calver preaching at Spring Harvest. He said, 'Are you so proud of the work you are doing in your church because it gives you a sense of purpose, that you are not taking the time to train up others so that they can take over when the time is right?'

That really challenged me. How will the next generation cope, if we are not prepared to spend time training and facilitating them for the future of our church and beyond? We can become so entrenched in our positions that pride won't allow us to let go and recognize that there are different seasons for our lives.

We need to seek God's purpose and place for us from day to day, in order to be effective for his kingdom.

Pray

Father, help me to know your purpose for me today.

Be Equipped

Fiona Castle

And you yourself must be an example to them by doing
good works of every kind.
Titus 2:7

As Christians, our behaviour should be above reproach, but whenever I think about that, I get into a downward spiral of self-examination. Do I always avoid gossip? Always demonstrate love? Remember to pray? Visit the lonely? The list is endless.

It's so tempting to wonder how God can love me when I do so many things wrong. But then I remember the disciples – they got a lot wrong, too! They often lacked faith – yet by the power of the Holy Spirit, they fulfilled Jesus' command to spread the Good News.

Yes, God can use us to do his work so long as we are willing to focus on him and not on our shortcomings. We are the means by which he can communicate his love in the twenty-first century.

So, we can be confident in the prayer from Hebrews 13:20–21: 'May the God of peace – who brought up from the dead our Lord Jesus, the great Shepherd of the sheep . . . equip you with all you need for doing his will.'

Pray

Father God, on my own I can do nothing, yet in the power of your Holy Spirit I know I can fulfil your will.

Be Beautiful

Fiona Castle

> Don't be concerned about the outward beauty of fancy hairstyles, expensive jewellery, or beautiful clothes. You should clothe yourselves instead with the beauty that comes from within, the unfading beauty of a gentle and quiet spirit, which is so precious to God.
>
> 1 Peter 3:3–5

Some time ago, I was invited to speak at a 'pampering' evening for young mothers. In various rooms around the church, the women were able to have their hair styled, nails painted, try new make-up and enjoy a massage or relaxation exercises.

The aim of my talk was to help them understand that their self-worth was not dependent on outward appearances.

Young women today feel under pressure to look as good as the models they admire – who lavish time and money on their appearance. Yet, however beautiful your ideal woman might be, if she were foul-mouthed or bad tempered you wouldn't want to spend much time with her, would you? There are more important qualities!

It's good to be reminded that we are all unique, with our own gifts and strengths. We should resolutely refuse to compare ourselves with others, and seek God's plan and purpose for us right where we are.

Pray

Lord, thank you that the beauty you value is not dependent on keeping away the wrinkles.

Day 241

Be Encouraging

Fiona Castle

> So encourage each other and build each other up, just as you are already doing.
> 1 Thessalonians 5:11

Recently, two close friends of mine, at different times, spoke to me about their perfectionist husbands, who find it difficult to talk about how they are feeling. It turns out that both of the men had similar childhoods, with parents who never praised or encouraged them. And no matter what they tried to do, it was never good enough. They were never affirmed or accepted.

So often, our attitudes are determined by our upbringing. If our parents constantly found fault with us, we're likely to find fault with others. If they looked for the good in us and praised it, they motivated us to live up to that – and taught us to look for the good in others.

Are you an affirmer or a critic? Do people feel better about themselves after spending time with you? If you think something good about someone, have the courage to say it. You could make their day! It's amazing how many people live with self-doubt and insecurity.

We need to encourage others to find their spiritual gifts as they grow.

Pray

Heavenly Father, help me to be an encourager, to help those with low self-esteem to know that they are loved and accepted.

Day 242

Be Strong

Mandy Catto

'So be strong and courageous! Do not be afraid and do not panic before them. For the LORD your God will personally go ahead of you. He will neither fail you nor abandon you.'
Deuteronomy 31:6

In this passage, Moses speaks some of his final words before his death. He knew that changes were coming for the people of Israel: a death, a new leader, a new land and a new home. Some of life's most stressful events were imminent, and God reminded his people that he would be right there with them. He gave them an early reassurance of his constancy and faithfulness.

When I had two young children, we moved abroad. Saying goodbye to our family and church was hard. Arriving at a new mega-church was overwhelming, and so different from our little Scottish parish that I felt afraid. The first Sunday the sermon was on my favourite psalm, Psalm 34 – the one I had requested for my wedding. The sense of God's comfort and presence was immediate. He had gone ahead of me and was right there in the midst of my anxiety. We were about to embark on a year of spiritual transformation and challenge, and God said, 'Be strong, my daughter. I have gone ahead of you. I am right here beside you.'

Pray

Thank you for your promise to go ahead of us and be with us. Through your Holy Spirit, give us the courage to live strong.

Be Comforted

Hayley Nock

'Dear woman, why are you crying?' Jesus asked her.
John 20:15

Mary had followed Jesus; he had changed her life. She had watched him be humiliated, tortured and killed. She could not do anything. Her whole world had now been shattered. Everything she relied on and loved was gone. She could not do for him what was normally done when someone was dying – even that had been taken from her. She went to the tomb to do the one thing she could do for him: care for his body, give him dignity and respect. But he was not there. So she was devastated again by yet another disappointment. Still she did not give up, but asked where the body was. And into this situation of pain and despair, Jesus calls her name and gives her hope.

In my life, I have had seasons where I have felt powerless and sad. Jesus has been my strength every time, even when I did not understand.

Are you feeling devastated by disappointment, and maybe not for the first time? Or is there someone you know who is disappointed?

Pray

Lord, you see my tears and disappointment. Please give me hope. Thank you that you call my name and that you know me.

Be Repentant

Fiona Castle

'Then if my people who are called by my name will humble themselves and pray and seek my face and turn from their wicked ways, I will hear from heaven and will forgive their sins and restore their land.'

2 Chronicles 7:14

When we repent, God turns to us with forgiveness, restoration and blessing. We have received his mercy. What a gift!

Forgiveness is not based on the enormity of our sin, but on the generosity of the forgiver's love. The whole basis of our Christian faith lies in receiving God's mercy through Jesus' act of love towards us. This was the ultimate gift of God, when Jesus paid the price for all we have done wrong through his death on the cross. He enables us to make a new start.

In this passage, God is speaking to Solomon about the people of Israel needing to turn their lives around, to seek his forgiveness and return to him.

Today let's pray, not just for ourselves and for one another but for our nation and the world. We are his people and need to be humble and repent of the damage our society has done, so that we may all be forgiven and that our world may be healed.

Pray

Father, I pray that those in our nation today who don't know you or have rejected you, might turn back to you and be changed, and know your salvation.

Day 245

Be Private

Rhiannon Goulding

'Don't do your good deeds publicly, to be admired by others,
for you will lose the reward from your Father in heaven.'
Matthew 6:1

Does anyone remember Friendster? It launched in 2002. It was followed by MySpace, then Facebook, YouTube, Instagram, WhatsApp, TikTok – and by the time you read this, there will be something new. The platforms may change but social media is now a part of our lives and our society.

For decades, children wanted to be astronauts or doctors. Now they want to be influencers: glamorous, rich and famous for being famous. The top tourist destination in Los Angeles is the pink wall in the Paul Smith shop – because it's 'an Instagram phenomenon'.

With the world pursuing 'likes', how can we as Christians see past all the airbrushed glamour and point to the one who is the Way, the Truth and the Life? How can we encourage our friends to look deeper?

If we've not done it unless it's been posted and praised or liked, how does that line up with the Bible's teaching on doing things in private that only God can see? In Matthew 6 Jesus talks about giving to the needy, praying, and fasting in private. And each section ends with the words, 'your Father, who sees everything, will reward you'.

Pray

Lord, help me be genuine: let me live for an audience of one – the only One who matters.

Day 246

Be Inquiring

Rhiannon Goulding

Dear brothers and sisters, don't be childish in your
understanding of these things. Be innocent as babies when
it comes to evil, but be mature in understanding matters of
this kind.
1 Corinthians 14:20

The 17-year-old asked me a big moral question and wanted an answer. I was happy to be able to give her a prompt reply – but, unfortunately, it was prompt because it was a glib parroting of what I'd been told at the same age.

'Is that in the Bible? Or is it just your interpretation? Is that culture, or prejudice, or what God says?' I was shocked – probably because she was right. When I thought about it, I was regurgitating stuff I'd been told, without ever really thinking about it. She was trying to work out her faith in her own way, and she wanted to understand.

If you've been a Christian for a long time, it's easy to respond automatically with a verse of Scripture or a phrase. Sometimes, taken out of context, that can be damaging or just plain wrong. It's better to take time to think before we speak, and not to be afraid to say we don't know. We need to give people space to ask honest questions, and be willing to get alongside them to examine their questions together.

Pray

Father God, help me to keep learning. Steer me away from easy answers and religious platitudes, and let the wisdom of Scripture bring me to a mature understanding.

Day 247

Be a Worshipper

Fiona Castle

There I will go to the altar of God – the source of all my joy. I
will praise you with my harp, O God, my God!
Psalm 43:4

Sometimes I don't feel like praying. Sometimes I don't feel
like reading the Bible. And sometimes I certainly don't feel
a bit like being loving and kind to anyone! But I thank God
that my faith is not based on feelings, but on the sure fact
of Jesus' death for me. In other words, my salvation is not
dependent on what I do for Jesus, but on what he did for me.

Psalm 22:3 says: 'O thou that inhabitest the praises of Israel . . .'
(KJV). Some translations are different, but I like this one. It
reminds me that as I start to praise God as an act of the will,
he lives in my praise, and my spirit lifts and my weariness
disappears. My whole attitude to my prayer time changes,
and my praise comes from my heart, not just my lips!

So, if today is 'one of those days' when you don't feel like
being anything but negative, begin to praise him. Soon you
will find your mood joins with your spirit as it soars towards
the Lord and brings joy to his heart.

Pray

Thank you, Lord, that though I am an imperfect human
being, you still love me and understand my failings.

Day 248

Be Natural

Rachel Allcock

'When you pray, don't babble on and on as the Gentiles do. They think their prayers are answered merely by repeating their words again and again. Don't be like them, for your Father knows exactly what you need even before you ask him!'
Matthew 6:7–8

I woke up to my husband shouting, 'Alexa, pause!' The oh-so-helpful voice assistant continued with her discordant beeping. 'Alexa, sleep!' (beeping continued). This is where I stepped in: 'Alexa, snooze!' Peace.

Those of you with a love-hate relationship with some form of 'smart' speaker/AI assistant will know all too well that you have to be specific. Unless you use the exact words, you don't get what you want. Hopefully, future readers will laugh at the current limitations of these things in much the same way my kids laugh when I show them how to rewind a VHS tape!

How amazing that God is omniscient (all-knowing). He doesn't need a certain magical sequence of words in order to spring into life. When we pray, we can be ourselves, we can be unrehearsed.

If you live in fear of being asked to pray out loud, don't try to do a fancy prayer. Practise praying aloud when you are at home so it doesn't feel so strange. Maybe you'll encourage Alexa to find out if there is more to life!

Pray

Holy Spirit, give me the words to say when I pray.

Day 249

Be Diligent

Fiona Castle

'Choose today whom you will serve . . . as for me and my family, we will serve the LORD.'
Joshua 24:15

At the time I became a Christian I was living a busy life. As a full-time mother of four, I was also involved with life in the local community, which took up any free time I might have had.

Within a very short time, God showed me clearly that I should give up all my outside activities in order to focus completely on my family and my marriage. I didn't find that easy. I knew that opting out of some of my voluntary projects would annoy and offend some people. However, because it was such clear guidance from God, I knew it was the right decision for me at this stage in my life, so I stood firm against opposition and didn't regret it.

At every season of life, we need to keep asking God what he wants of us. For some of us our calling is to go out into the world, for others it is to stay close to home and do the tasks that present themselves there. And sometimes we move from one to the other, as our calling changes. Whether God calls us to work in the home, the community, the church or the workplace, we know we are working for him.

Pray

Wherever I go and whatever I do, help me to remember, Lord, that I am serving you.

Day 250

Be Forgiving

Fiona Castle

'If you forgive those who sin against you, your heavenly
Father will forgive you.'
Matthew 6:14

Recently someone close to me erupted in anger. It had obviously been smouldering for a while! I took it on board and said very little in response, and decided later that I should just shrug it off and forget it. But God showed me that I needed to forgive her in my heart, so I did so, and sent her a loving little note. And that was the end of it.

But the next time I went to communion, I asked God to show me any areas where I needed to ask forgiveness, and suddenly I realized I was still brooding.

Then God showed me a picture of myself as a fortress. I had lifted the drawbridge to prevent the hurt from touching me – in other words, my defences were up! I sensed him telling me that I had to open the gate to allow his love to come in and heal me, so I could be totally free.

That experience reminded me afresh of what a wonderful, caring God we belong to, and how he longs for us to respond to his healing love.

Pray

Father God, thank you for your forgiving and healing love, setting me free.

Be an Example

Rhiannon Goulding

Dear brothers and sisters, pattern your lives after mine, and
learn from those who follow my example.
Philippians 3:17

I was having a tough time at school, so my mum drove a
12-mile round trip every day to have lunch with me. I wish I
could say I was grateful, but I was an angry teenager.

One day she suggested we stop at a shop to pick up
sandwiches. I knew Mum's habit of getting into conversation
with everyone, so I said moodily, 'OK, but you can only talk to
two people.' By the time she'd chatted to a couple of people
I was already fuming. Then she saw a little old lady trying to
reach a tin on the top shelf.

'Hello, Miss Evans,' she said, ignoring my cross face. 'Let me
get that for you.'

Now, years later, I'm no longer the grumpy teen with a bad
attitude; I'm the woman saying 'Hello, can I help you with
that?' Mum's lessons of love and kindness didn't fall on deaf
ears – even though it may have seemed like it at the time.
The life lessons we learn from those we love sink in deeply,
past the feelings of 'now', and form our characters for ever.

Pray

Lord, let me never tire of doing good, even when people
around me get cross or don't understand. Help me to notice
the ones who need a helping hand, and give me the courage
to offer it.

Be a Witness

Mandy Catto

'For you are to be his witness, telling everyone what you have
seen and heard. What are you waiting for?'
Acts 22:15–16

In our law courts people play different roles as judges, lawyers, defence and prosecution. All are important and essential for a fair trial.

We read many times of legal vocabulary in the Bible. God is often described as the ultimate judge – fair and just. Christians are sometimes notorious for their reputation for acting as judges on the behaviour and beliefs of others. In Luke 6:37 Jesus tells us not to judge others.

What does God ask us to be instead? Witnesses! Witnesses of Jesus and of faith. A good witness is someone who tells the truth and talks of what they know – no hearsay, no judgement, but simply their own account of what they saw and what happened.

In Acts 22 Paul tells the story of his conversion. A persecutor of Christians, he was stopped in his tracks by a blinding vision of Jesus. In Damascus, a brave believer called Ananias met Paul and commanded his sight to return. He explained to him that God had called him to be a witness for Jesus. His life's work after that day was to share the Jesus he had encountered, and convince others of the truth of salvation by his personal witness.

Pray

Lord, help me to talk with authenticity of what I know to be true. May I be a witness for Jesus today.

Be Loved

Fiona Castle

No one has ever seen God. But if we love each other, God
lives in us, and his love is brought to full expression in us.
1 John 4:12

I was standing in the arrivals area of Heathrow Airport,
waiting for my daughter's flight, fascinated by all the busy
comings and goings around me. People came through the
doors laden with luggage, and I had fun trying to match
them up with those waiting in the hall. It was a pleasure to
see the joy on their faces as they greeted one another! Looks
didn't matter. They were loved by the people meeting them,
with a love that went beyond mere appearances.

How wonderful it is to know that God loves us just as we
are, because he created us. He looks at what's inside – our
thoughts, feelings and motives.

My daydreaming ended as my daughter appeared – and she
was quite the most beautiful of all those I'd seen! Of course
she was, to me, because she's mine: I know her intimately
and I love her. And she could trust me to be waiting for her.

Let's be grateful for God's love, which we can always depend
on and which, in turn, teaches us how to love.

Pray

Lord, I'm so grateful for your constant love for me, just as I
am. Help me to love others that way too.

Day 254

Be Prayerful

Hayley Nock

One day Jesus told his disciples a story to show that they should always pray and never give up. 'There was a judge in a certain city . . . A widow of that city came to him repeatedly, saying, "Give me justice in this dispute with my enemy." The judge ignored her for a while, but finally he said to himself, "I don't fear God or care about people, but this woman is driving me crazy. I'm going to see that she gets justice, because she is wearing me out with her constant requests!"'

Luke 18:1–5

I had wanted some traditional weighing scales for a long time. Then, one day, we found some in a charity shop, with the full set of weights as well. I was delighted – though carrying them home was hard work!

There was a learning curve, too: using these scales takes a different technique. You put the weights on one side, and keep adding the ingredients bit by bit on the other side until the arm is balanced. You never know when the balance will tip.

There was a particular issue I'd been praying about for several years, and I'd lost heart to continue. Then I was reminded of this story that Jesus told of a persistent widow. It's a bit like my scales: you just have to keep going and at some point, the balance will tip.

Pray

Lord, help me not to give up. Thank you that my prayers make a difference.

Day 255

Be a Messenger

Fiona Castle

'I am praying not only for these disciples but also for all who
will ever believe in me through their message.'
John 17:20

Anniversaries are often a time for celebration, but they can
also be sombre. Every year the anniversary of my husband's
death brings me mixed feelings: sadness, but also immense
gratitude for a happy marriage that was filled with laughter
and blessings.

When my husband knew he was dying he insisted that we
would not be sad or complain. 'We've had such a privileged
life, we mustn't ever grumble, just be grateful,' he said. I've
tried to remember that.

When we set out on our Christian walk, we have no idea of
the path God has planned for us. As I look back, I can only be
grateful as I recognize God's hand guiding me through the
various circumstances of my life.

It was only because a friend took the time to tell me about
new life in Jesus that I came to know his peace and security.
In today's verse, Jesus prays not just for his disciples but for
all those they share the Gospel with. We are indebted to all
the Christians who have faithfully gone out into the world
and shared the Good News.

Pray

Dear Lord, help me to take every opportunity to make the
message of the Gospel known to those around me and
beyond.

Day 256

Be Honest

Fiona Castle

Cling to your faith in Christ, and keep your conscience clear.
For some people have deliberately violated their consciences;
as a result, their faith has been shipwrecked.
1 Timothy 1:19

D.L. Moody said, 'Character is what you are in the dark' – a very powerful and challenging statement!

If two people were talking honestly about you, what would they say? Your character is unique. You build your reputation by how you live and behave and by the example you become to others, whether by kindness, thoughtfulness and generosity, or the opposite.

We might gain a reputation through having a powerful, important job and earning a large salary, but isn't it more important to measure our value by the faith God has given us to be his follower in all our circumstances? Jesus is our ultimate example of integrity, openness and honesty at all times.

Integrity means sticking to our principles rather than being swayed by popular opinion or the demands of the moment; it means ordering our lives and our responses to situations according to God's will, rather than what will make money or keep us in our comfort zone.

Pray

Teach me, Lord, to shape my conscience according to your example, and to live with the integrity that will honour you.

Day 257

Be Prayerful

Jaz Potter

Pray in the Spirit at all times and on every occasion. Stay alert
and be persistent in your prayers for all believers everywhere.
Ephesians 6:18

I have to admit I'm not the world's greatest prayer! I'm not
one of those people that can go into a room alone and spend
hours on my knees. I truly admire all who are able to do this,
and it's something I aspire to. But I'm much better praying
with other people. It keeps me on track and focussed.

However, I do spend a lot of time praying: I set up little
prompts for myself. For example, I was desperate to see a
breakthrough for a couple I knew, so I committed to praying
for them every time I drove past their door. I had to pass by
several times a day, so they got a lot of prayer! My prayers for
them weren't lengthy or elegant, but they were real and full
of compassion.

I love how this verse frees us to pray any time, anywhere and
on any occasion. I am so grateful that God is everywhere all
of the time, and Jesus has reconciled us to God so we can
talk to him with complete ease.

Pray

Dear God, thank you that you hear our cry from wherever we
are. Help us to keep talking to you – not just for ourselves, but
for others, too.

Be a Teacher

Rhiannon Goulding

Tell your children about it in the years to come, and let
your children tell their children. Pass the story down from
generation to generation.

Joel 1:3

My daughter was doing a school project about 'Family', and she asked each of us what family meant to us. The answers came back: somewhere we feel safe and loved, where we have fun together. She was surprised by my answer: 'Family is the place where you build people up to be more than yourself, and create something that doesn't just last your lifetime, but eternity.'

The fact is that in two generations' time my descendants probably won't even know my name. But my prayer is that my faith, my character and ethos will be within my children, and in turn their children, just as part of my mum's character and my grandma's is within me.

What do we give our children? Holidays and new toys bring pleasure for a while, but the stories of faith, the Christian ethos of our family life, the experience of trusting God and our prayers for our children outlive us, and can last for eternity.

Let's show all the young people around us what it means to follow Jesus in a real way. Let's teach them so they can teach others of God's love and faithfulness and purpose for our lives.

Pray

Father, help us to pass on the message of your wonderful love to the next generation.

Day 259

Be Determined

Rhiannon Goulding

With all these things in mind, dear brothers and sisters, stand firm and keep a strong grip on the teaching we passed on to you both in person and by letter.
2 Thessalonians 2:15

'Head down keep going, head down keep going, head down keep going.' This was the chant in my head as I faced my nemesis, the hill that I just could not run up. The more I ran the longer it got, and every time I tried to conquer it, I just couldn't reach the top. But not today; today I was going to win, I was going to make it. Head down keep going, head down keep going, one foot in front of the other . . . imagine how good it will feel when you beat this hill . . .

How often does life feel like that? Sometimes when things are tough we have to just keep doing what we know is right, remember what we've been taught in podcasts, preaching, studies and traditions, and just keep going. Because like me on that run, one day you will beat your nemesis and conquer that hill, and it really will be an amazing feeling when you do.

Pray

Lord Jesus, give me the strength to persevere as I follow you.

Day 260

Be Fair

Rachel Allcock

> Isaac loved Esau because he enjoyed eating the wild game Esau brought home, but Rebekah loved Jacob.
>
> Genesis 25:28

Rebekah and Isaac are a warning for family life, to prioritize fairness and communication. Before the twins Esau and Jacob were born, God told Rebekah that the older would serve the younger (Genesis 25:28).

Yet as Isaac reached the end of his life, he called for his older son, Esau, to bless him as the firstborn (Genesis 27:4). Why hadn't Rebekah told her husband what God had said to her about them? Maybe she had; maybe Isaac had refused to listen.

Whatever happened, the family developed a rift. Rather than speaking to Isaac about the blessing, she sent Jacob to trick Isaac into blessing him instead.

After this deception, it took years for Jacob to make peace with who he was. When he had to flee from his angry brother, he was leaving his family's land of promise, and all the safety of his homeland. But God was with him – he reaffirmed his blessing of Abraham and applied it to Jacob (Genesis 28:10–22).

Twenty years after all the lies, his brother was still alive and so was his father! Jacob wrestled with God and received a new name, and the courage to face his family again (Genesis 32:28).

Pray

Lord God, thank you that, in time, you heal, restore and bless your people. Help us to be fair in our relationships, avoiding favouritism and deception.

Day 261

Be a Teacher

Fiona Castle

'And be sure of this: I am with you always, even to the end of the age.'
Matthew 28:20

'It's just a phase – he'll grow out of it.' Most parents have said that at some point. We've certainly had our fair share of phases in our family. Once we even bought a poodle to help our daughter when she was terrified of dogs. She came out of that phase a week later – my husband Roy said we could have rented one and saved a lot of trouble!

Another time one of the boys was afraid to be upstairs on his own. We reasoned with him, we prayed with him and we prayed for him, to no effect. Bedtimes were a misery. But then I noticed that he'd started going up alone to fetch something sometimes, whether or not the lights were on. Gradually the fear left him. Just a phase?

Eventually I asked him why he was happy to be alone upstairs. He grinned and pointed upwards. 'I knew it was all right because I was being looked after.'

I praised God for bringing that reassurance to a little boy.

We try to teach our children Bible truths and think it has all fallen on stony ground. What an encouragement it is to see that it's bearing fruit!

Pray

Lord, help us to remember that your ways are not our ways. Give us opportunities to help others discover that your ways are right; your ways are eternal.

Be Determined

Fiona Castle

So we don't look at the troubles we can see now; rather, we fix our gaze on things that cannot be seen. For the things we see now will soon be gone, but the things we cannot see will last for ever.

2 Corinthians 4:18

We often feel like victims of our circumstances. Life can be tough and painful and we can look at others and think, 'It's all right for them – they have no idea what life is like for me!' However, it's not so much what happens to us but how we handle it that's important.

No one can ruin a day for us without our permission. We can choose our attitude to our circumstances. We can allow them to overcome us with grief and anguish, and sometimes self-pity, or we can rise up and stand firm, trusting the Lord, knowing that he understands what we are going through and has promised never to leave or forsake us.

There will always be times when we are unable to understand why things are happening the way they are, but God calls us to be courageous amidst our trials. Remember, tomorrow is another day!

Pray

Dear God, help me to remain strong in the armour you provide for me when life gets tough.

Be Unanswered

Rachel Allcock

Job lived 140 years after that, living to see four generations of his children and grandchildren. Then he died, an old man who had lived a long, full life.
Job 42:16–17

I don't cope well with even minor pain! However, once I know the reason for it, the worry (and often the pain) diminishes. That pain in my hip is because I need to strengthen some tendons. That headache is because I'm dehydrated, and so on.

When suffering comes our way we, like Job and his friends, try to find a reason for it. God allows Satan to test Job. He loses everything in an instant – his animals are stolen, his farmhands and servants killed, his sheep and shepherds are burned, his house collapses, and his children die (Job 1:12–19). And this is only Job's first test!

The unsettling drama continues, but Job remains steadfast and praises God, in spite of everything. No fully satisfying explanation can be found as to why Job is suffering. Then, after 42 chapters, we read today's wonderful verses about his remaining 140 years of life. Hundreds of years later, James writes of Job, 'You can see how the Lord was kind to him at the end, for the Lord is full of tenderness and mercy' (James 5:11).

Pray

Lord, help us to remember that a larger story is playing out behind our unanswered prayers and inexplicable suffering. Help us to be inspired by Job's steadfast praise.

Be Diligent

Fiona Castle

Endurance develops strength of character, and character
strengthens our confident hope of salvation. And this hope
will not lead to disappointment. For we know how dearly
God loves us, because he has given us the Holy Spirit to fill
our hearts with his love.

Romans 5:4–5

To be honest, most of what we do on a daily basis is not exciting! It can be repetitive, but necessary. Sometimes it can be stressful and exhausting and we need courage to see it through. Much of what we do is unnoticed and unappreciated and very often taken for granted, and so we have to be careful not to allow ourselves to be dragged down into self-pity. Rather, we need to remind ourselves to be grateful for the strength and ability to do the work we have been given.

Often, the difficult, boring, unrewarding tasks can underpin everything: the major achievements may belong to others, but without our work in the background they would not be possible. And the glory of both belongs to God.

God sees our hearts and all the work we do.

Pray

Dear Lord, please enable me to cope with whatever work comes my way today and remind me that I am serving you, so that I work with a loving heart.

Day 265

Be Loving

Fiona Castle

He took the humble position of a slave and was born as a
human being.
Philippians 2:7

I was singing Charles Wesley's lovely hymn 'And Can It Be?' when one line seemed to jump from the page. Jesus 'emptied himself of all but love'.

I stopped to think. Jesus was God – the Son of the Creator of all. But he gave up everything to identify with us. He allowed himself no rights. He was totally obedient to his Father's will.

As I sang, I thought of all that I have left in me which is not love, and I realized just how far short I fall from God's ideal. I like to think I'm humble – but if I'm ignored completely my pride takes over and demands to be noticed. I think I'm long-suffering – but put me in a traffic jam for a few minutes and I become tense and irritable. I think I'm thankful – but if things go wrong, I start to consider my rights.

So when I think of how much Jesus gave up I realize how much I have to learn. In the words of another hymn, 'Love so amazing, so divine, demands my soul, my life, my all.'

Pray

Lord, take my life and let it be, always, only, all for you.

Be Willing

Fiona Castle

We ask God to give you complete knowledge of his will and to give you spiritual wisdom and understanding. Then the way you live will always honour and please the Lord, and your lives will produce every kind of good fruit.
Colossians 1:9–10

God wants to use us to serve his purposes in our world. This isn't necessarily to take up an important position, but to seek his will and to give ourselves entirely to him, wherever he wants us to be.

When we stop telling God what we want, and start listening to him and watching out for his guidance, then he is able to use us. As the Methodist Covenant Prayer says, 'I am no longer my own but yours' – and that is when our lives 'will produce every kind of good fruit', and we will always 'honour and please the Lord'.

When we know he holds the future we needn't be afraid.

Pray

Lord, I trust you to direct my path. Help me to listen to you so that I make the most of every opportunity you give me.

Be Less Busy

Fiona Castle

Oh, that I had wings like a dove; then I would fly away and rest! I would fly far away to the quiet of the wilderness.
Psalm 55:6–7

Have you ever felt like that? I remember learning a song in the school choir which included those verses and I have never forgotten it! Later in life, whenever I was exhausted, with an over-busy schedule, when people were making too many demands on me, I would sing that song.

I felt I wanted to escape from the pressures of life and disappear to a place where no one could find me. Sadly, there's no escaping from the life we have created for ourselves. We have to work our way through all our commitments before we can take even a short break. Perhaps it would be good, when the opportunity arises, to take stock of our busyness. Is what we are doing worthwhile, necessary and sensible? Are we doing what we are doing for the right reasons, or to try to win the approval of others? Ask God for his answer.

If you're too busy to do all the things you feel you ought to do, then you're busier than God wants you to be!

Pray

Lord, help me to plan my days under the banner of your loving wisdom.

Be Re-Started

Rachel Allcock

'But I will confirm my covenant with you. So enter the boat –
you and your wife and your sons and their wives.'
Genesis 6:18

One of my first memories of being on a big stage was of sharing a piano stool with my big sister at the Burton Music Festival, messing up our duet and calling down to the serious-looking man, 'Can we start again, please?'

In which areas of your life do you just want to 'start again'? By Genesis chapter 6, God's perfect world was so corrupt that he had to start again.

Starting again has to be a good thing. God chose to use community and friendship to help him start again. He entrusted Noah with building the ark, gathering the animals and protecting each living thing. God knew we would mess things up but he still wanted to start again.

The story of God's people is all about starting again and again. So don't be disheartened. Get a friend to help you, or be a friend to someone else. And if you haven't done so yet, speak to Jesus and ask him if you can start again, please. Unlike that steely-eyed adjudicator all those years ago, he won't make you feel as if you're taking liberties by asking.

Pray

Thank you, Jesus, that you are ready and waiting for me to start again.

Be a Seeker

Fiona Castle

'O Father, Lord of heaven and earth, thank you for hiding these things from those who think themselves wise and clever, and for revealing them to the childlike.'
Luke 10:21

I love receiving Christmas cards! I like to pray for each sender – though that mainly happens after the rush of Christmas is over. I sort through and choose my favourites, keeping the finalists to one side until my card of the year is selected. It may be that the sender is very special, or the message has been thoughtfully and lovingly composed. Perhaps the picture captures the imagination.

This year my favourite card was chosen not for the picture but for the words. The colours were harsh, showing a desert scene with camels crossing the sand dunes in the foreground. The words said simply 'Wise men still seek him.'

It made me think of the words of Jesus above. We don't have to be intellectuals to understand how our names can be written in the book of life! I am so grateful to God for that, because otherwise I wouldn't have stood a chance. People are wise if they simply seek after God.

Let's pray today for the wisdom to trust our Lord and Saviour.

Pray

Lord, help me to display your love to others, so that they will seek and find you.

Day 270

Be Thoughtful

Fiona Castle

'All right, but let the one who has never sinned throw the first stone!'
John 8:7

This was the response of Jesus to the Pharisees, about the woman caught in the act of adultery. It is, to me, one of the most challenging ways Jesus taught – by making people think about their own behaviour.

In the press, we constantly read criticisms and condemnations of people who, in the critic's eyes, don't meet the required standards. But there are always two sides to every story.

Do I always do right, no matter what the pressures that have been placed upon me? Am I without sin? Do I have a right, therefore, to judge someone else without understanding their background or behaviour?

Jesus saw the sin and recognized the wrong that had been done, but he challenged the self-righteous accusers. He was encouraging them to think differently by looking at their own lives. He then set the sinner free, telling her to go on her way but to sin no more.

We are all sinners, accepted and forgiven by the grace of God, through Jesus.

Pray

Jesus, teach me not to be judgemental, but rather to be thoughtful and careful in my attitude towards others, knowing that I'm a sinner, saved by grace.

Day 271

Be Focussed

Rhiannon Goulding

Look straight ahead, and fix your eyes on what lies
before you.
Proverbs 4:25

As I sat in ICU next to my husband, I was texting, calling, organizing . . . and frazzled. Had I made everyone else feel OK? Had I organized everyone? Had I, had I, had I . . . ? At which point I heard a small voice say, 'Let the main thing be the main thing.' I was so busy looking at my phone and organizing, I'd missed spending time with the main thing, my husband.

I reached out, held his hand and kissed it. I didn't know what was going to happen, but I knew this was the main thing, to sit and to pray. Over the next few weeks, as he was in recovery, every time I felt my organizing brain taking over, the gentle voice reminded me, 'Let the main thing be the main thing.'

How many times have we missed the moment trying to capture the moment? How many times have we missed the face-to-face because of the screen? Let's work to recognize our main things, and not let small things block them out.

Pray

Lord Jesus, help me to see the wood for the trees today, and help me to put you at the centre of all I do.

Day 272

Be Adventurous

Fiona Castle

'This is my command – be strong and courageous! Do not be afraid or discouraged. For the LORD your God is with you wherever you go.'
Joshua 1:9

How important it is for us to be adventurous and courageous in our lives, in order not to waste time and opportunities and end up with regret.

If we stand strong in our faith, doing the right thing for the right reason, we can be bold enough to face whatever situations may come our way. This doesn't mean being reckless, but rather having the courage to try something new, perhaps taking a new direction in life – a more exciting job or a scientific experiment never tried before!

We can make excuses in order to stay within our comfort zones, thinking that in time we might make the effort when things are easier, but we can wait a lifetime for a 'when' that never comes.

Are you prepared to face the fears that prevent you from having an adventure? Are you prepared to risk failure and not be afraid?

Years may wrinkle the skin, but giving up wrinkles the soul! Activate, don't vegetate!

Pray

Give me an adventurous spirit, Lord, with the determination to take every opportunity you show me, without being afraid.

Be Loving

Fiona Castle

'If any of you wants to be my follower, you must give up your
own way, take up your cross daily, and follow me.'
Luke 9:23

Some years ago, a friend nursed her husband through a severe mental breakdown. When I told her how loving she had been to keep caring for him, in spite of the abuse he hurled at her, she said: 'But I didn't feel loving. In fact, I felt guilty because I hated it. I had to keep reminding myself that it was just the illness making him behave like that.'

It's the greatest love of all to keep on acting lovingly in spite of your feelings. Most mothers can remember nights when a child has been sick. We don't feel loving as we change the sheets for the fourth time while everyone else is sleeping soundly! But we make sure the child feels loved and secure. Our commitment to the child goes way beyond one night's exhaustion.

So take heart if you're going through difficult times with loved ones. It's not what we feel but how we act that's important, and God sees and rejoices in our attempts to act in a Christlike way.

Pray

Father, I pray that you would give me your heart of love when I deal with tricky situations.

Be Still

Mandy Catto

'Be still, and know that I am God! I will be honoured by every nation. I will be honoured throughout the world.' The LORD of Heaven's Armies is here among us: the God of Israel is our fortress.

Psalm 46:10–11

What does it look like to 'be still' in our busy lives today? As we fill our days with events, challenges, duties, work, and visiting, even our quieter moments of waiting are often filled with checking messages on our phones. Perhaps we reject still moments as being unproductive, or leaning towards some kind of mystical state of numbness.

The psalmists were not asking us to stare into space. They offered us this call to 'be still' in the middle of a reminder that God will be honoured by every nation. He is the Lord and he is among us: this is why we can 'be still'. He is the one in charge, with the big picture covered from every side – our regrets about our past, our worries about today and our fears for the future. Once we catch this vision, even just a glimpse of who God really is, then our right response is to pause. Be less frantic. Be unafraid.

Pray

Father God, help me to pause. Give me eyes to see that you are my God and you are among us here today. Give me the vision to know you. May I be still and know that you are my God.

Day 275

Be Delightful

Mandy Catto

'He led me to a place of safety; he rescued me because he
delights in me.'
2 Samuel 22:20

What do you delight in? Warm chocolate sauce poured over
fresh vanilla ice cream? A bright orange sunset over the
ocean? All these are delightful, but temporary and purely
sensual. Maybe a deeper, longer-lasting delight would come
from sharing laughter with a good friend, or seeing the face
of a child light up with a smile. Delight is deeper when it is
linked to a relationship. And so we read repeatedly that God
delights in us – weak, fallen and prone to mistakes as we are.
God chose to create us, to love us and to delight in who we
are and the relationship we have with him.

This loving delight leads our Heavenly Father to carry us out
of danger into his protection and a safe place. He rescues us
from danger, from those who would harm us and maybe
from ourselves! Just as a parent hovers over their vulnerable
children with constant, protective care, so our Father looks out
for us, ready to lead us to a place of rescue. What does it mean
for you to know that God delights in you, just the way you are?

Pray

Father God, thank you for your love for me, and that you
delight in me. Rescue me today and lead me to safe places.
May I always live close to you in the centre of your will and
protection.

Be Filled

Jaz Potter

*I will study your commandments and reflect on your ways. I
will delight in your decrees and not forget your word.*
Psalm 119:15–16

Once, when I was going through a particularly tough time,
God showed me I was like a cactus – which doesn't sound
that flattering! It was a tough season, when I felt I could say
all the right things but I didn't feel them inside. I felt like
a fake.

A cactus, though, flourishes in arid conditions. It stores up
all it needs, and releases nutrients as required. God showed
me that all through my Christian life I had been storing up
all I needed to sustain me in drier seasons. That even though
things looked tough on the outside, he had been preparing
me on the inside, so I could still flourish when it didn't seem
possible.

In the season of Covid-19, I had similar moments where I
didn't feel close to God but, once more, he reminded me I
was like a cactus. It's OK to feel a bit parched, but everything
stored inside will keep directing me to God, who sustains me.

Spending time in the word, praying, reflecting and meeting
with God builds you up, so you have enough stored for the
tougher times.

Pray

Dear God, help me to delight in your work. Help me to
remember your words and store them in my heart, so I never
forget them.

Be at Home

Rhiannon Goulding

'So he returned home to his father . . . Filled with love and compassion, he ran to his son, embraced him, and kissed him.'
Luke 15:20

When we were children, travelling home after a family outing, Dad would make us a bed in the back of the car. No seat belts in those days: he'd drop the back seats and make us cosy with coats and cardigans. The engine noise would send us into a deep, uninterrupted sleep for the whole journey home. Yet magically, however long and deeply we'd slept, we'd all wake up the moment we turned into the drive of our home.

I was reminded of this recently when our children, who'd been silently asleep in the car for two hours, woke up as soon as we turned into our road. It made me think of the prodigal heading back to his father, back to home.

Each of us has the opportunity to turn our family house into a family home – a place of warmth, encouragement and strength. Now my children are almost ready to leave home. But I'm still determined that whenever they head for home, they'll experience those same feelings of comfort and love. And as children of God, our fellowships are like families – and our churches, whenever people return to them, should offer the same warm welcome.

Pray

Dear God, give me a heart of understanding and compassion for others, to welcome them and show them your love.

Day 278

Be Indiscriminate

Sarah McKerney

'Still other seeds fell on fertile soil, and they produced a crop.'
Matthew 13:8

A few years ago, I started a vegetable patch. I was a complete novice. I am also a rule-follower. I prepared the soil carefully and planted the seeds according to the instructions on the packet – if it said 'Sow 20cm apart' then I was there with my tape measure. Yet in this parable, the seed was sown broadcast-style, scattered by hand in all directions while the sower walked up and down the field. This seems strange to me: surely, to get the best harvest you sow in prepared ground.

Jesus was the expected, anticipated Messiah, as prophesied in the Old Testament. So it was logical that the best place for Jesus to sow seeds of faith would be where he was expected, in the religious places. The seed was sown but it didn't grow there; they shut the door on Jesus. The seemingly 'good soil' was not good soil at all.

The New Testament tells us that Jesus sowed seed indiscriminately (broadcast-style) even in the least promising places. He didn't seem to have a plan, he just sowed everywhere he went. Likewise, we are to spread the Good News indiscriminately everywhere we go. Because good soil can be anywhere. We simply have to be faithful with the seed.

Pray

Lord Jesus, help me to sow the seeds of faith in you everywhere I go.

Day 279

Be Grateful

Fiona Castle

So now there is no condemnation for those who belong to
Christ Jesus.
Romans 8:1

One of the things which amazed me when I became a
Christian was that I was able to stop striving, let go and allow
Jesus to lead me.

I'd spent years struggling to become 'good enough' to be
acceptable to God. I really believed I could earn my way to
heaven by good deeds, rather like a boy scout collecting
badges. Then one day I really looked at the traditional Easter
hymn 'There is a Green Hill' by Cecil Francis Alexander: 'There
was no other good enough to pay the price of sin; he only
could unlock the gate of heaven, and let us in.'

'He only' could mean that the only thing Jesus could do was
to unlock the gate of heaven, but if we reverse those two
words, 'only he' brings out a whole new emphasis. Only he
was obedient to the Father, so it's only through him that we
can be saved.

It was his perfect obedience that paid the price for our sin, and
gained access to heaven's holiness for all of us. The only condition
for this wonderful hope is that we open our hearts and let him
in to be our Lord and Saviour. I'm so thankful for that!

Pray

Thank you, Jesus, that you were willing to pay the price for
my sin. Help me to remember your sacrifice each day, with
gratitude.

Be Fit

Rhiannon Goulding

Physical training is good, but training for godliness is much better, promising benefits in this life and in the life to come.
1 Timothy 4:8

I walked into my kitchen and made myself a cup of tea, and I don't even remember doing it. This made me think: I want to have better muscles. Not so that I can lift a bigger kettle – I mean better muscle memory.

We do things every day on autopilot: drive a car, ride a bike, get dressed. We don't have to think about every step in the process – it comes automatically. If you play a musical instrument, you know about training your muscle memory so your fingers can play a phrase or a whole piece without stopping to think about each note.

I want to live for God and in my community with muscle memory – when acting in godly ways is so much a part of my day-to-day life that I do it without even thinking. I want my first response to be always 'Yes, God,' and to be so ingrained in my life that it's automatic.

To build that muscle I need to exercise it, to practise every day, in every part of my life.

When muscles are growing there's stretching and pain, but you have to keep focussed on the end result. So I'd better get training.

Pray

Lord, help me to exercise the muscles of my faith, so I can be fit enough to do your will.

Day 281

Be a Sharer

Fiona Castle

'Each generation tells of your faithfulness to the next.'
Isaiah 38:19

This verse indicates a great responsibility to pass on to the next generation everything we have learned. Our God is faithful and we have benefited from his faithfulness to us, therefore we must encourage others to discover it for themselves. If we are not willing to tell others about our faith, how will they know?

Jesus prayed to his Father for us by saying, 'I am praying not only for these disciples but also for all who will ever believe in me through their message' (John 17:20). What a blessing to be prayed for by Jesus! And what a responsibility we have, to continue to make the Good News of Jesus known to the coming generations.

In order to share that Good News, we have to be faithful in the way we live – so that we tell people about him not only with our words but also in our lives, so that we can be living examples of his faithfulness.

Pray

Lord, I pray for the next generation, that they will know and love your name.

Day 282

Be Confident

Fiona Castle

And we are confident that he hears us whenever we ask for
anything that pleases him.
1 John 5:14

Some verses in the Bible make it sound as though we will
get anything we want, if we ask God for it; but this verse
explains that he hears our prayers as we pray according to
his will. Prayer is not a magic formula to make things happen
the way we think they should; rather it is trusting God for his
answers, whatever they might be.

A beloved former pastor of my church, Jim Graham, gave
wonderful advice when he said, 'Prayer is not getting God
into my world to meet my needs, but getting me into his
world to serve his purposes.'

This makes sense. How do we serve God's purposes, even
when our most passionate prayers are not answered in the
way we wanted, expected or hoped? Does prayer entice God
to manipulate circumstances on our behalf? No, but we must
trust him to bring his purposes to pass, whatever the answer.

He has the whole world in his hands.

Pray

Lord, when I pray with passion and longing, help me to
understand that you have the right answer, even when it
doesn't meet my human expectations.

Be a Guest

Rachel Allcock

'Don't carry a traveller's bag with a change of clothes and sandals or even a walking stick. Don't hesitate to accept hospitality, because those who work deserve to be fed.'
Matthew 10:10

In this verse, Jesus told the disciples to take only the shirt on their backs. It was a real test of their faith.

I'm a 'just in case' packer. Pride prevents me from packing light. I love the recognition I get from being the one with plasters, a change of clothes for everyone if they get muddy, and a fully loaded snack box in the boot of the car. Maybe I need to check the second part of today's reading: 'Don't hesitate to accept hospitality.'

In today's culture, it's hard to ask for things, hard to feel worthy enough to take up someone's time and space: phoning rather than texting feels like such an invasion of a friend's day! Yet Jesus was quick to point out that the disciples were to find someone suitable and stay with them until they left town (Matthew 10:11). For us, it's simpler to be anonymous in a hotel.

Whenever we've travelled for an Activate event, the best meals have been shared in someone's home, and amazing connections have been made. Let people share their gift of hospitality!

Pray

Lord, help us to be better at receiving help, hospitality and time. Help us to be willing to share our lives and possessions with new friends.

Be Trusting

Fiona Castle

> Therefore, since we have been made right in God's sight by faith, we have peace with God because of what Jesus Christ our Lord has done for us.
> Romans 5:1

There is a well-known saying that, 'You won't find many atheists in a shipwreck!'

When life's going well, people feel self-confident and satisfied, but when trouble comes and life seems out of control and they feel they're drowning, they cling on to anything that might save them. That's very often the moment when even non-believers call out to God to help.

As Christians, we're not too different. We know that God is there, holding out his hand to lift us out of our desperation and providing peace, through our trust in Jesus. This doesn't mean that all our troubles immediately disappear and life is easy again. It means we can trust him through the turbulence, knowing we are safe in his grip. It is faith, not our perfection, which gives us strength in difficult times.

When we believe this, we have a responsibility to share our faith with those we meet, who may be in difficulties. We can build friendships, pray for them and show them what a life of faith means. Look out for those who may be struggling in life's storms today, and reach out.

Pray

Thank you, Father, that through Jesus, we can trust you through all the turbulence of our lives.

Day 285

Be Brave

Rhiannon Goulding

Jesus was sleeping at the back of the boat with his head on a cushion. The disciples woke him up, shouting, 'Teacher, don't you care that we're going to drown?'
Mark 4:38

It's 3.16 a.m. I'm in a tent and a yellow weather warning has been issued. Wind and rain are gusting, and the tent's threatening to free itself from its moorings and launch into the night sky! Within minutes, I'm hammering in the extra-long tent pegs and tightening ropes. Then comes the tense, nervous bit . . . sitting and hoping your pegs will hold and the wind will subside.

I wonder how the disciples felt, desperately trying to control their boat amidst the lashing rain and roaring sea. How hard would it be to choose between trust and action? I think I'd have wondered, 'Is it up to me to save this boat and contend with the storm, or do I ask the Master to deliver a solution?'

Perhaps I'd have been the one slightly frustrated and greatly worried that when it seemed we needed him the most, the Master was asleep in the boat! The truth is that there are always pegs we can hammer and ropes we ought to tighten, but the Master is never far away. And however inactive or dismissive we might imagine him to be, he is only ever a prayer away.

Pray

Thank you, Lord, that you have promised that you will never leave me nor forsake me.

Be Bold

Mandy Catto

And so, dear brothers and sisters, we can boldly enter heaven's Most Holy Place because of the blood of Jesus. By his death, Jesus opened a new and life-giving way through the curtain into the Most Holy Place. And since we have a great High Priest who rules over God's house, let us go right into the presence of God with sincere hearts fully trusting him.

Hebrews 10:19–22

We know that God is holy and we are not. Sometimes our sins and failures can overwhelm us and cause us to hide, just as Adam and Eve hid from the presence of God in the Garden of Eden.

And yet – we have Jesus. Believing in him means that God looks on us and sees his perfect Son. This makes all the difference! We don't have to hide or withdraw from God. We can step confidently into his presence. We can walk daily with him, confident that he loves us and accepts us.

What difference will this knowledge and confidence make to you today? If you can walk boldly even into the holiest of places because of your salvation, then live boldly everywhere! In your church, in your home, at your workplace and in your community.

Pray

Lord, show me that I am saved and made holy through Jesus. Help me to walk boldly with you today, in confidence and without fear because I walk with you.

Day 287

Be a Thinker

Rachel Allcock

> But now you have been united with Christ Jesus. Once you were far away from God, but now you have been brought near to him through the blood of Christ.
>
> Ephesians 2:13

How do you explain why Jesus died for us? My daughter's Year 7 RE homework required us to sort reasons into order of importance.

I remembered the diagram of one cliff ('God'), a gap ('sin'), and another cliff ('mankind'). Christ's cross was drawn as a bridge, to allow us to reach God. It's a simple but effective illustration. Here's the conclusion we wrote:

'Jesus died to bridge the gap between us and God. That gap had come about when Adam and Eve sinned. People had never been good enough to get back to a close relationship with God, even when they kept the Law and performed all the sacrifices instructed in Leviticus. So Jesus was a sacrifice for all our sins – he died to bring us eternal life. There were other reasons why people wanted him dead at the time, many of which relate to the fact that they didn't realize he was the promised Messiah. However, the main reason that matters throughout all of history is that he allowed us to get close to God again, by wiping out our sin.'

What would you write? Do you agree?

Pray

Lord God, may we be forever awestruck by your amazing plan to redeem mankind.

Day 288

Be Sensitive

Fiona Castle

'God blesses those who mourn, for they will be comforted.'
Matthew 5:4

Blessed are those who do not use tears to measure the true feelings of others.

Blessed are those who stifle the urge to say, 'I understand', when they don't.

Blessed are those who do not expect the bereaved to put into the past someone who is still fresh in their hearts.

Blessed are those who do not always have a quick 'comforting' answer.

Blessed are those who do not make judgements on another's closeness to God, by their reaction to the loss of a loved one.

Blessed are those who allow the sorrowing enough time to heal.

Blessed are those who admit their discomfort and put it aside to help others.

Blessed are those who do not give unwanted advice.

Blessed are those who continue to call, visit and reach out, when the crowd has dwindled and the wounded are left standing alone.

Blessed are those who know the worth of each person as a unique individual, and do not pretend that they can be replaced or forgotten.

Blessed are those who realize the fragility of sorrow and handle it with an understanding shoulder and a loving heart.

Pray

Lord, help me to be sensitive to the needs of others.

Day 289

Be Hospitable

Becky Burr

Cheerfully share your home with those who need a meal or a place to stay.
1 Peter 4:9

Before I married, I dreamed of a lovely home, perfectly tidy and clean, with matching plates and dishes, and me cooking up a storm and inviting over our most fabulous friends for a lively dinner party! Just a few months later, all I wanted was a simple plate of pasta with a few people who I could serve through conversation and not the tidiness of our lounge.

There's a huge difference between entertaining and hospitality. Entertainment is all about the fancy food and matching dishware. It rules out those who house-share, the culinarily challenged, the busy mums whose dining table is covered in washing, the low-income households who can't afford to create a Michelin-star dish.

Other translations of this verse say 'offer hospitality without grumbling'. The Greek word for hospitality means 'love of strangers'. Hosting means welcoming others into our home and serving them just as Jesus would, so that strangers become family. As Christians, we host the Kingdom of God. When we open up our door to others, we are opening the door for them to meet Jesus also and join his family.

So don't worry about the mess, invite them over anyway!

Pray

Lord, help me to host the kingdom of God. Show me who I should invite round for a simple meal or cup of tea, so I can love and serve them.

Day 290

Be Beautiful

Fiona Castle

The sun has one kind of glory, while the moon and stars each have another kind. And even the stars differ from each other in their glory.
1 Corinthians 15:41

Beauty comes in all sorts of shapes and sizes, as well as preferences. We all have different ideas of what we think is beautiful. But there is one model for beauty within the context of God's word, which is the kind of beauty we exhibit to others. This is not dependent on hairstyle, make-up or fashion, but rather on how we behave.

I found a lovely illustration of this by Elisabeth Kübler-Ross, who once likened people to stained-glass windows. When the sun shines they look bright, but in the darkness you can only see their beauty if they are lit from within.

Our physical beauty will fade with age, but an inner sparkle lasts, so long as we don't lose our enthusiasm for life.

Which of your friends, relations or even public figures come to mind when you think of this kind of beauty? The person I'm thinking of has a beauty that has transcended all the seasons of her life, and the light within her has shone on every occasion. In spite of much sadness and difficulty, her faith has remained strong.

Pray

Lord, help me keep my zest for living in your world, to serve your purposes.

Be a Worker

Mandy Catto

'And now get to work, for I am with you, says the LORD of Heaven's Armies. My Spirit remains among you, just as I promised when you came out of Egypt. So do not be afraid.'
Haggai 2:4–5

God had a specific task for Zerubbabel and Jeshua, to rebuild the Jerusalem Temple. He encourages them to get on with his work as he promises to be with them. He reminds them that his spirit has been among them for many centuries and that he rescued them from slavery in Egypt. Because of this past protection and present presence, they can proceed without fear. In the short book of Haggai, he asks for obedience and promises blessing.

What is the task that God has for you in this season of your life? Has he spoken to you of a job he wants you to do, a ministry to continue with, a person who needs your support? Perhaps he is nudging you to get to work on something new? It may not be building a temple, but it might be building up his church. We are all asked to be witnesses and get on with the work of telling others about Jesus.

Pray

Lord, you have promised me that your Holy Spirit is within me. Show me the work you want me to do, and help me to get on with it with courage and determination.

Day 292

Be Assured

Rhiannon Goulding

I praise your name for your unfailing love and faithfulness
. . . As soon as I pray, you answer me; you encourage me by
giving me strength.
Psalm 138:2–3

Horatio Spafford lost his 4-year-old son in a fire. He faced financial ruin in 1873. His wife and daughters travelled to England on the SS *Ville du Havre*, and all four of his daughters died in a collision at sea. What pain, what anguish, what loss. But in the most horrendous of circumstances, he wrote the well-known hymn 'It is Well With My Soul'. This hymn has carried many believers through difficult times. It's amazing that out of such loss came such assurance. The line that hits me is this: 'When sorrows like sea billows roll; whatever my lot, thou hast taught me to say, "It is well, it is well with my soul."' This hymn encourages us to go on trusting that God will get us through, as he has in the past.

Where do you turn during times of pain and anguish? Which worship songs help you to focus on God's promises and assurance? If you don't have verses and songs to turn to, it might be worth listening out for some that resonate with you. In challenging times, they become a lifeline and help us focus on the one who saves us.

Pray

Father, you have brought me through so much. Help me to go on trusting you.

Be Loving

Fiona Castle

'Your love for one another will prove to the world that you are my disciples.'
John 13:35

Being a Christian comes with certain expectations, one of them being that we love our neighbours as ourselves. This isn't always easy! But if we can love others when they are difficult or unappreciative, it proves that we understand the love of God for us, when we're being equally difficult and unappreciative!

Those of us who are mothers love our children unconditionally, though when they have tantrums or behave badly, we probably don't feel very loving towards them. But God calls us to show loving discipline. This is for their long-term benefit and doesn't mean we love them any less. In fact, it demonstrates that we love them and want the best for them.

Sometimes we can be so busy, coping with so many jobs, that we fail to enjoy leisure and play time with our children, yet this is a part of showing love too. It is said that children spell love T-I-M-E. Perhaps this is a lesson to safeguard our time and get our priorities right, by loving our friends and family through spending focussed and intentional time with them.

Pray

Help me, Lord, to love others as you have loved us.

Be a Comforter

Fiona Castle

Now may our Lord Jesus Christ himself and God our Father,
who loved us and by his grace gave us eternal comfort and
a wonderful hope, comfort you and strengthen you in every
good thing you do and say.
2 Thessalonians 2:16–17

When we are going through loss or difficulties, we need someone with love and compassion to stand beside us to give us comfort in our time of distress.

Such comfort is not necessarily expressed in words – in fact words, unless given with sensitivity, can have the opposite effect! Someone who says, 'I know exactly how you feel,' almost certainly doesn't! Every situation is different and we can only try to imagine how someone might be feeling. The important thing is for people to feel they are not alone in their struggles, but that you are standing beside them and with them, to uphold them at such times.

God is our ultimate comfort when we grieve, when we are discouraged, when we are afraid, persecuted or rejected. When we know God has comforted us, we are able to comfort others.

Pray

'All praise to God, the Father of our Lord Jesus Christ . . . the source of all comfort. He comforts us in all our troubles, so that we can comfort others' (2 Corinthians 1:3–4).

Day 295

Be Hopeful

Fiona Castle

Faith shows the reality of what we hope for; it is the evidence of what we cannot see.
Hebrews 11:1

The word 'hope' is generally used in a fairly casual way, in phrases like, 'I hope you have a lovely day,' or 'I hope you'll soon be feeling better.' The dictionary definition is 'a feeling of expectation or desire'. However, the eternal meaning is much more encouraging and important. It tells us that we can be assured that this life is not the end. Rather, because of our faith and trust in the Lord Jesus, whatever life throws at us, we can be hopeful of eternal life in heaven, where suffering and pain and sorrow will be finished.

When we know Christ and all he has done for us, our outlook on life is so different. It's so much more positive, because even if things don't go as we hope or want, we have the ultimate eternal hope. People who dismiss faith in Christ have nothing to hold on to apart from their own confidence.

Our eternal perspective gives us hope, even through the darkest times.

Pray

Lord, I thank you for the eternal hope we have in you, today and always.

Be Missional

Fiona Castle

'Just as you sent me into the world, I am sending them into the world. And I give myself as a holy sacrifice for them so they can be made holy by your truth.'
John 17:18–19

Jesus prayed for his disciples that they would go into the whole world to preach the Good News. It was because of their obedience that this Good News has been passed down to us through the generations. Now he calls us to take every opportunity to share his love with those who don't know him, so they will be able to understand the gift of life in all its fullness. Our mission is to build friendships with people in a truly relational way, rather than preaching at them.

St Francis of Assisi is commonly attributed as saying, 'Preach the gospel at all times, and if necessary use words.' Let us not use the church as a building where we can gather and have a cosy time, but rather as a missional group of people reaching out towards the lost.

C.T. Studd wrote, 'Some wish to live within the sound of church or chapel bell. I want to run a rescue shop within a yard of hell.'

What are your plans for today?

Pray

Dear Lord, give me a missional heart for the lost, so that they might find you.

Day 297

Be Loving

Esther Tregilgas

'For the LORD your God is living among you. He is a mighty saviour. He will take delight in you with gladness. With his love, he will calm all your fears. He will rejoice over you with joyful songs.'
Zephaniah 3:17

My 2-year-old has taken to saying, 'I love you too.' Not just when we say we love her: she'll just randomly hug you and say it unprompted. She's so secure in her knowledge that she's adored by the whole family.

This made me think how much God would love us to say that to him, knowing we're loved more than we could possibly imagine, so much that he rejoices over us.

On the London underground a few weeks ago, I noticed signs on every train that said something like this: 'If you feel unwell please do not stop the train. Get off at the next stop and seek assistance there.' In other words, London won't stop for you if you need help. Don't hold up the rest of us!

God sent Jesus to die for you and me. He would absolutely want us to stop the train, to hold everyone up if it were necessary for our salvation.

He asks us to come like little children, like my daughter, knowing we don't have to hear the 'I love you' to respond, 'I love you too.'

Pray

Father, help me to understand how great is your love for us, and help me to love you in return.

Be Obedient

Rhiannon Goulding

'But I say, love your enemies! Pray for those who persecute you! In that way, you will be acting as true children of your Father in heaven.'
Matthew 5:44–45

The orange plastic sandwich box sat on my lopsided kitchen worktop next to the unevenly plastered wall. It was the property of the builder who'd left our renovations in ruin and us out of pocket. As soon as I saw it, I wanted to bin it and forget the whole thing, and him. On the way to the recycling bin, I felt God saying, 'Keep it, use it for dishwasher tablets, and every time you use it, pray a blessing on him and his family.' Really, this was the last thing I wanted to do. With a big family, that means I will see that hideous upsetting box twice a day!

It was hard to pray for him and his family. Over a year later, I still do it every time the dishwasher goes on, and it's still hard. We're not called to love and pray only for people we like. We're called to pray for the people who are against us, who wrong us or upset us. It's tough and that's why we need God's help, God's love for others running through us, and his eternal eyes on our temporary situations.

Pray

Father, give me grace to be obedient to your will, even when it's hard.

Day 299

Be Patient

Mandy Catto

Rejoice in our confident hope. Be patient in trouble, and
keep on praying.
Romans 12:12

When Paul writes to the believers in Rome, he ties two important ideas together in one verse. We can be joyful because we have confidence in our relationship with Jesus. We know he is with us, has saved us and will bring us to heaven. This gives us joy, and out of this flows patience in times of trouble. When we see the big picture and how the story ends, then the troubles that come our way have less power to rob us of peace. Trouble is still trouble, and pain and hurt will happen. But when we hold on to what we know – that God's got us covered – and when we remember to fill our days with prayer, then we can be patient.

The group Mercy Me have a beautiful song that helps us to focus on being patient in hard times. 'Even If' shares the experience of going through the worst of times – of being held to the flame and not seeing God step in. They sing that even if we can't see an immediate answer to our prayers, our hope is in God alone because he has been faithful all of our days. These words give us hope to be patient, based on the sure knowledge of his unchanging character.

Pray

Lord, help me to be patient as I trust in my hope in you.

Day 300

Be Dedicated

Fiona Castle

Don't you realize that in a race everyone runs, but only one person gets the prize? So run to win! All athletes are disciplined in their training. They do it to win a prize that will fade away, but we do it for an eternal prize.

1 Corinthians 9:24–25

Years ago, my husband Roy hosted a TV programme called *Record Breakers*. Its signature tune was a song about the need for 'dedication' if you want to achieve your aims.

Nowadays dedication appears to be a forgotten concept. People want to be famous, but not for anything in particular. The really dedicated people – expert musicians, athletes, academics, etc. – are sometimes seen as obsessive. Most of us stick with things while we enjoy them, but when the going gets tough, we quit!

It is easy to begin well, but it is finishing well that is of ultimate importance, and only those who abide by the rules win the prize. Many of us started the Christian life with great energy and enthusiasm – but is our commitment wearing thin? Let's rededicate ourselves to the Master's service.

Pray

Heavenly Father, I dedicate my life to your service today. Help me to be obedient to your calling, wherever it takes me.

Be an Illuminator

Rachel Allcock

> He is the God who made the world and everything in it.
> Since he is Lord of heaven and earth, he doesn't live in man-made temples, and human hands can't serve his needs –
> for he has no needs. He himself gives life and breath to everything, and he satisfies every need.
> Acts 17:24–25

I've highlighted this verse in my Bible. I love it because it's a very respectful comeback to the Athenians who describe Paul as a 'babbler' with 'strange ideas'. They ask him to explain all these strange things he has 'picked up'.

Paul starts from the Athenian position and beliefs, noticing that they are very religious and have shrines. He explains that the 'Unknown God' they worship is the one he is telling them about, the God he describes in today's verse.

When we highlight or annotate verses of Scripture in our Bibles, we bring them to life. Have you seen medieval illuminated manuscripts? Beautifully copied Scripture was embellished with luminous colours, especially gold. We may not be as skilled in calligraphy or illustration as those monks and nuns. Still, when we share our favourite verses, maybe written over a beautiful photograph, we continue a centuries-old tradition of bringing the text to life.

Pray

Lord, help us to be creative and honouring in the way we bring your word to life. Whether we speak, write, tweet, post or comment, may we throw light on who you are.

Day 302

Be Persistent

Fiona Castle

> Let us strip off every weight that slows us down . . . And let us run with endurance the race God has set before us.
>
> Hebrews 12:1

Many years ago, I heard a story about a very successful sportsman. Someone remarked that he was lucky to have done so well, and he replied, 'That's true. And do you know, the harder I work, the luckier I become!'

Every time there are sporting events on television I think about all the hours of determined and dedicated practise the competitors have put in to get this far. It doesn't happen by chance or luck.

At the age of 61, I ran in my first London Marathon. I never expected to win – I just hoped to finish. My family asked if the finishing line had been cleared away by the time I arrived! Well, not quite, but it had taken months and years for me to build up enough endurance to even take part. There are many things we struggle with in life, but we have to endure if we are to accomplish God's purpose for our lives.

If we want to win the race of life, we have to remain faithful to God's instructions, whatever the reasons and whatever the consequences.

Pray

Lord, help me faithfully to run the race you have set before me, so that I finish well.

Day 303

Be a Friend

Fiona Castle

A friend is always loyal, and a brother is born to help in time of need.
Proverbs 17:17

Real friends are very special and very important to us – they can sometimes be closer to us than family. A true friend can be trusted with our greatest secrets, our problems and our needs. No wonder we appreciate them!

How friendly are we in our churches? Do we look out for those we haven't met or seen before? Do we try to make them feel welcome? They might be new to the area and know no one. Do we extend friendship to those in need in our neighbourhood, in our place of work, or at the school gate?

I heard the story of a woman who went for counselling because she was lonely and had no friends. The counsellor asked her the qualities she needed in a friend. Her reply was that she needed someone who accepted her; someone she could trust; and someone with whom she could share her hopes and dreams. The counsellor's advice was to go and be that kind of friend to other people.

If you want a friend, be one.

Pray

Thank you, God, for the friends you have given me. Make me a friend to the friendless.

Day 304

Be Truth-seeking

Rachel Allcock

'You must not testify falsely against your neighbour.'
Exodus 20:16

'I think the people next door are annoyed we drove over their grass the other day.' 'I know she was judging me for making fish fingers and chips again.' 'Your mum thinks I can't keep on top of cleaning the house.'

When you feel worried that someone is mad at you, or that you're not good enough for someone, ask yourself, 'Who told you that?' Usually you'll realize that you don't have any evidence to back up your belief. You've spent too long ruminating on something and have made up a scenario in your head.

How often have we 'testified falsely' against our friends, family or neighbours? It's a poisonous habit, and I, for one, have to watch it. Once our over-active imaginations cause us to make statements like those above, we are lying to ourselves, and to our families, without giving the accused an opportunity to defend themselves! That neighbour you think is annoyed, probably worries you are mad with them about their dog barking. That mum you felt was judging you on your limited culinary ability is probably in awe of how you juggle work, family and kids. And your mother-in-law doesn't see the dust, she sees her grandchildren's smiling faces.

Stop ruminating! Life is too short.

Pray

Lord, help me seek truth, stop ruminating and use my creativity in ways that are more beneficial!

Day 305

Be Sad

Rhiannon Goulding

For his anger lasts only a moment, but his favour lasts a lifetime! Weeping may last through the night, but joy comes with the morning.

Psalm 30:5

Last week I didn't want to go on the family walk I'd arranged the day before. I'd had a bad morning, and I felt sad and tired as I walked up the steep path beside the lake. With my head down, looking at my muddy shoes, I started complaining to God about all the things that were wrong, and it was a long list.

Then I felt God say to me 'Look up!' As I did, I found myself at the top of the hill. The sun was shining across the water and the rain had stopped. It was breathtakingly peaceful. My eyes filled up as I heard him say, 'Look to the hills where my help comes from.'

In a world where happy is the aim and smiles are expected, it's hard when you just feel sad. But God gave us our wonderful assortment of emotions, and sadness is one of them. The next half of the walk was different. I was still sad, but I also took the time to be grateful for what I did have and to reflect on how blessed I truly was. I felt loved in my sadness, and a sense of contentment over where I was, because morning is coming and joy will return.

Pray

Thank you, Father, that I am always accepted by you.

Day 306

Be Faithful

Mandy Catto

Be sure to fear the LORD and faithfully serve him. Think of all the wonderful things he has done for you.
1 Samuel 12:24

What does it mean to be faithful? In today's fast-moving post-millennial culture, we tend to move on quickly and embrace new fads as our emotions lead us. Being faithful and consistent in our beliefs, relationships and ministry is not highly valued.

Why should we be faithful? The prophet Samuel asked the people to fear the Lord and continue to serve him and gave them the reason: because God had been faithful to them. Can you take a few minutes today to look back and see God's hand in your life? Reflect on the moments, events, relationships and circumstances when you have seen God move and protect you. Write them down in words or draw pictures if this will help you. Take a moment to thank God for his faithfulness to you, and decide if this will make a difference in how you serve him today.

Pray

Lord, thank you for your faithfulness to me and the way you have blessed my life. Give me a fresh perspective today that will enable me to reflect your faithfulness in my relationships, my beliefs and my serving.

Be Trustworthy

Fiona Castle

A gossip goes around telling secrets, but those who are
trustworthy can keep a confidence.
Proverbs 11:13

In the age of the internet, stories and comments (whether truthful or not) can be put on social media or Wikipedia in seconds. This can have disastrous effects on young people, who are vulnerable to other people's opinions: they may find themselves the subject of gossip, or of stories caused by jealousy or arguments.

Gossiping may be caused by boredom, when people have nothing better to do than tell stories about other people, which may be hurtful or damage their reputation. I imagine most of us have been guilty of gossip occasionally, but the Bible condemns any slanderous talk.

We can stop gossip by simply refusing to listen to it. Proverbs also encourages us to know when to keep a confidence and not to share secrets.

We should only talk about others in a way we would be happy for them to hear!

Pray

Father, guard my tongue and help me resist negative chatter.

Be Obedient

Fiona Castle

Work hard to show the results of your salvation, obeying God
with deep reverence and fear. For God is working in you,
giving you the desire and the power to do what pleases him.
Philippians 2:12–13

It may surprise you to realize that obedience to God actually frees us up to enjoy life as he intended, rather than leaning towards ways that distract us and lead us in the wrong direction. Not long after the war, when times were still hard, I was sent to a boarding school. Discipline was strict but the habits of hard work and consideration for others were ingrained for life.

We went to chapel every morning and, among other things, recited the school prayer: 'The Prayer of St Ignatius Loyola'. I've never forgotten it and thought you might like to read it, so it's included as the prayer for today. Don't let the archaic language put you off! The focus is to serve, give and work without looking for a reward. I've always appreciated it as an important way to live each day.

Pray

Teach us, good Lord, to serve thee as thou deservest: to give and not to count the cost; to fight and not to heed the wounds; to toil and not to seek for rest; to labour and not to ask for any reward, save that of knowing that we do thy will.

Day 309

Be Discerning

Fiona Castle

You will show me the way of life, granting me the joy of your
presence and the pleasures of living with you for ever.
Psalm 16:11

In a Bible study once, I was asked to discern the difference
between living 'for' Jesus and living 'with' Jesus. This might
seem rather vague, but I was very challenged by the difference
these two words can make.

With shame I realized I was a person who always lived *for*
something rather than *with*. As a mother of four children, I
was constantly motivated to doing things *for* them, in order
just to reach the end of the day and have everything done.

It took a long time for me to realize and understand the
importance of being *with* my children, enjoying them, rather
than simply being there for them to take care of them.

This applies not only to family, but also to those around us, such
as work colleagues and friends; but most of all, acknowledg-
ing the importance of being *with* Jesus, rather than feeling
that we always have to do things *for* him, to gain his approval.

This is illustrated by Mary, who benefited more by simply
being with Jesus than Martha, who was anxious to please
him by her industrious efforts to cook a meal for him.

Pray

Dear Lord Jesus, help me to realize the joy of simply being
with you as my Lord and Saviour.

Day 310

Be Whole

Fiona Castle

No power in the sky above or in the earth below – indeed,
nothing in all creation will ever be able to separate us from
the love of God that is revealed in Christ Jesus our Lord.
Romans 8:39

I've often told the story of how, even when I had everything
I thought I needed in life, I still felt unfulfilled. Yet once I
discovered a personal relationship with Jesus my life took on
new meaning. My whole life was transformed as a result.

All the material benefits in the world can't help you to
be whole, but with Jesus you can be whole even when
the material benefits are removed. We see this over and
over again: storms cause devastation; chaos on the stock
market leaves people bankrupt; disasters show us our utter
defencelessness. They are beyond our power to control.

But when Jesus rules our lives, let the storms blow us as they
will, let our money be washed away in the floods, still we
know that our lives are intact and whole: we are secure in
the love of our Lord.

Pray

Because you rule my life, Lord, I am grateful that nothing can
separate me from your love.

Be Sure

Jaz Potter

It is God who enables us, along with you, to stand firm for Christ. He has commissioned us, and he has identified us as his own by placing the Holy Spirit in our hearts as the first instalment that guarantees everything he has promised us.

2 Corinthians 1:21–22

When our children were small, we thought it was funny to tell them that the ice cream van tune meant the ice cream had run out. They are adults now and are still not entirely sure what the tune means.

However, we also had a code with them: if we ever used the word 'promise', it was always an absolute truth. If 'I promise' was added to any sentence, the longed-for hope would be a certainty. We rarely used it, and we have never broken a promise to our children.

They also worked out that if they asked, 'Do you promise?' and we said no, their desire was not going to be met. I'm not sure why they never asked about the tune on the ice cream van . . .

We felt it important to use the word 'promise' seriously, because we wanted to reflect the nature of God. He never breaks his promises to us. If he has said it, it will happen, because he does not lie, and therefore we always have hope.

Pray

Dear God, thank you that I can always trust you, because you will never break your promises to me.

Day 312

Be Thankful

Fiona Castle

But each day the LORD pours his unfailing love upon me,
and through each night I sing his songs, praying to God who
gives me life.
Psalm 42:8

Psalms express every emotion and situation we will ever go through, whether it is joy, praise and thankfulness, or fear, anxiety, grief and pain.

What are you going through at the moment? How are you feeling today? Take time to look through the psalms until you find one that expresses your feelings. God encourages us to talk through our emotions, whether anger, or pain, or joys or triumphs, because he is a compassionate God who understands our feelings.

I was astounded to discover Psalm 32, telling my life story, which I read after I had invited Jesus into my heart. 'Oh, what joy for those whose disobedience is forgiven, whose sin is put out of sight . . . I said to myself, "I will confess my rebellion to the LORD." And you forgave me! All my guilt is gone . . . The LORD says, "I will guide you along the best pathway for your life. I will advise you and watch over you."'

Thanksgiving and praise to him for ever.

Pray

I thank you, Lord, that you have given me life in all its fullness.

Day 313

Be in Awe

Mandy Catto

I have heard all about you, LORD. I am filled with awe by your amazing works. In this time of our deep need, help us again as you did in years gone by.

Habakkuk 3:2

What surprises and delights you most about God? Is it the wonder moments when he moves in miraculous ways? When 'God-incidences' stun you into suspending all doubt and knowing for sure that God has intervened? Or is it his faithfulness and consistency over the years – when you can look back and know with certainty that, despite others letting you down and despite difficult circumstances, God is faithful and consistent and always to be trusted?

When I was a new Christian, I think it was the unexpected moments that caused me to stop and stare upwards in awe and wonder. As I grow older, I think it is more often the security of knowing that God can always be trusted. His unconditional love and steady presence fills my heart with love and banishes anxiety.

Perhaps we need both of these to live a life in awe of God. There are sure to be times when we are in deep need of God, his presence and intervention. Don't be afraid to look back for reassurance, but at the same time, look forward and expect miracles!

Pray

Lord, help me to pray big prayers and expect you to act. Help me to remember your faithfulness and all the support you have given.

Day 314

Be Open-handed

Sarah McKerney

Then the LORD asked him, 'What is that in your hand?'
Exodus 4:2

My Auntie Anne was the most wonderful woman. She was a farmer's wife, who had a remarkable skill when it came to baking. She was incredibly shy. She didn't preach to thousands, she was never in church leadership, she didn't petition parliament, nor did she go as a missionary to remote parts of the world. She spent her whole life in a small Lancashire village. But she loved God and she loved people. She was welcoming, inclusive and always had an open door and a seat at her kitchen table.

When she died, it became clear what an impact her life had made. Her funeral was held in a local village church, and it was packed. Hundreds of people came to pay their respects to a woman who changed her community with her listening ear and open door. She was, quite simply, faithful with what she had in her hand – her 'ordinary'.

Sometimes we equate greatness with heroism or extravagant acts of service. But what we see in the Bible is that again and again God uses what ordinary people already have in their hands. When we give God what we have, he works a miracle in our 'ordinary'.

Pray

Lord, open my eyes to see what ordinary things I have in my hand that can be used by you.

Be a Delegator

Rachel Allcock

It is useless for you to work so hard from early morning until
late at night, anxiously working for food to eat; for God gives
rest to his loved ones.
Psalm 127:2

Does laundry take over your life? The bulging odd sock bag used to taunt me as I stepped through a cluttered utility room to retrieve yet another load from the drier. That was until I got talking to a feisty French woman who told me in no uncertain terms that odd socks were not my concern. After each wash they need to be handed straight back to the owner, who must keep them in their own sock drawer and be responsible for matching the pair when the lost one turns up.

I'm sure you have your own examples of times when you carry other people's stress. We're often so busy picking up the pieces and solving their problems that we don't even get enough sleep. I think this verse is telling us to stop trying to fix everything. It's pretty hard for control freaks, who make it our business to carry the anxieties of the family, to give in to sleep. But it is God's blessing and we must rest. If you're like me, gather all the tips you can on how to simplify your life, and shove those odd socks back in the kids' drawers. Don't underestimate the importance of sleep.

Pray

Lord, help me today to manage my time and prioritize rest.

Day 316

Be a Returner

Mandy Catto

Return to the LORD your God, for he is merciful and compassionate, slow to get angry and filled with unfailing love. He is eager to relent and not punish.

Joel 2:13

I was never good at reading maps, always turning the map round to make sense of it. I'm very grateful for satnav systems that can now guide me. My favourite button on the satnav is 'take me home'. However lost you may be, however many miles away, and however dark the road, just press that little button and you will be guided safely back home.

In the book of Joel, the Israelites had disobeyed and wandered far from God. They had just experienced a plague of locusts and Joel warned them that they would soon face further consequences of their sin, with an invading army approaching. He urged them to turn around and follow God's commands and directions. Joel highlighted the merciful nature of God, his never-ending love and forgiveness.

God is our true 'home'. He promises an eternal perfect home in heaven, but he is our home right now, because it's only in him that our identity and purpose can flourish. If you feel that you are far from God, facing the wrong direction or moving away from what is right, then resolve now to return to him.

Pray

Lord, I turn to you. May your Holy Spirit guide me and 'take me home' so that I can be close to you.

Be Real

Rhiannon Goulding

We can say with confidence and a clear conscience that we have lived with a God-given holiness and sincerity in all our dealings.
2 Corinthians 1:12

I was chatting to my grandad about Sunday school and the different teachers we'd had, laughing as we recalled happy times. I remembered that one of them always had peppermints. Then Grandad said a strange thing: 'Don't smell of mints.' I stopped laughing and looked at him with puzzled eyes. 'What do you mean?' I said.

Apparently, that Sunday school teacher used to smoke, and would eat mints to try to disguise the smell. Smoking wasn't the issue; it was the fact that he was trying to hide it and pretend to be someone he wasn't.

We have to live an authentic life, right where we are. We're not perfect, and we don't have to be. If we pretend to have everything sorted, other people feel they can't be real with us or share how they're feeling. I want to be me: faults, failures, highs, lows and all.

So that's why we should never smell of mints!

Pray

Lord, it's difficult to be genuine with people and allow them to see our failures and struggles. Help me to find friends who encourage me to be truly honest, so that I can work on areas of my life I need to work on, and not feel I need to hide anything.

Day 318

Be Forward Thinking

Fiona Castle

I focus on this one thing: Forgetting the past and looking forward to what lies ahead.
Philippians 3:13

It is easy to dwell on the past and regret our failures and wrong choices, but we have all made mistakes. No one's life has been perfect, whether in work, in relationships, or through illness, bereavement or loss. Paul was in prison when he wrote these words, yet he constantly focussed on how he could become more Christlike in all his circumstances.

We all know people who are always filled with self-pity and blame their situations for the way they feel and behave. We also know those who are determined to move forward, no matter what disasters they have endured. Which type would you prefer to spend time with?

The more we concentrate on Christ and his purpose for our lives, the more we learn that we can endure, whatever our difficulties. We belong to Christ and he alone gives us the determination to press on and not give up – and some of us have to remember that we mustn't use old age as an excuse!

Look forward. Look to the future, knowing that in Christ we have already won the race.

Pray

Dear Lord, thank you for the assurance that whatever we go through in this world, our future is secured in you, so we don't need to be afraid.

Day 319

Be Reassured

Rachel Allcock

I want to do what is good, but I don't. I don't want to do what is wrong, but I do it anyway.
Romans 7:19

Have you ever been the subject of your own nightmare? My daughter experienced this the other night. She dreamed that she opened the door to another version of herself, and she couldn't convince people that she was the real girl.

I wonder why this sort of idea is so horrifying. I wonder if our subconscious is playing with all the efforts we make to project different versions of ourselves in front of others.

I'm troubled by how awful I really am on the inside, in the version nobody sees. But I'm comforted that this troubled Paul too. We may genuinely want the best for our friend, but our sinful nature causes us to be jealous of her new house or her successful new business. And it's not just sometimes, or when we 'fall away from God'. If we're anything like Paul, it continues: 'I do it anyway'.

The good news is that Paul goes on, in Romans 8, to explain that this infuriating situation is overcome by Jesus. We don't have to battle our sinful nature alone.

Pray

Dear Lord Jesus, thank you for Paul's honesty about our sinful nature. Help us to comprehend the magnitude of your sacrifice.

Be Caring

Fiona Castle

> Dear friends, let us continue to love one another, for love comes from God. Anyone who loves is a child of God and knows God.
> 1 John 4:7

There are so many unmet needs in the world, and God knows that we can't help everyone. But on a daily basis, how can we make a difference?

There is a saying, 'If you see someone without a smile, give them one of yours!' I make a point, when I go out, to smile at the passers-by. If I'm in a commuter area, I often notice that many people are so focussed on their mobiles that they don't even see me! But then I think, what are their problems? What struggles are they going through? As they pass by, I pray for them and ask God to become real to them and bless them.

Similarly, when I'm on a tube train, I look around at the expressions on people's faces and pray for peace in their hearts. On rare occasions, an opportunity for conversation happens and I can even ask God to bless them. A caring attitude can make a difference to someone's day – or their life.

Pray

Lord, give me a caring heart towards those who are struggling with life's pressures today.

Be Peaceful

Mandy Catto

May the LORD bless you and protect you. May the LORD smile on you and be gracious to you. May the LORD show you his favour and give you his peace.

Numbers 6:24–26

I was watching my lovely nephew, baby Luke. He was eating his lunch and looking out at friendly faces, but he began to fret when he lost sight of his mum. The carrot sticks were abandoned and tears turned into cries of anguish. As he looked around, he spotted his mum, and as soon as that known and loved face came into view, he reached out and pulled gently on her hair until she was looking directly at him. The distress disappeared, smiles returned and peace reigned.

If we lose sight of our loving heavenly Father, we can become overwhelmed by circumstances and events. We can feel as lost as a newborn. Focussing our eyes back onto our ever-faithful God, and remembering the graciousness of his forgiveness will give us a true sense of his blessing washing over us. Take some time out today to let these words of blessing rest on you.

Pray

Father God, thank you for your blessing and your presence. Help me to look up into your face and be peaceful because you are gracious to me and will protect me. Help me to remember that you are smiling on me today.

Be Fruitful

Fiona Castle

'A tree is identified by its fruit . . . A good person produces
good things from the treasury of a good heart.'
Luke 6:44–45

The fruit God desires from us has nothing to do with outward appearances or trying to be seen to be good, but rather living out his purpose for our lives. This will be different for everyone, as every person is unique, with different talents and gifts. The most important thing is that we are where God wants us to be, doing what he wants us to do.

What are your gifts? Have you spent time praying and asking the Holy Spirit to show you where you can be most effective for the Kingdom? We are not all called to be preachers, but we are all called to go into all the world and make disciples. There are many ways of going about this, because we all have different skills and we all have different spheres of influence. You may have the opportunity to touch many lives, or a ministry to pray quietly for one or two. God calls us to be fruitful wherever we are.

Knowing that will give you peace of mind and heart.

Pray

Purify my heart, Lord, cleanse me and remove from me all that gets in the way of your love.

Day 323

Be Forgiven

Fiona Castle

'No one is righteous – not even one' . . . For everyone has
sinned; we all fall short of God's glorious standard. Yet God,
in his grace, freely makes us right in his sight. He did this
through Christ Jesus when he freed us from the penalty for
our sins.
Romans 3:10,23,24

A preacher recently said, 'You don't have to approve of
yourself before you can accept yourself. God accepted you
before he approved you.'

That helped me. Sometimes we feel like hopeless failures
because we don't come up to the standards we set ourselves.
How lovely to remember that God is quite the opposite. He
sees our failures but declares us 'not guilty' – not because he
approves of us, but because of Jesus, whose sacrifice is the
basis for our redemption.

There have been so many times in my life when I have
inwardly cringed at the things I have done or said that have
caused hurt and misunderstanding. So often, I've hated the
way I have behaved, and I can't forgive myself. But, oh, the
release when we know Jesus as our Lord and Saviour – he
forgives us as soon as we repent. We don't have to carry the
burden of guilt around any more. We are forgiven!

Pray

Thank you, Lord Jesus, that you love and accept me, even
when I fall short and feel a failure.

Day 324

Be an Anchor

Rhiannon Goulding

'I'm not asking you to take them out of the world, but to keep them safe from the evil one.'
John 17:15

A while ago, I heard that the local amusement park had closed its doors for the last time. The news brought back fond memories. I recall one visit when my children were smaller, when they went on the pirate ship about twenty times. Despite their appeals, I told them I was quite happy simply to sit and watch, and be there when the ride was finished.

Now, many years later, I still find myself watching as they ride the rollercoaster, not of a pirate ship but of life, with all its complex decisions and emotional challenges. 'I can't join you on that ride or take it for you,' I tell them, 'but I can advise, and I will always be here when you get off.' Sometimes that has meant watching them stumble and fall, still insisting that their way was the better option. I've learned to sit patiently while they take that ride, ready to chat, comfort and advise before they gear up for the next ride.

Walking with your children like this is a little like the way God walks with us. Jesus prayed not that we would never experience difficulty, but that we'd be kept, secured and strengthened in all our troubles.

Pray

Thank you, Lord, that you are with us and promise to keep us safe. Help me to be an anchor for those who need me.

Day 325

Be Available

Fiona Castle

Always work enthusiastically for the Lord, for you know that
nothing you do for the Lord is ever useless.
1 Corinthians 15:58

When my husband, Roy, died, there was a lot of media attention – he had been a star. But I was horrified when I heard I was to be interviewed on television. I didn't do TV – that was Roy's job, not mine!

I panicked. And then I prayed. 'God, I can't do this. I'll make a mess of it.' The reply came immediately: 'Rise to the challenge.'

Then I realized that one day I would have to answer to God for everything I'd done – or not done. I didn't want him to say, 'Where were you when I needed you? I gave you all these opportunities and you didn't take them.'

Nothing I've done since has been quite as scary as that, but I've tried to always be available to go where God has led me. I've often failed, but I have made the effort.

I believe it is better to try and fail than not to bother, so that at the end of my life I won't have to face 'What ifs' and 'If onlys'.

Pray

Lord, help me always to rise to the challenge of the opportunities you give me.

Be in Awe

Mandy Catto

> For the LORD is the one who shaped the mountains, stirs up the winds, and reveals his thoughts to mankind. He turns the light of dawn into darkness and treads on the heights of the earth. The LORD God of Heaven's Armies is his name!
>
> Amos 4:13

Living in California is a blessing, with many days of beautiful sunshine. But wildfires are springing up in many areas this year, so we are living under smoke-filled skies. And last night an earthquake woke me up with loud noises, jolting windows and rolling floors. I am reminded that this is a fallen world and I live on a planet that is groaning. At times, it feels out of control – yet God is the one who created it and he stirs up the weather. Does he cause fires, floods and earthquakes? Or does he allow them to happen as part of his created but fallen world, marred with sin?

I don't have the answers, but I know God does, and that ultimately he is in control. These words from Amos remind us that he is the Lord God of Heaven's Armies. What a beautiful, powerful title. How reassuring that he treads on the heights of earth. How incredible that this is the God who reveals his thoughts to us.

Pray

Lord God of Heaven's Armies, thank you that you created the world and you are sovereign over it. I am in awe of you.

Be Purposeful

Fiona Castle

Even in old age they will still produce fruit; they will remain vital and green.
Psalm 92:14

Age is just a number! Attitude is far more important. But we need to try to remain as healthy as possible through all the seasons of our lives, in order to be effective for the Kingdom. Even as we grow older and maybe are unable to be as active, we can still remain young at heart. We can have a positive attitude, because we know that God has a purpose for us at every stage of our lives.

We mustn't give up because we can't do the things we were able to do decades ago!

Ecclesiastes 5:19 says, 'To enjoy your work and accept your lot in life – this is indeed a gift from God.'

As we grow older, we don't want to look back with regrets about things we didn't bother to say or do. How important it is to make the most of the moment at every stage of our lives so that we can look back with thanksgiving.

Pray

Thank you, Lord, that you give us a purpose at every stage of our lives.

Be Helpful

Fiona Castle

> God has given each of you a gift from his great variety of spiritual gifts . . . Do you have the gift of helping others? Do it with all the strength and energy that God supplies.
> 1 Peter 4:10–11

A helpful person has a servant's heart. Some people have a special gift for helping others; others don't feel so good at it. We all live in different communities – whether in a town or village; we all have different opportunities to communicate with others – at the school gate, in the workplace or at the supermarket. We should be constantly watching out for those in need in one way or another, to see how we can make their lives easier through our thoughtfulness.

Sometimes a crisis can bring out the best in people. In a flood, or fire or earthquake, some people will rush to supply food, hospitality, medication or clothing to those in need. However, it doesn't take a crisis to seek out someone who needs our help.

Is someone you know in need today? Think of some small way to help and encourage them, whether it's a phone call or a bunch of flowers. And if that isn't possible, there is something you can always do – pray for them.

Pray

Lord, give me eyes to see and wisdom to know when I can be helpful to those in need.

Be in Relationship

Fiona Castle

It is no longer I who live, but Christ lives in me.
Galatians 2:20

What would you say to a younger you? Hindsight is a wonderful thing, but if I had to write a note to my former self, I'd explain the reality of Jesus.

'Fiona, faith isn't a ritual, it's a relationship,' I'd say. 'You don't have to try to live up to God's expectations. He loves you as you are. Jesus was willing to die in your place to give you new life. He says, "Come to me and I will give you rest." He doesn't say, "If you work harder, I might accept you."'

If I'd learned this truth earlier in life, I would have felt comfortable in my own skin, without the need to be a people-pleaser. It would have saved me from being completely devoid of self-worth until I found Jesus for myself, aged thirty-five. I'd always believed in God, gone to church and thought I was a Christian, but no one had ever told me of the joy and miracle of inviting Jesus into my life. It changed my attitude to everything.

If only that could be my note to the whole world!

Pray

Lord, keep me close to you, and let my life reflect your love.

Day 330

Be a Romantic

Rachel Allcock

'I am your servant Ruth,' she replied. 'Spread the corner of
your covering over me, for you are my family redeemer.'
Ruth 3:9

I love introducing my daughter to the heroes of my youth:
Mr Darcy, Gilbert Grape, Norman Warne! There's something
about chivalry with vulnerability, or bravery with humility,
that makes these men so attractive.

When I first met my husband, he spoke tenderly about the
needy kids he'd cared for over the previous summer. From
that moment, I could tell that his qualities matched those I'd
admired in all those on-screen heroes of mine.

I love Boaz in this story. When he finds Ruth – at the end of his
bed, all dressed up in her nicest clothes and best perfume – he
acts chivalrously and doesn't take advantage of her. He acts
humbly, recognizing that she could have gone after a younger
man, but she chose him. He knows there is another family
redeemer and he assures her that he will check first whether
this man wants to marry her. Then, the next morning, when
he meets this man, he carefully omits how pleasant, faithful
and hardworking she is! Instead, he points out the burden it
would be to marry a foreigner as well as buy the land. In this
way, he fights for her and proves his love for her.

Pray

Lord God, thank you for all the men in our lives who are godly
and honourable. Help me, too, to live with integrity.

Day 331

Be Clean

Fiona Castle

Let us strip off every weight that slows us down, especially the sin that so easily trips us up.
Hebrews 12:1

One of my favourite household chores, believe it or not, is spring-cleaning! It takes me a little while to get round to it, but once started, I become quite ruthless – clearing out, cleaning and rearranging!

Sometimes I find I get so used to deterioration in my home that I cease to notice it. Chipped paintwork, peeling paper, worn patches on the settee become comfortably familiar – until I remember that visitors are coming to stay! Then suddenly I see my home through their eyes and realize that some urgent repair work is necessary.

This doesn't just apply to the home, but to all sorts of situations in our lives. We get so used to our familiar rut that we don't notice that our habits aren't necessarily helpful ones. The writer to the Hebrews encourages us to have a spiritual spring-clean: something we need to do regularly. Let's look hard and prayerfully at our lives, and ask God to show us what he wants us to do.

Pray

Father, please open my eyes to see my own life clearly, and show me the things I need to change.

Be Salty

Fiona Castle

'You are the salt of the earth. But what good is salt if it has lost its flavour? Can you make it salty again? It will be thrown out and trampled underfoot as worthless.'

Matthew 5:13

Salt is what adds flavour to food – and stops it going off! We can be like salt among the people we know, helping them to find life in the real sense. Perhaps a good illustration is that we should be 'door openers' to help people enter into life in all its fullness.

In Isaac Watts's famous hymn 'When I Survey the Wondrous Cross', there are some very powerful words:

> Forbid it, Lord, that I should boast,
> Save in the death of Christ my God.
> All the vain things that charm me most,
> I sacrifice them to his blood.

What do we need to sacrifice and lay aside in order to be effective as salt in this world? If the people in our lives had to write a definition of Christianity from what they see and hear from us, what would they write?

If we allow ourselves to be distracted by worldly things, we lose our ability to affect the flavour of life. Let's focus on the things of the kingdom!

Pray

Heavenly Father, show me what I need to lay aside today in order to be salt and light in this dark world.

Be Unqualified

Rachel Allcock

God chose things despised by the world, things counted as nothing at all, and used them to bring to nothing what the world considers important. As a result, no one can ever boast in the presence of God.
1 Corinthians 1:28–29

Years ago, I helped at a summer camp in Canada. I wasn't qualified in anything of much use. All the sporty, life-guard-trained leaders sprinted off to their posts whilst I was assigned 'Cloud Watching' and 'Frog Catching'! One day, however, I found myself teaching archery. I could describe the technique, but I couldn't get that arrow to fly when I demonstrated it!

The good news is, God calls the unqualified. It's precisely because of our lack of qualifications that we can give all the glory to Jesus, who provides what we need. I'm not suggesting unqualified archery instructors are a good idea, but you don't need a degree or a certificate to share the story of what God has done in your life. Each time you feel unprepared and unqualified to help in ministry, you'll come out the other side knowing you have only done it in God's strength.

To some of those kids at camp, it meant a lot to see a non-sporty, clumsy girl have a go at something, fail, laugh and keep going. I wasn't there to excel at archery, I was there to get alongside the children and love them.

Pray

Lord God, thank you for choosing the unqualified to glorify you.

Day 334

Be Accepting

Rhiannon Goulding

Be patient with each other, making allowance for each other's faults because of your love.
Ephesians 4:2

Titles somehow hold expectations, we make assumptions based on books, films or comparison with others. Maybe we think all grandmas should be welcoming, generous and cuddly. Our sister should have heart-to-hearts with us. When our real-life relatives and friends don't meet the unattainable standards our culture has brainwashed us to expect, disappointment is inevitable.

My mother-in-law is a lovely person, but she is not a typical grandma. At the start of my marriage, this caused tension, and a few arguments. My expectations of her were not fair. If I put the title 'Grandma' next to her, I was disappointed. But when I saw her just as she was, we got along well and really liked each other.

Two of my children are adopted and their biological mother holds the title 'Mum'. This puts pressure on both her and the relationship.

We may have unrealistic expectations of 'pastor'. We might want a 'friend' to be something impossible. A 'perfect friend' wouldn't have time for any other role – the clichés about 'always being there' would make it a high-pressured, all-encompassing job!

Is there anyone in your life who might need releasing from your impossibly high expectations? By dropping the title, you might see them in a kinder light.

Pray

Lord, please help me to see the people in my life clearly, with the eyes of your love.

Day 335

Be Loud

Mandy Catto

Then Jonah prayed to the LORD his God from inside the fish.
He said, 'I cried out to the LORD in my great trouble, and he
answered me.'
Jonah 2:1–2

Jonah's story is one of adventure, rebellion, courage and anger! When he first hears the request from God to warn the people of Nineveh, he runs fast in the opposite direction. When the storm hits and he ends up thrown into the sea, he calls out to God and realizes that it is God who rescues him. He then has the courage to go to Nineveh and shout out warnings and as a consequence, the people repent and are saved. Rather than celebrating the success of his mission, Jonah is very angry and complains to God that he has been too merciful. He has no hesitation in expressing all that he feels. God questions his anger and teaches him a lesson about love and mercy with a tree and a worm.

Jonah is loud! He is courageous when he shouts warnings of destruction. He is honest and authentic when he tells God what he feels. He is rebellious and impulsive, and yet God uses him to save a city. And after all of this, he is brave enough to tell his story to others, so that we can learn from it today.

Pray

Lord God, even when we sometimes go the wrong way, may we be loud in speaking up for you, and always honest and open in our prayers to you.

Be Assured

Rachel Allcock

> All glory to him who alone is God, our Saviour through Jesus Christ our Lord. All glory, majesty, power, and authority are his before all time, and in the present, and beyond all time! Amen.
>
> Jude 1:25

Jude didn't hold back when he wrote against false teachers. He starts his letter explaining that he wants to write about the salvation we all share (Jude 3). However, he has to tackle another issue first: 'some ungodly people who have wormed their way into your churches, saying that God's marvellous grace allows us to live immoral lives' (Jude 4). Jude compares them to clouds that produce no rain and stars wandering in darkness. Jude's brother, James, was also quick to point out that teachers in the church will be judged more strictly (James 3:1).

It makes for unsettling reading, and these verses certainly keep me in check when I start feeling a little smug. The warning is as relevant today as it was then.

However, today's verse is a bit like the phrase I taught my kids to say after a nightmare: 'In Jesus' name, bad dream, go away!' Jude ends with a powerful prayer of praise, assuring us that God is able to keep us safe, even through the dangers.

Pray

Mighty God, may we build each other up, pray in the power of the Holy Spirit and await the mercy of our Lord Jesus Christ, who will bring us eternal life (Jude 20–21).

Day 337

Be Content

Fiona Castle

Not that I was ever in need, for I have learned how to be
content with whatever I have. I know how to live on almost
nothing or with everything.
Philippians 4:11–12

There is a vast difference between what we need and what
we want. We in the developed world always seem to be
striving to attain more. Money and possessions are worldly
aspirations that are never satisfied. We look for comfortable
and luxurious lifestyles, but however successful we become,
it seems there's always more to be achieved. We become
prisoners of our possessions.

Why? Are we trying to impress others? Are we competing
with the lifestyles of others? Does this help us feel content?

True contentment is not dependent on wealth, but neither
should it be ruined by poverty. Our contentment comes
through trusting the Lord, in whatever circumstances we
find ourselves, not through owning a lot. If he is guiding our
lives and we follow that guidance, we need not be afraid.

Fulfilling God's purpose in our lives is far more beneficial to
our spirits than how much we possess.

Pray

Lord, I thank you for all you have faithfully provided for me
over the years. Help me to strive to be content throughout
my life, as you lead and guide me through all circumstances.

Day 338

Be a Blessing

Fiona Castle

And God will generously provide all you need. Then you will always have everything you need and plenty left over to share with others.

2 Corinthians 9:8

When J.K. Rowling was a single mother living on benefits, she often struggled to pay the bills. Then one day, out of the blue, a friend gave her a cheque for £4,000. She didn't expect ever to be able to repay that kindness. Recently a presenter on my local radio station, hearing that story, asked listeners to ring in with their own tales of unexpected kindness. The switchboard was swamped with calls!

People told of losing wallets or handbags which were returned by honest passers-by; of people stopping to help when a car broke down; of friends who came every day when someone was discharged from hospital. The presenter spoke of the 'rush of joy' and the 'gift of happiness' that such acts produced.

It made me wonder: what have I ever done to make someone feel like this? How aware am I of other people's needs? What have I ever done that has 'blessed someone's socks off'?

I resolved to look out for more opportunities to be a blessing to others.

Pray

Dear God, make me a blessing to others by the way I treat them and care for them.

Be Wise

Mandy Catto

How wonderful to be wise, to analyse and interpret things.
Wisdom lights up a person's face, softening its harshness.
Ecclesiastes 8:1

When you think of wisdom, who comes to your mind? There's a person who comes straight to mine. She passes on her considerable life experience gently, without ever issuing judgement or wishing for the old days. She is endlessly positive and calming in a group, and others look to her for her quiet lead. She never pushes her opinion on others, but offers words of peace that gently guide.

Wisdom, however, does not necessarily just belong to those who are older, or highly educated or in positions of authority. My son is also wise. I like to talk things through with him because he listens well and brings a kind and fresh perspective to a discussion without trying to 'quick-fix' a solution. As young and inexperienced as he is, I can see that others look to him for advice, as he begins to step into leadership.

When I picture both of these wise people, I see the light in their faces, reflecting their kindness and their godly characters.

Pray

Father God, you are the giver of wisdom. Thank you for friends in my life who share their wisdom with me. Please help me to listen, analyse and interpret well, no matter who I meet today. May my face light up with kindness as I speak with words of wisdom.

Day 340

Be Persistent

Fiona Castle

We can rejoice, too, when we run into problems and trials, for we know they help us develop endurance. And endurance develops strength of character, and character strengthens our confident hope of salvation.
Romans 5:3–4

I remember our first family skiing holiday. The children loved skimming down the mountain slopes, exhilarated by the speed and the sense of achievement when they arrived safely at the bottom! The downhill journey was speedy, but the trek back to the top took much longer.

I couldn't help comparing our spiritual lives. Those 'mountain-top' experiences – when things are going well and we feel close to God – fill us with joy. We feel that nothing can stop us, and we set off full of confidence. But often we land at the bottom with a bump, and the trudge back up feels like one step forward and two back.

There isn't always a chair lift! We aren't always offered an easy route back to joy. But if we trust in Jesus, we can go through the tough times knowing that he is beside us, catching us if we start to slip back, and keeping us on the safe path.

Pray

Dear Lord Jesus, thank you that you have promised never to leave or forsake us. It fills me with joy!

Day 341

Be Teachable

Rhiannon Goulding

Cry out for insight, and ask for understanding. Search for them as you would for silver.
Proverbs 2:3–4

I got into houseplants during the first lockdown. One of my first plants was a parlour palm, which I killed very quickly with too much water and somehow scorched in the searing north-of-England sun!

I decided I needed to learn, so I joined an online group that provided help and advice from people who are much more knowledgeable. They have made the same mistakes, so can offer solutions, praise and encouragement on my new plant-rearing journey. I've lost count of the number of times I've said, 'I didn't know how much I didn't know.' This ignorance has cost many poor plants their lives!

How true is this on our faith journey? On our own, we stumble and fail to bring things to life. We need that community of believers. We need to be really grounded in the word of God. We need to surround ourselves with teachers and encouragers, and keep learning and growing.

Pray

Lord, help me to be willing and eager to learn from others, so that my life may be fruitful for you.

Be a Cheerleader

Rachel Allcock

Her children stand and bless her. Her husband praises her:
'There are many virtuous and capable women in the world,
but you surpass them all!'
Proverbs 31:28–29

Thankfully nowadays, books, TV programmes, blogs and articles are rewriting what it means to be a girl. We can help, too, by asking questions about dream jobs, books or food (instead of headbands, dresses, or shoes).

It's been interesting revisiting Proverbs 31 over the past 20 years, seeing how interpretations differ. Recently, my friend preached on this passage and explained that it isn't a scale of wifely perfection to measure ourselves against. Instead, it was written by King Lemuel's mother, to guide her son towards certain qualities and values. The passage refers to a woman who works hard, lives generously, and provides for the needs of her family. It reminds us that the biblical view of women is anything but weak and submissive.

The husband's compliment relates to the wife's noble actions. That is where her beauty lies. Which women in your life need a compliment like that? Next time you contact a friend, try one of these meaningful compliments: 'You make me feel better', 'You're a good listener', 'You inspire me'. When value is placed in attributes, rather than clothes and style, that compliment fits for ever.

Pray

Father, help me to develop a different attitude when speaking to the women in my life, valuing their bravery, hard work, and strength.

Day 343

Be Brilliant

Mandy Catto

Those who are wise will shine as bright as the sky, and those who lead many to righteousness will shine like the stars for ever.
Daniel 12:3

Daniel offers a picture of two different ways to shine. There is the brightness of the day, with the strength of the sun that shines in all its intensity, representing wisdom. And there is the vast brilliance of the night sky, with its endless stars. Not the faint twinkling that we see when we look out over a light-polluted city, but the jaw-dropping celestial majesty of the galaxy that we can see when we take time to look up in dark, remote places. This canopy of endless brilliance is the picture presented by Daniel for those who witness, who lead others to righteousness.

Your authentic faith will be a story obvious to those who meet you, who spend time with you as you share openly what a difference Jesus has made in your life. Weave your beliefs and your love of God into every aspect of your life, as you show love in action to those around you.

Pray

Lord, as I look up at the brilliance of the sun today, may I be wise and shine for you. Give me the words, actions and courage that will lead others to faith in you. Let my legacy last as long as the stars, because I have brought friends to eternal life in heaven.

Day 344

Be Joyful

Fiona Castle

'When you obey my commandments, you remain in my love, just as I obey my Father's commandments and remain in his love. I have told you these things so that you will be filled with my joy. Yes, your joy will overflow!'
John 15:10–11

I once read the comment that a joyless Christian is a contradiction in terms. A salutary statement!

Christ himself is the source of our joy. He teaches us that we are cherished and valued and loved by him, which he proved through his sacrifice for us. If we accept that joy from him, it persists, regardless of life's circumstances. It doesn't change.

How can we express that joy to others? Joy isn't just some kind of cheerful mood, it's a deep-seated contentment and we can know it even when times are difficult. It's true that we can lose sight of it, and then our bad moods can take over – but we need to recognize that and refocus on Jesus.

Joy in our hearts is not a reward for success or perfection. It remains constant simply because we know our future is assured.

Joy is what the world desperately needs, so whatever you do, don't fail to spread the joy!

Pray

Dear God, fill my heart with your joy every day, so that it overflows to all I meet.

Day 345

Be Free

Rhiannon Goulding

Loving God means keeping his commandments, and his
commandments are not burdensome.
1 John 5:3

My head was spinning, my mind racing: my daughter was having a meltdown and was making me look bad . . . Stop! Wait! What? Did I just think that? She was making *me* look bad? At that moment, I realized I was parenting out of fear: fear of failure, fear of what others would say about me, fear of my reputation being spoiled.

I walked away and started to pray, and that is when I was given the answer to parenting. She is not my handbag! She's not alive to make me look good or bad! She's her own person with her own life; her failures and her successes are hers. I love her and I parent her the best I can in a fallen world. She was given to me for a time to cherish and love, but she hasn't been put here simply to enhance my image or boost my ego.

If you're living with guilt over parenting or struggle with what others think, learn to let go. Our children are a gift from God, and his gifts are not burdensome but a pleasure. So enjoy the journey, let them find their own path and love them anyway! And if your concern is not a child but some other worry: don't take responsibility for what's not yours.

Pray

Lord Jesus, teach me your values and help me to see things with your eyes.

Be an Opportunist

Fiona Castle

'This is my commandment: Love each other in the same way
I have loved you.'
John 15:12

I was once asked to speak at a meeting about five people who'd had a positive influence on my life. I suppose my choices were fairly predictable – my mother, my husband, the person who led me to Christ, my pastor, and an author whose books have had a great influence on me.

It struck me that this could be a good theme for an evening with neighbours and friends. Invite them to talk about two or three people who have influenced their lives, in just five minutes. It will be amazing how much you will learn about them!

This gives Christians an unthreatening way of gently telling the story of how they came to Christ and the difference it has made to their lives.

At that first meeting, I was able to talk in depth to several of the visitors, and for some it was the beginning of a rethink about what was important in their lives. Just setting up that framework for the evening created openings for everyone to talk at a personal level.

Pray

Lord, I pray that I might see people with your eyes, and take opportunities to reach them with your love.

Be Prepared

Fiona Castle

So, my dear brothers and sisters, be strong and immovable.
Always work enthusiastically for the Lord, for you know that
nothing you do for the Lord is ever useless.
1 Corinthians 15:58

It's good to know that when we work for God, we never work in vain. But what about when we think we're doing his work, but it doesn't work out?

Sometimes I've been convinced God is telling me to visit someone – and when I get there, they're out! I wonder if I've got my wires crossed! Once I started a quiet time and I was interrupted by a visitor. I prayed frantically for an escape, but I felt God saying, 'Her need to talk to you is greater than your need to be quiet.' I did feel frustrated – but to God that wasn't as important as my willingness to be obedient.

We all have seasons of life when we seem too busy, constantly dashing from one commitment to the next and somehow convincing ourselves that we don't have time to carry out God's work. Instead, let's remember how Paul urged Timothy to be prepared 'whether the time is favourable or not' (2 Timothy 4:2).

Pray

Lord, remind me to be prepared to work for you, even when it's not convenient.

Day 348

Be a Speaker

Mandy Catto

'O Sovereign LORD,' I said. 'I can't speak for you, I'm too young!' The LORD replied, 'Don't say "I'm too young," for you must go wherever I send you and say whatever I tell you. And don't be afraid of the people, for I will be with you and will protect you.'

Jeremiah 1:6–8

When God first called Jeremiah, he was very reluctant to step up. I have felt out of my depth when others have used their years of experience or clever words to make fun of my faith. Emergency arrow prayers, like the one Jeremiah used, are a great tool in the middle of a conversation: 'Lord, give me the words. Help me to be brave.'

Sometimes the Holy Spirit will give you a verse or truth and the conversation will turn in a positive direction. At other times, it may feel as if you have failed or lost an argument. We are not required to always have the last word; it may be better to listen with love, and admit that we don't know the answer. Soul-winning conversations are rarely one-time battles with clever winning retorts. Tentative loving words, and questions that invite future opportunities for sharing together are usually the best plan.

Pray

Sovereign Lord, be with me and protect me as I look for opportunities to speak for you today. Give me confidence beyond my years. Help me share Jesus with love.

Day 349

Be Present

Fiona Castle

See how very much our Father loves us, for he calls us his children, and that is what we are!
1 John 3:1

I recently heard a speaker ask what qualities we expect from a good father. Suggestions included fairness, patience, understanding and love. But the one which most struck me was 'being present to his children'.

As a mother, I've been present 'with' my children, making sure they were safe and secure and well cared for; but was I always present 'to' them? I have read that it's important to have eye contact when communicating with children. How many times did I reply to their questions without lifting my eyes from the cooking or the washing-up? Even if I didn't say it, my posture showed that I was too busy to take them seriously. I seem to remember saying 'in a minute' a lot! It's a good thing we have a forgiving God.

They say that failed relationships with our earthly parents can affect the way we think of our heavenly Father. If a troubled past causes you to doubt your heavenly Father, just read the first epistle of John and you will see how many times he tells of God's love for us.

Pray

Thank you, Father, that you repeatedly assure me of your love for me. May I give others the assurance of that love too.

Day 350

Be Trusting

Fiona Castle

Now all glory to God, who is able, through his mighty power at work within us, to accomplish infinitely more than we might ask or think.
Ephesians 3:20

I've just walked round our garden on a bright spring morning. One corner is ablaze with hundreds of crocuses of different colours. It's beautiful! We've never had so many before. I planted a few last year and they've multiplied beyond belief.

They reminded me of Abraham: God promised him more descendants than there were stars in the sky. Abraham trusted and believed, although he would never live to see them.

Do we do the same? We pray, but when nothing seems to happen, we start to believe our doubts rather than God's promises.

But I never saw those crocuses coming! All winter the ground looked dead and cold, with nothing happening. But hidden beneath the earth life was waking and growing, ready to burst through at the first sign of spring.

So with our prayers. We have to trust that God is working his purpose out – though the answer may not always appear where or how we expect.

Pray

Lord, even when you seem silent and I hear no answer to my prayers, I will trust you in the silence.

Day 351

Be at Peace

Fiona Castle

Don't worry about anything; instead, pray about everything.
Tell God what you need, and thank him for all he has done.
Philippians 4:6

Where do you stand on worry? I know some people seem to think it's a good thing – they think it shows they are taking their problems seriously. Others disagree: surely you can show concern without becoming anxious. The passage above goes on, 'His peace will guard your hearts and minds as you live in Christ Jesus.'

What an abundant life we can live if we believe the promises of the Bible!

Sometimes I find myself chewing over a problem, trying desperately to work it out on my own, and feeling that there's no possible solution. Then I realize what's missing: I haven't handed it over to the Lord. The moment I do this, I feel better. I may not get an instant solution, but I can trust God for the outcome.

'Now all glory to God, who is able, through his mighty power at work within us, to accomplish infinitely more than we might ask or think' (Ephesians 3:20).

How can we ever worry about anything in the light of these wonderful promises?

Pray

Remind me, Lord, that your peace will keep my heart quiet and at rest at all times.

Day 352

Be Uninhibited

Rachel Allcock

I will put my hope in God! I will praise him again – my Saviour and my God!
Psalm 42:5–6

I spent April 2020 desperate to see people. In those first few weeks of lockdown, I took every opportunity to holler out of the window to greet anyone I vaguely knew.

As lockdown restrictions eased, I didn't feel that urgent desire to connect. I had settled into a routine and learned to live a smaller life. I had become slightly embarrassed by the memory of that frantic version of myself – the person who raced out onto the drive for a quick, socially distanced chat.

Do you ever look back on past emotional encounters with Jesus in a slightly sheepish way? Do you feel embarrassed by times when you sang, cried or poured out your heart to him? I have to admit, I sometimes do. I've doubted whether a spiritual experience was real. At these times, it has been a relief to me that I kept a journal. I recorded what happened, what God said to me, and how I felt.

It's easy for the passion we once felt to disappear as we settle into the familiarity of a smaller life. Re-reading what God has done in your life will remind you of an urgency you once felt. It's good to re-live milestone moments in your relationship with Jesus, taking stock and re-cultivating a desire to connect with God. Why not spend some time today re-living important moments in your journey with God?

Pray

Lord God, my Saviour, I put my hope in you and praise you.

Day 353

Be Loyal

Fiona Castle

My life is worth nothing to me unless I use it for finishing the work assigned me by the Lord Jesus – the work of telling others the Good News about the wonderful grace of God.
Acts 20:24

We have all been given different assignments in life and we should be faithful in carrying them out. All our opportunities and lifestyles are different, so it's important that we don't look at others with envy if they seem more productive or worthwhile. I love the reply of Jesus to Peter, who was questioning him about John's life, when he said, 'What is that to you? You follow me.'

We have to be loyal to our particular assignment, and each will be different. The actors in a play are noticed with admiration by the audience, but the play couldn't happen without those who provide the lighting, the sound, the costumes and the scenery. They are not seen or applauded, but they are loyal to their contribution to the play's success.

Wherever God has placed us, our loyal obedience to him is love in action.

Pray

Lord, I thank you that you have never given up on me, even when I have failed. Help me to be faithful and loyal to you in my everyday life, whatever the circumstances.

Day 354

Be Present

Fiona Castle

'So don't worry about tomorrow, for tomorrow will bring its own worries. Today's trouble is enough for today.'
Matthew 6:34

Before I became a Christian, my husband Roy often used to say to me, 'You don't enjoy today because you're so busy worrying about tomorrow.' How true! I wasn't just thinking and planning, I was worrying and fussing, too. What a waste of energy . . .

I have a favourite chorus: 'Because he lives, I can face tomorrow' (written by Bill and Gloria Gaither). I remind myself that before I knew Jesus I was fearful and tense. Once he was in my life, Jesus gave me the courage and strength to face each day.

Of course, there are still moments when I find it hard to face tomorrow. Then I remember that God holds the future. If we belong to him, we will spend eternity with him. What a wonderful future to look forward to! How can we be afraid of anything that happens in between?

Billy Graham's wife, Ruth, had a little sign on her desk which said: 'Don't be afraid of tomorrow – God's already there!' What reassurance – that God is outside of time and already knows our pathway for tomorrow.

Pray

Thank you, Jesus, that because you live I can face whatever the future holds, without fear.

Day 355

Be Thankful

Fiona Castle

Give thanks to the LORD, for he is good! His faithful love endures for ever.

1 Chronicles 16:34

When my husband died, I realized early on that there's no blueprint for bereavement. Everyone is different.

A defining point came one day when I arrived at Heathrow Airport. I was passing the usual row of people waiting for friends, when a woman in front of me rushed into a man's outstretched arms. I started to sob uncontrollably: I would never again be met by anyone who loved me like that. All I had ahead of me was a lonely drive home to an empty house.

Suddenly, I realized these were tears of self-pity, not sadness: poor old me!

'Pull yourself together, woman,' I said out loud. 'Be grateful that you've had 31 years of a wonderful marriage. Now, get back to the car and go home.' And I did!

From that moment, I determined that I would have a heart of gratitude rather than despair. I recalled the old hymn, 'Count your blessings, name them one by one . . .' From then on, I did so. I found if I thanked God for all he had given me my heart would start to sing.

Pray

Heavenly Father, your love and provision for me makes my heart sing, whatever my circumstances.

Be Unselfish

Fiona Castle

Don't be selfish; don't try to impress others . . . Don't look out only for your own interests, but take an interest in others, too.
Philippians 2:3–4

It's easy to become so engrossed in the pressures and activities of our own lives that we fail to listen to or care about the needs of others.

This can happen in marriage, when each partner has a stressful work life and returns home in the evening only to pour out complaints and difficulties without any concern for the other. We hear the resulting comments: 'He never . . .' or 'She's always . . .' Of course, there are always two sides to every story, but when our friends talk like this we can easily imagine the scenario. Such selfishness can destroy relationships and tear families apart.

The most valid, and possibly the hardest lesson, is to learn to put others first. Think about Jesus. He was willing to put us first by giving his life for us, so that we might know the assurance of God's love, which is not just for this life, but is everlasting.

Pray

Thank you, Lord Jesus, for your selfless love for mankind, providing new life and eternal life through your willingness to die for us. Help me to remember to put others first.

Be Forgetful

Sarah McKerney

'But forget all that – it is nothing compared with what I am
going to do.'
Isaiah 43:18

What's interesting here is that in verse 16 Isaiah starts out speaking of the 'former things'. He reminds the Israelites of the Exodus, centuries before, when God led them out of slavery in Egypt. Isaiah acknowledges that their current situation is similar to the past. It's as if he's saying, 'As a nation we've been here before, but remember the great things God did then. God saved us and rescued us, so have hope!'

But although he starts by talking about the past, he then says, 'Forget the things I've just reminded you of.'

I wonder if Isaiah recognized that though the past can give us hope for the future, equally, it can become a place we get stuck in or a place we idealize as 'the good old days', where we retreat to when the future becomes too frightening.

Past disappointments and struggles can constrain us. Isaiah doesn't want Israel to focus on the slavery and hardships of the past, but rather to remember that the wilderness has been conquered before. There is hope. We can choose whether to allow our past pain to paralyse our present, or to let it shine hope into our future.

Pray

Mighty God, thank you for bringing us safely through past problems. Help us to hold on to the hope that Jesus offers us.

Day 358

Be Grateful

Fiona Castle

> He was led like a lamb to the slaughter. And as a sheep
> is silent before the shearers, he did not open his mouth.
> Unjustly condemned, he was led away.
> Isaiah 53:7–8

Long ago – before the days of electronic payments – I had an embarrassing experience at the supermarket checkout. For some reason, my payment for groceries wouldn't go through. I had to stand aside while the shop assistant served several other customers, as I waited for a confirming phone call from my bank. Eventually, the problem was sorted out and I rushed home, humiliated and feeling like a criminal.

I asked God what he was trying to teach me from the situation. He pointed me to Jesus, who faced the death penalty without cause. He stood before his accusers, knowing he had done nothing wrong. God allowed him to suffer in order to redeem wretched people like me.

My problem that day was trivial, but Jesus suffered the agony of knowing what lay ahead of him. He was prepared to face it on my behalf. It reminded me to put aside my wounded pride, and instead to focus on my gratitude for his sacrifice. What a wonderful Saviour.

Pray

Father, I am amazed and humbled every time I think of Jesus' willingness to suffer and die, to save a wretch like me.

Day 359

Be a Believer

Fiona Castle

'I am the way, the truth and the life. No one can come to the
Father except through me.'
John 14:6

If you'd asked me at the age of 5 whether I was a Christian,
I would have said, 'Yes'. Our family went to church and said
grace before meals and prayers at bedtime. I didn't think
much about it for years.

It was only when life seemed pretty much perfect – I was
married, with a loving husband, healthy children and a
comfortable home – that I fell apart. I had no idea why I felt
so low. That was when I asked God to help me, and he did –
by sending a friend who gently explained the Gospel to me.

Since that day, life hasn't always gone my way, but Jesus didn't
say it would. However, he has always been with me, helping
me through many different circumstances. Someone once
described my dilemma as having a God-shaped hole inside
me. No matter how I tried to fill it, whether with possessions,
pleasures or comforts, nothing fitted, because it was the wrong
shape. Only God, through Jesus, could bring satisfaction.

Since that day, my longing has been to share that wonderful
news with other people. So many people struggle with the
difficulties and stresses of life. Isn't it worth investigating?

Pray

Jesus, help me to direct people to understand that only you
are the way, the truth and life who can bring real fulfilment
into their world.

Day 360

Be Hopeful

Rhiannon Goulding

We are pressed on every side by troubles, but we are not
crushed. We are perplexed, but not driven to despair.
2 Corinthians 4:8

Our camping trip had been cut short. Heading down the M6
in the storm, I could feel the trailer swaying and threatening to
dislodge from the tow bar. I let my speed drop to an embarrassing
30 mph as bemused and frustrated drivers overtook us.

The back of the car was a muddled heap of wet tent, soggy
sleeping bags and a litter of pots, cups and plates. The smell
of damp was overpowering, and not just from our little dog:
both my son and I were wet through, having hastily thrown
all our gear into the car during a downpour. Driving was not
pleasant. My hands ached and I realized I'd been gripping
the steering wheel with increasing intensity.

Suddenly, in the midst of the relentless weather, I saw a
glimmer of sunlight. 'Look, Bob,' I said to my son. 'Sunlight,
just over the hills!'

Immediately, I felt my anxiety calm and my fear dissolve. My
hands relaxed their grip on the wheel and, in that moment,
the world seemed a more ordered place. Life will and does
place us in many storms, but there is always sunlight . . .
waiting . . . just over the next hill!

Pray

Please, Lord, remind me that whatever difficulties I go
through, there is always sunlight over the hills. Thank you
that my hope is in you.

Day 361

Be Loving

Fiona Castle

'So now I am giving you a new commandment: Love each other. Just as I have loved you, you should love each other. Your love for one another will prove to the world that you are my disciples.'

John 13:34–35

This command of Jesus to his disciples is such a challenge to us today. If we are his disciples, we are called to love each other, as a witness to the world that Jesus is the true path to life in all its fullness. In other words, we should be 'infectious' Christians – with something that people are eager to catch!

Disagreements invariably happen, but the way we resolve our conflicts is very important. Different denominations of the Christian faith can indicate rifts and differing viewpoints, which is why it is such a positive witness when churches in communities get together, finding common ground, making an effort to support local activities, showing love for one another.

Instead of focussing on the negative, let us focus on the truth and that common ground, so that we, as less than perfect people, love each other, because Christ loved us and gave his life for us.

Pray

Lord Jesus, help me to show your kind of love to others.

Day 362

Be Cheerful

Fiona Castle

So you see, faith by itself isn't enough. Unless it produces
good deeds, it is dead and useless.
James 2:17

I'm ashamed to admit that in the days before I became a
Christian, I was very moody! My children have since confessed
that they would say to each other, 'Don't go near mother
today, she's in a foul mood!'

I recognized this attitude in myself when Jesus changed my
life, and I realized that a priority for me was always to maintain
a happy atmosphere in my home, no matter what was going
on. I wanted my children to feel confident that whenever they
invited friends into our home they would always be welcomed,
and know it would be a time of enjoyment and laughter.

Our lifestyle displays our faith, and I wanted my children to
be influenced by my attitude. Making an effort to control my
feelings lifted the mood of the whole house. The best part
was the joy it brought to me as well!

'As a face is reflected in water, so the heart reflects the real
person' (Proverbs 27:19).

Pray

Lord, challenge us to work to make sure that those we invite
into our homes, for whatever reason, will be welcomed with
warmth and love.

Day 363

Be Clothed

Mandy Catto

> Since God chose you to be the holy people he loves, you must clothe yourselves with tenderhearted mercy, kindness, humility, gentleness, and patience.
>
> Colossians 3:12

I love clothes shopping! Whether it's gazing into the windows of shops that are too expensive, browsing the aisles, diving into the bargain rail, thrifting in charity shops or clicking online, there's excitement in choosing an outfit that fits, is the right colour and fills a particular need. In the January sales, I once bought a pair of red jeans that cost four pounds. Every time I wore those trousers, I felt like a new person. If I needed to feel confident when I went out, all I needed to do was to put on my red jeans.

When Paul wrote to the new Christians in Colossae, he seemed to understand this. He encouraged them to put on positive attributes as if they were putting on different clothes. He tells them this is a necessity and gives them the reason why: they are loved, chosen and called to be holy. Paul knows that patience and mercy don't come easily or naturally, so we must put on these attributes afresh each day – just as regularly as getting dressed.

Pray

Father God, thank you for loving me and calling me to be holy. Clothe me with patience, gentleness, kindness, tenderhearted mercy and humility today.

Day 364

Be Rooted

Fiona Castle

Let your roots grow down into him, and let your lives be built on him. Then your faith will grow strong in the truth you were taught, and you will overflow with thankfulness.

Colossians 2:7

We live in an age of fast food. We buy instant noodles and soups, and frozen pre-cooked meals. These foods may satisfy our hunger pangs, but they often lack nutritional value.

In the same way, we look for instant blessings from God. Sometimes I feel envious when others tell me what the Lord has been doing in their lives. Why can't I feel like that?

But when I consider it carefully, I realize that we can't exist for long on mountain-top experiences. The air and the soil are thin there. We need the richer soil lower down the slopes to grow our food, and the richer air to breathe to exert ourselves. Just as we have to tend the soil for food, so we have to dig deep into God's word for spiritual nourishment.

I know I find it easier to be busy than to take time to be alone with God, studying his word. But he is faithful and ready to feed me whenever I'm hungry – and with food which never fails to satisfy.

Pray

Thank you, Father, that your word provides the nourishment I need to keep me strong, even when circumstances are difficult.

Day 365

Be Hopeful

Mandy Catto

Yet I still dare to hope when I remember this: The faithful love of the LORD never ends! His mercies never cease. Great is his faithfulness; his mercies begin afresh each morning.

Lamentations 3:21–23

What does daring to hope look like? Hoping even when circumstances are overwhelming. Continuing to have hope when others have given up and turned to cynicism. It is more than having an optimistic personality – it is actively choosing to remember that God has been faithful in the past. It is focusing on his character, his love and goodness in the present. And it is looking towards his forgiveness and mercy for each new day.

God invented night and day to give our bodies physical rest. But he also knew that we need a fresh start each morning to wake up and have hope. Every single day, however bad, has an end point at midnight. God's mercies begin afresh as the new day reboots in the morning. God's never-ending faithful love for us underpins the fresh confidence that can be ours as we wake up.

Pray

Lord, thank you for your faithfulness and mercy to me. Give me the strength to dare to hope this day, to wake up knowing that you love me and offer me a fresh start. Great is your faithfulness.

Afterword

We hope you've been inspired by these Be-attitudes! If you'd like to find out more about the authors, please visit activateyourlife.org.uk.

We've all been drawn to Activate Your Life through our passion for friendship evangelism – in other words, sharing God's love through making and keeping friends. It's as simple – and as difficult – as that. The more friends you make and keep, the more people you influence. Your influence is powerful. When you follow Jesus, you reflect him in the way you live and interact with everyone. Conversations happen at book groups, at the coffee machine or in the playground. You may be the only Christian your friend comes into contact with, and if you can help her take even a tiny step in the right direction, you are engaging in friendship evangelism.

During some seasons of your life, it's easy to make connections. At other times, it's incredibly hard. But remember, you are uniquely placed to reach those around you. We hope this book has opened your eyes to the fact that this doesn't have to be a burden. If you'd like to be encouraged and inspired to reach others, our website is full of resources. You'll also find details of our latest events and ways to connect or contact us.

Now that you know a little about us, we hope to find out a little about you, too! We'd love to meet you at one of our weekends away or Activate days. If you'd like to hear more from a particular author, why not invite her to speak at your event? You can request this through the website. We have Activate supporters and groups all over the country. Get involved and have fun!

About the Authors

Fiona Castle – President of Activate Your Life, Fiona guides the team in their mission to equip women in friendship evangelism. Fiona is a retired dancer and was married to TV entertainer, Roy Castle. She has authored numerous books and was awarded an OBE for her charity work in 2004. Fiona enjoys helping at a toddler group at her local church.

The friends Fiona encouraged to contribute to the book are all part of the Activate team:

Mandy Catto – university teaching professor and director of Activate. Mandy loves reading and being by the sea.

Rhiannon Goulding – director and Events Coordinator for Activate. Rhiannon loves spending time with people and paddle boarding.

Rachel Allcock – Project Manager and writer for Activate. Rachel loves chatting, shopping, and playing games.

Sarah McKerney – on the leadership board for Activate. Sarah loves preaching, dog walks and podcasts.

Esther Tregilgas – Social Media and Day Events Coordinator for Activate. Esther loves being creative and wild swimming.

Jaz Potter – a pastor with a passion for bringing people to faith. Jaz loves making beautiful things.

Hayley Nock – a nurse who loves her local community and any gardening project.

Becky Burr – a charity worker involved in planting Christian communities in Africa. Becky enjoys cooking and hosting.

Sarah Jones – a pastor who also speaks at conferences. Sarah loves walking on the beach.

Thanks to our editor **Jan Greenough** who took us through the project with kindness and wisdom.

We are thankful for the women who have developed and supported Activate over the past 55 years and those we are yet to meet!

Find us at activateyourlife.org.uk

A Beautiful Tapestry

*Two ordinary women,
one amazing God,
many lives transformed*

*Tracy Williamson
with Marilyn Baker*

Being blind, Marilyn's childhood was one of increasing isolation whilst Tracy's was marked by deafness and low self-esteem. Yet from these most unlikely of origins, God brought these two remarkable ladies together in the most hilarious fashion and gave them a joint vision to work together through Marilyn Baker Ministries.

Through their work in prisons, concerts, retreats, conferences and prayer ministry, they have seen many lives transformed by the power of God's love. Many of those testimonies are included in this book, showing that God is indeed weaving a beautiful tapestry in all our lives. Each individual strand of yarn isn't much in itself, but when woven together an amazing picture emerges as he uses us in our weakness to show the beauty of his love to others.

978-1-78893-156-4

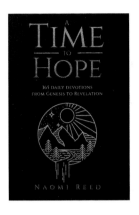

A Time to Hope

*365 daily devotions from
Genesis to Revelation*

Naomi Reed

A daily devotional that provides an accessible way into the whole Bible story. Many of us have favourite Bible verses that we draw comfort from, but we don't always know their context or understand how they fit into the main story arc of the Bible. Tracing the big picture of God's story through the key themes and events from Genesis to Revelation allows us to see the abundant riches in the Word of God. As you read the unfolding story, day by day, you can encounter God in all his glorious holiness and faithfulness and lift your eyes again to his plans and purposes for the world and be reminded that Jesus is, indeed, the hope of the world.

If you have ever struggled to read the Bible from cover to cover, then this devotional will help you to find a way into God's big story and help you fall in love with Jesus all over again.

978-1-78893-144-1

A–Z of Prayer

Building strong foundations for daily conversations with God

Matthew Porter

A–Z of Prayer is an accessible introduction that gives practical guidance on how to develop a meaningful prayer life. It presents twenty-six aspects of prayer to help you grow in your relationship with God, explore new devotional styles and deepen your daily conversations with God.

Each topic has a few pages of introduction and insight, an action section for reflection and application and a prayer to help put the action point into practice. There are also references to allow further study.

978-1-78893-062-8

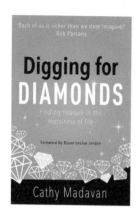

Digging for Diamonds

Finding treasure in the messiness of life

Cathy Madavan

What is hidden always shapes what we can see. In this book, Cathy Madavan encourages us to dig deeper and discover more of the life-transforming treasures of our identity, strength, character and purpose that God has already placed within us – right where we are.

Cathy explores twelve key facets which point the reader to a deeper understanding of their unique, God-given raw material and how God wants to transform them to live a valuable, purposeful life that will also unearth precious potential in others.

978-1-78078-131-0
Devotional: 978-1-78893-152-6

God Conversations

*Stories of how God speaks and
what happens when we listen*

Tania Harris

Stories of God talking to his people abound throughout the
Bible, but we usually only get the highlights. We read: 'God
said "Go to Egypt,"' and then, 'Mary and Joseph left for
Egypt.' We're not told how God spoke, how they knew it was
him, or how they decided to act on what they'd heard.

In *God Conversations*, international speaker and pastor Tania
Harris shares insights from her own story of learning to hear
God's voice. You'll get to eavesdrop on some contemporary
conversations with God in the light of his communication
with the ancients. Part memoir, part teaching, this unique and
creative collection will help you to recognize God's voice when
he speaks and what happens when you do.

978-1-78078-188-4

God Speaks

*40 Letters from the
Father's heart*

Ruth O'Reilly-Smith

Ruth O'Reilly-Smith helps us to slow down, listen to God and
respond to him in this beautiful devotional journal.
God speaks. If we take the time to quiet our racing thoughts
and be still for a moment, we can hear him. He is speaking all
the time.

Draw closer to God as you listen to 40 messages of love
straight from the Father's heart, reflect on Bible verses and
learn to talk to him with guided questions and prayers. As you
write your thoughts in the journalling space provided, you will
create a precious record of how God speaks to you that you
can always treasure.

Deepen your walk with God as you listen and respond to him
speaking to you in this beautiful devotional journal.

978-1-78893-222-6

Blood, Sweat and Jesus

The story of a Christian hospital bringing hope and healing in a Muslim community

Kerry Stillman

What is a Christian hospital doing in a remote Muslim area of Cameroon?

Kerry Stillman shares her own experiences of working as a physiotherapist in a sub-saharan village hospital. A vivid impression of daily life is painted as the team deal with the threat of terrorism, the attitudes of local people towards Western medicine, their patients' health issues, and the challenge of sensitively sharing the gospel in a different culture.

Passionate, intriguing and uplifting, this is a colourful interweaving of cultures, beliefs and the power of prayer alongside modern medicine.

978-1-78893-148-9

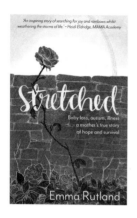

Stretched

Baby loss, autism, illness – a mother's true story of hope and survival

Emma Rutland

Real, raw and candid, *Stretched* will encourage anyone struggling with baby loss or parenting challenges.

Emma Rutland shares her very honest account of a faith that is tested to the limit when faced with the reality of living with children with special needs and the pain of baby loss.

Stretched is a story of fear and loss, hope and strength, reality and acceptance and, ultimately, the victory of living an unexpected life with a faithful God.

978-1-78893-039-0

Authentic

We trust you enjoyed reading this book
from Authentic. If you want to be
informed of any new titles from this author
and other releases you can sign up to the
Authentic newsletter by scanning below:

Online:
authenticmedia.co.uk

Follow us: